"Dr. Miguel De La Torre addresses systemic issues of justice-making while confronting biblical texts that have long been misinterpreted. By addressing the interlocking and systemic nature of sexism, heterosexism, racism, and ethnic discrimination, Dr. De La Torre rightfully challenges readers to embody a stance that will more faithfully serve the needs of the world and of our churches. This is an integrative work that is desperately needed in today's culture of hate and violence."

— Joretta Marshall, Brite Divinity School, Author of *Practicing Care in Rural Congregations and Communities*

"Miguel De La Torre's *Liberating Sexuality* is grounded in biblical scholarship and takes on such topics as masturbation, God beyond gender, and ethical S & M. Without providing easy answers, De La Torre presents biblical texts and characters that both confirm and subvert patriarchy, sexism, machismo, heterosexism, and racism. This book forces the reader to engage the Bible and sex deeply and thoughtfully in the movement for justice."

— Marie Alford-Harkey, President and CEO, Religious Institute

Contents

Preface

My academic fascination with sex has less to do with its enjoyment than with how it has historically and religiously been used to control bodies, and by extension, society. What we call sexism preludes all forms of oppression (racism, classism, heterosexism, and ethic discrimination), where all lacking race and class privilege are relegated to a feminine space so as to be housebroken. All forms of oppression are identical in their attempt to domesticate those who fall short of the privileged white male ideal. The sexist, who sees women playing a lesser productive role than men, transfers to their Others effeminate characteristics, placing everyone within a feminine space. Women must be kept in their place, because once they are liberated, all types of other groups would want to be liberated as well.

Any struggle for liberation must truly begin with a discussion on sex, specifically its usage to domesticate all occupying feminine spaces. If justice is lacking between the sheets, then we should not be surprised that a more egalitarian social structure is absent within society. In a very real sense, I would argue, we as a society must deal with our sexism if we ever hope to make progress with all the other oppressive "isms."

Obtaining my doctorate in social ethics in 1999, I have, from the time of this writing, been in academia for sixteen years. During this period, I have published over thirty books and hundreds of chapters and articles. All of my works have a common thread running through their pages: a thread that consistently examines, explores, and explains sexism, racism, classism, heterosexism, and ethnic discrimination. This book is but a sliver of those writings focusing solely on sexuality.

I am grateful to Brad Lyons from Chalice Press who approached me with the book concept. When I was asked if I would be interested in publishing some of my contributions to the discourse concerning sexuality and faith, I feared the task would be arduous. I am grateful to Kristian Diaz who served as my research assistant and spent countless hours correlating published articles, chapters, and blogs. And finally, I would like to thank Victoria De La Torre, who spent hours proofreading this text.

What follows are some of my writings concerning sexuality and faith, with an eye toward how to engage in more liberating sex. Although not prudish, the main thesis of this book is not advocating great sex for its own sake. My concern lies more with how oppressive social structures, rooted in a two thousand-year-old misunderstanding of Christian sexuality, prevent us from a more just social order. To that end, liberating sex means more than simply liberating sex from bad theology and poor biblical hermeneutics; liberating sex is also an ethical call for a more justice-based society. This compilation of essays and other works on sexuality and faith is my humble attempt in assisting Christian readers to think deeper about their faith and how its implementation might help move us closer to justice.

ultimate purpose; for while sex is the source for future generations, it is also the source of extreme pleasure.

And yet, since the founding of Christianity, an attempt has been made to equate sex with the forbidden fruit. For Augustine, sex became the reason for Adam and Eve's expulsion from the garden. Adam covered his genitals with fig leaves not out of a sense of modesty, but rather because Adam, according to Augustine, was sexually aroused. By linking shame and sex to the Christian doctrine of the Fall, Augustine argued that the aroused sexual organs of humans signify human will toward the flesh, over and against the spirit.[4] The erect male sex organ symbolized man's rebellion to God, hence, for Augustine, redefining sex as the cause for expulsion from Paradise. To desire or participate in sex today links us to Adam, who chose the things of this world rather than the spiritual realm of God.

Augustine's interpretation of the role sex played in the garden reduced sex to an act involving nothing more than the genitals, with an emphasis on whom one engages in sex and the sexual act itself. Sexual ethics is reduced to a fear-driven discourse. Have sex and you will get someone pregnant, you will die of AIDS, you will catch some sexually transmitted disease, or, if female, you will get pregnant or be seen as a "fallen" woman unable to marry a godly man. Yet this verse in Genesis states that sex is blessed by God. Rather than a "just say no," knee-jerk reaction to sexuality, this verse encourages creation's focus on relationships where sex can and should occur.

Frustrating our ability to interpret a pro-sex, pro-body reading of this verse is that for the past two thousand years Christianity created a false dichotomy between the sacred (spirit) and what was defined as profane (the body). Crucial to Christian thought is the concept that the soul and the flesh struggle against each other for supremacy of the individual. Early Christian writers were highly influenced by this antagonistic body/soul dualism, stressing the danger new believers faced if they succumbed to the mortal body, as opposed to the immortal soul. That which is of the flesh was conceived as being corruptible, while only that which is of the spirit could expect to inherit the eternal. Or as St. Paul reminded us, "flesh and blood cannot inherit the kingdom of God, nor does the perishable inherit the imperishable" (1 Cor. 15:50). Even though some will argue that the way Paul defined flesh and spirit is not necessarily supportive of the argument in favor of the flesh-spirit divide, this divide still became a salient characteristic of Christianity, with Paul's words being appropriated to justify this divide.

This understanding of a flesh-spirit divide is foreign to the Hebrew Bible; nevertheless, it became a prominent feature of early Christianity through the influence of Neoplatonic thought and stoic philosophy and its proclivity for devaluing the body. The emphasis on obtaining inner peace through the human will's ability to control passions contributed to the overall pessimism regarding desire, specifically sexual desire. For the Stoics in particular, marriage became the means by which self-control was practiced. The rational reason for engaging in sex became procreation. While many modes of understanding gender and sexual reality developed during Christianity's early years, the body/soul cosmic split was among the most prevalent characteristics of that era. As early Christian scholar Tertullian succinctly stated: "Flesh is an earthly, spirit a heavenly, material."[5]

To argue that the flesh is inherently sinful alienates believers from their bodies and, in turn, from their sexuality. Redemption came to be understood as a flight from the body—the material toward the spiritual—an understanding that continues to influence faith communities today. For those seeking spiritual purification, hope for spiritual wholeness was, and continues to be, found in the process of freeing oneself from the sinful influences of one's body or for Christians, crucifying one's sinful flesh to Jesus' cross. Earthly pleasures like sex are forsaken in remembrance of Christ's ultimate sacrifice. What develops from this body/soul dichotomy is a very anti-body perspective, where the body, in and of itself, is evil. But contrary to the body/soul dichotomy constructed by Christianity, this verse stresses that God blesses sex and declares it good.

2

Unmasking the Biblical Justification of Sexism[1]

As a field researcher conducting interviews in Patterson, New Jersey during the mid-1990s, I was responsible for observing church life in predominantly poor congregations. Part of my task was to interview Latina/o church members, specifically Christians who attended a Pentecostal church. I remember a particular interview I conducted with an elderly woman, probably in her eighties. In many northeastern Pentecostal churches, women are very careful about the way they dress. In many cases, skirts come down to the ankle (even during the summer) and shirt tops are baggy so as to conceal the upper curves of the female body. I asked her why she dressed in this matter. Without much thought she quickly responded, "So as not to tempt the men." Frankly, I didn't have the heart to tell this eighty-year-old woman that she need not worry about this. Nevertheless, what I found fascinating about her comment was the way she saw herself—that is, through the eyes of the men of her church. Her activities, including the way she dressed her body, were molded by this viewpoint. From the pulpit, for all of her life, she has heard men preach about the sinful nature of women's bodies. It is the woman who leads men astray, so she must be hidden from sight. Pious Christian women impose upon themselves their own subjugation by dressing the way men expect them to dress so that these same holy men do not fall into temptation. In my mind's eye I could just see her walking up to the female teenagers of the church to lecture them about their "improper" attire, thus maintaining a dress code established by men and perpetuated by the church women, who have been taught to see themselves only through the eyes of men.

For many churches, any not-biblical sanctioned sexual activity between men and women becomes the fault of the woman. How many times have you heard the same questions raised, at times by women, upon hearing of a rape? What was she wearing? What was she doing at that party? Why did she go out with those boys? How was she acting?

Did she drink too much? What can you expect if she was asking for it? These questions, and many like them, underline a major component of patriarchy: women's bodies are evil, and as such lead righteous men to sin, hence the Bible grants authority to these holy men to protect and confine female bodies from sin. For the good of the community, for the purity of women, men must rule, a concept justified by how some men read the biblical text.

Justifying Patriarchy

At seminary I attended a class where the professor would begin each session by asking the students to call out their favorite biblical verse. This being a class full of future ministers and theologians, you can imagine the types of verses that were typically called out—John 3:16, Psalm 23, Romans 3:23, and Ephesians 2:8, to name a few. One day the professor looked in my direction and asked what was my favorite verse. Without hesitating I responded Genesis 2:25, "And they were both naked, the man and his wife, yet they were not ashamed." I was not trying to be funny. I am attracted to this verse because I can find no better depiction of God's intention concerning human relationships, relationships where participants stand totally vulnerable before each other yet feel no shame. Nonetheless, the Bible is seen as patriarchal by many women who read the text.

Any examination of the biblical justification of patriarchy should begin with Genesis: "To the woman [God] said, 'I will greatly increase your sorrow in your childbearing, you shall bear children in sorrow, and your desire shall be for your husband, and he shall rule over you'" (3:16). Reading through the eyes of patriarchy, the passage is quite straightforward. God has ordained men to rule over women. Historically, men have always cited the Bible to counteract women's attempts to advance in society. The Bible has been used to condemn female actions toward empowerment as unbiblical. In particular, many men have interpreted Genesis 3:16 to mean that because women first ate the mango (or apple) from the forbidden tree, they were punished by God. Their eternal sentence was to be subservient to men.

Yet, the words spoken by God in Genesis 3:16 occurred after the fall of humanity, after the disobedience of Adam and Eve, after the entrance of sin into the cosmic story. The question that should be raised is if it is God's will for women to be ruled over by men, or if it is God simply foretelling what the consequences of sin will be for humanity, specifically women, in this verse. The next two verses might shed some light upon this question. In them, God turns to man and curses the ground, stating that from now on man would have to till the cursed soil, only to produce "thorns and thistles." The garden, and the effortless fruits it produced, will be gone. Only through the sweat of the brow will

Adam be fed. Again, does this mean that it is the will of God for Adam and all of his descendants to work and labor in sorrow? No, of course not. It is God's will for Adam to continue living in the garden, being one with his wife and his Creator.

By the same token we ask if it is God's will that women be ruled over by men. Again, using the same reasoning, the answer must be no. It is God's will to return women to the garden, where "they were both naked, yet they were not ashamed," where the relationship between the man and woman was vulnerable, yet safe, because no power relationship existed between them. Genesis 3:16 does not describe God's curse on women, any more than Genesis 3:17 does not describe God's curse on men. In both of these verses, God is foretelling the consequences of sin. Both the man and woman wanted to be like God, so they ate the mango; both desired the power that came with being God. Instead, they have fallen to a state where social structures are created to deny them the power they sought: subservience to economic structures (agriculture as a way of surviving) for men, and sexist relational structures for women. It is not that God ordains, approves of, or condones these new structural relationships, but rather, that their development is part of the natural evolution of humanity's fall.

But doesn't Genesis 2:18 say that the woman was created for the man to be his helpmate? "And Yahweh God said, 'It is not good for the man to be alone, I will make for him a helper suited for him.'" The Hebrew word used in the text, *ezer*, usually translated as helpmate, comes from the root word meaning "support" or "help." But the usage of *ezer* does not imply subordination or inferiority for the one who is doing the helping. For example, in Exodus 18:4, God is referred to as the "God of my fathers [who] was my *helper*." In Psalm 10:14, the psalmist proclaims God as being the "*helper* of the orphans," and in Psalm 118:7, the psalmist declares, "The Lord is with me, God is my *helper*." In none of these cases, nor in any of the other places throughout the Bible where God is referred to as our helper, does *ezer* imply subservience. Why then do we assume it when *ezer* is used to describe the woman? Several female biblical scholars insist that a better translation of *ezer*, as used in the Genesis passage, is the word "companion," which connotes woman as a counterpart to man.

What then is God's desire for the relationship that should exist between men and women? For this, we turn to the first creation story, specifically Genesis 1:27.[2] "And God created the *adam* in God's image, in God's image God created it, male and female God created them." Most Bibles translates the Hebrew word *adam* as "man," hence rendering the verse as "God created man in God's image." Yet, the word *adam* can have three different meanings. It can mean Adam, a proper name, in this case, Adam the husband of Eve. Or the word *adam* can be translated as man, a male-gendered individual, as opposed to the word "woman." Finally, the word can also mean mankind, as in all of humanity.

If we translate *adam* to mean a man, as opposed to a woman, we must ask if this created man was both male and female? No, of course not.[3] What if we were to translate *adam* to mean humanity? Is humanity male and female? Yes, both males and females make up humanity. Thus, I suggest that God created humanity in God's own image, male and female God created them. The image of God is both male and female, for both sexes find their model in the Deity.

Both Jews and Christians have historically proclaimed that their God has no bodily form, hence no gender. The masculine pronoun attributed to God has less to do with "correct" theological thought, and more to do with the patriarchal bias of biblical writers who attribute a "he" to God. Yet, to solely refer to God in the masculine limits and confines the mystery that is God to a human-made image. God is both male and female and thus God is neither male or female.

If God created male and female in God's own image, then both the man and the woman are equal within God's eyes because both are patterned after God. Women cease to be a copy of a man, an appendix to a story centered on the man's need for companionship. The fall of humanity, due to Adam and Eve's action, changed this mutually equal relationship. One of the consequences of sin was its manifestation in the form of sexism, where the woman ceased to be a person in the image of God and became instead a possession to be owned by the man. The transformation of women into objects for possession is reflected throughout the Hebrew Scriptures. The tenth commandment demonstrates how a woman, like a house, slave, ox, or donkey, is a possession of the male.

> You shall not covet your neighbor's house; you shall not covet your neighbor's wife, or his male slave, or his slave girl, or his ox, or his donkey, or anything which belongs to your neighbor. (Ex. 20:17)

Women as possessions were a means by which a man's honor within society could be lost. The taking of another man's woman brought shame to the household and family name of the man whose possession was taken. Consequently, adultery only applied to the married or betrothed woman who engaged in sexual relationships with anyone other than her husband. If a woman was caught in the act of adultery, she could face a death sentence. John 8:3–11 tells the story of a woman, "caught in the very act of committing adultery," who was brought to Jesus. It is interesting to note that the man with whom she was adulterous was not called to task. Why wasn't he also brought before Jesus? Because it was her sin, not his.

In the Hebrew Scriptures, a man was guilty only if he has sexual relationships with another man's wife, that is, another man's possession. With this one exception, a married man was free to engage in sexual relationships with nonmarried women. When King David was punished for his adulterous relationship with Bathsheba, it was not because he engaged in a sexual relationship outside of marriage. David's sin was against Uriah, Bathsheba's husband, because David took his possession, his wife, Bathsheba. This is made clear in the prophet's condemnation of David in which he compares the king to the rich man with an abundant flock who steals the only lamb of a poor man. Bathsheba, like the lamb, was the object taken from the "true" victim, Uriah (2 Sam. 12:1–4).

As possessions, women could also be given as ransom for men. This happened more than once, as in the city of Sodom, where Abraham's nephew Lot lived. One night, when Lot has received unknown visitors, the men of Sodom surrounded his house and banged on the door, crying out, "Where are the men who came to you tonight? Send them out to us that we may abuse and rape them!" But Lot went out to them and said:

> My brothers, please do not act evilly. See now, I have two daughters who have never known a man. Please let me bring them out to you, and do to them as you see fit. Only do not do a thing to these men, because they have come under the shadow of my roof. (Gen. 19:7–8)

In Lot's mind, his daughters were worth far less than the two strangers, only because the strangers were men.

There is a similar scenario in the book of Judges 19–21. On his journey home, a Levite, along with his concubine, stopped in the town of Gibeah, which belonged to the tribe of Benjamin. An old man of the town offered hospitality to the Levite and welcomed him to his house. When night fell, the men of the city came banging at his door, demanding that the Levite be sent out so that the town men could have their way with him. The old man went out to meet them, and like Lot, offered his virgin daughter and the Levite's concubine as a ransom, insisting that the men of the town do with them whatever they saw fit. They took the concubine, raped her and left her lying at the door of the house where the Levite slept. The next morning the Levite arose to find his concubine lying on the floor. He placed her on his donkey and continued his journey home. When he arrived at his house, he took a knife and cut her into twelve pieces, sending her dismembered body parts to the borders of Israel. When the rest of Israel saw what occurred, they were outraged at the wickedness of the people of Gibeah, from the tribe of Benjamin, because they had violated the Levite's possession.

All of Israel then went to war against the tribe of Benjamin. After winning the battle, the rest of Israel swore never to give their daughters to the Benjamites as wives. Yet they regretted their oath, for it meant the loss of one of the twelve tribes. In the end, the other tribes of Israel, after great bloodshed, captured four hundred virgins from Jabesh-gilead who were then given as wives to the six hundred surviving Benjamites. The rape of one has now become the rape of four hundred. However, there were not enough virgins to go around, so they instructed the Benjamites to lie in wait in the vineyards of the town of Shiloh, and when their young maidens come to dance during the Lord's feast, the Benjamites were to catch a wife for themselves and take them back to their land. Hence the kidnaping and subsequent rape of these young maidens resolved the honor of the men who swore not to give their possessions (daughters) in marriage to the Benjamites.

This story is disturbing for several reasons. First, the Bible is silent about the identity of the concubine. She is remembered only as an unnamed object. As a possession, her name, identity, or story are unimportant. The narrative never reveals her voice, or her humanity. Second, the giving of the virgin daughter, and the "seasoned" concubine indicate the low station of women. Rape of men by men was considered a vile thing but rape of women by men was more acceptable. Third, conflicts between men, whether between the old man and the Gibeah townsmen, or between the tribes of Israel and the survivors of the tribe of Benjamin, could be resolved through the sacrifice of women. Fourth, rape of the woman was not the crime that defined the wickedness of the Benjamites; rather, their sin was the violation of the Levite's property. Fifth, the Hebrew text does not state whether the concubine was dead or alive after being raped all night. The silence of the text indicates that it really didn't matter if she was alive or dead, for, after all, her owner could dispose of his possession as he chose. Like Christ, her body was broken, and literally given for many. Sixth, the battle that ensued from the rape of one concluded in the offering of six hundred maidens to be raped by the surviving Benjamite soldiers and the taking of two hundred more maidens. Finally, the most disturbing aspect of the narrative is the silence of God. Nowhere does the text provide comfort to the abused women or to the reader of the story. Nowhere are we informed of how God viewed these atrocities. No reassuring words demonstrate God's contempt for such actions. The unnamed concubine is neither the first nor the last example that demonstrates how women were reduced to objects within the Hebrew Bible.[4] Women like Tamar, the daughter-in-law of Judah; Tamar, the daughter of King David; the unnamed daughter of Jephthah; or the virgins of the town of Midian who were taken as booty on Moses' order—all provide disturbing narratives of female marginality.

Because of patriarchy, a woman who belonged to one man, yet was used by another, brought shame to the honor of the man who owned her. Hence, to protect his honor, the man confined the woman to the household where she was secure from dishonoring her husband. By the same token, if her husband's authority was to be challenged by a political or social rival, the best way to announce the challenge publically was by taking control of his possessions, specifically his women. This concept is demonstrated in 2 Samuel 15–16. In these passages, David's authority as king was challenged by his son Absalom. Absalom mounted a rebellion that forced David to flee Jerusalem. Upon entering the city, Absalom, on the advice of his counselor Ahithopel, thought of a way in which Absalom could consolidate his power and authority. The solution: he pitched a tent on the palace's housetop, in the sight of all Israel, and raped all of his father's concubines. This was not a sexual act motivated by lust; rather, women were the means by which Absalom could wrestle authority from his father. Absalom literally provided public notice that he had taken his father's place and was now in control of his father's possessions.

A survey of the Law clearly shows how patriarchy is anchored in the Bible. According to the Law: (1) If a Hebrew man was sold into slavery he served for six years at which time he could leave with no compensation due. Female Hebrew slaves had to be bought back (Ex. 21:1–11). (2) A man who seduced (raped) a virgin had to either marry her or pay her father a fixed sum. Additionally, the victim of the seduction was not the virgin, rather it was her father, and so it was he who received compensation for the "spoiling" of his property (Ex. 22:15–16). (3) The firstborn son (or male animal) was consecrated unto the Lord; not so for the first-born daughter (Deut. 15:19–23). (4) Three times a year only the menfolk had to present themselves before God during the great national feasts. Women did not do so (Ex. 23:14–19). 5) Women could not serve as priests, and priests could only marry virgins (Lev. 21:1–9). (6) A woman's parents had to prove their daughter was a virgin when she climbed into her new husband's bed (Deut. 22:13–21). No such requirements of sexual purity were expected of men. (7) If a man made a vow to God, he had to keep it; but if a woman made a vow, her father or husband had veto powers that could void the vow (Num. 30:1–17). (8) Women were frequently excluded from participating in Temple rituals and festivals due to the "uncleanliness" of their menstruation cycle (Lev. 15:19). (9) Only if a man died without having any sons would his inheritance pass to his daughters (Num. 27:8–9). (10) Women could be taken as war booty (Deut. 21:10–14). (11) A woman who gave birth to a boy was "unclean" for fourteen days, but if she gave birth to a girl, she was unclean for twice as long (Lev. 12:1–5). (12) Men could have multiple sex partners, even to the point of maintaining a harem. Women could only have one sex partner (Lev. 18:18). (13) A husband who suspected his wife of infidelity could have her ingest a bitter elixir before the priest—if she survived, she was faithful; if she was afflicted, she was guilty of adultery (Num. 5:11–31). Men did not need to drink such brews.

Probably the most blatant abuse of sexism was the determination of the value of a person dedicated by a vow to God. According to Leviticus 27:1–8, the value of men between the ages of twenty and sixty years was fifty silver shekels while a woman was only worth thirty. If the men were over sixty years of age, then their worth dropped to fifteen shekels, while the worth of women dropped to ten. One is left questioning if these laws were indeed the will of God, or if these were the laws of men who attributed the regulations to God in order to protect their power and privilege within patriarchy. If these regulations came from God, then God stands accused of sexism.

It appears that the Bible advocates patriarchal structures. At the very least, it has been used to justify sexism. How can liberation be found in what feminist biblical scholar Phyllis Trible calls these "texts of terror"? We are told that King Solomon, the wisest man who ever lived, had three hundred wives and six hundred concubines. Can a biblical case be made for polygamy and concubinage? Of course not—we automatically assume that these particular social structures are not relevant for the modern era. Additionally, we consciously or subconsciously make a distinction between the Bible advocating a particular social structure and the Bible simply describing the social practices of its time. Yet, how do we justify in our own minds the rejection of social structures like polygamy and concubinage while still advocating the overall foundation of patriarchy? Is patriarchy also a structure that the liberating Good News of Jesus demands that his disciples flatly reject? To answer this question, we turn to the New Testament.

Sexism from the Margins

One of the regulations of the Law not mentioned above deals with divorce. According to Deuteronomy 24:1–2, a husband could dismiss his wife simply by serving her with a written bill of divorce. The grounds for divorce could be minor, based on something she did that was considered improper or even a general dislike of her. By the time of Jesus, the practice had developed where a husband was able to divorce his wife for whatever reason he chose, yet no Levitical law existed that allowed women to initiate divorce procedures. Divorce was a male privilege. Matthew 19:3–9, however, provides a model for interpreting patriarchal passages like Deuteronomy 24:1–2, as well as the other biblical verses that contribute to the marginalization of women. The

Matthew passage reads as follows:

> And the Pharisees approached [Jesus] tempting him by saying, "Is it lawful for a man to dismiss his wife for whatever reason?" And he answered them, "Did you not read that God made them male and female from the beginning? And God said, 'For this reason a man shall leave his father and mother, and be joined to his wife, and the two shall be one flesh.' So they are no longer two, but one flesh. What God has yoked together, let no one separate." They said to him, "Why then did Moses command to give a bill of divorce, and put her away?" He said to them, "In view of your hardheartedness, Moses allowed you to put away your wives, but from the beginning it was not so. And I say to you, that whosoever puts away his wife, with the exception of fornication, and marries another, commits adultery. And the one who marries a divorcée, commits adultery.

In the above passage, Jesus dismisses the Deuteronomic law because of the social context in which it was written, a context in which the "hardheartedness" of men who benefited from sexism took preference over the intended will of the Creator expressed in the first two chapters of Genesis. Laws like Deuteronomy 24:1–2 are, according to Jesus, the product of men establishing sinful patriarchal hierarchies, rather than God's perfect will that men and women coexist as companions.

Can Christians follow Jesus's example and dismiss biblical verses, like the ones previously mentioned, if they cause oppression? The entire Bible should be read through the lens of the gospel message, specifically passages like John 10:10, where Jesus states "I came that they may have life, and have it abundantly." If verses within the Bible advocate the subjugation of one person to another and hence prevent life from being lived abundantly by a segment of the population, then those verses are anti-gospel and must be reinterpreted in light of the fullest revelation of God found in Christ. Insisting to read the text solely through the eyes of men violates the gospel message of liberation as women are forced to conform to patriarchal traditions that rob them of their dignity. Women who read the text with their own eyes are simply no longer willing to accept biblical interpretations constructed by men as normative for their lives. In short, as demonstrated in Matthew 19:3–9, Jesus becomes the model by which Christians read, interpret, and accept (or dismiss) verses that appear to justify oppressive social structures.

Feminism among Women of Color

Women of color face multiple oppressors. They must learn how to survive in a society that privileges Euro Americans as well as a society that privileges men. Like their Euro American sisters, they struggle for genuine respect of their personhood. As a result, they emphasize their social location while valuing their experiences as a source and lens for reading the biblical text. Yet, unlike their Euro American sisters, they must also face racial and ethnic discrimination from the dominant culture along with sexism from within their own marginalized group, where all too often Euro American men and men of color agree on the so-called biblical mandate that subordinates women. In addition, their Euro American sisters who also confront sexism may very easily become their oppressors as they achieve some equal opportunities with men in certain roles, roles that privilege the dominant culture at the expense of those existing on the margins of society....

Women of color often question some feminist approaches toward liberation, fearing that the term is being used to mean equality with white middle- and upper-class males. Such equality means equal opportunities in employment and education and being viewed as equals before the law. Although inequality in opportunities is unacceptable, oppression (or discrimination) and liberation can never be limited to Euro American definitions. Then liberation is reduced to political maneuvering within society where marginalized groups attempt to create new power bases and often struggle against each other. Such movements ignore the disproportionate distribution of wealth and overall racism existing in society. This is why women of color challenge Euro American feminists to resist becoming another group competing for their respective rights within a balance of power based on conflicting interests, interests that at times collide with those of people of color (both female and male).

The failure of some Eurocentric feminist groups to distinguish between liberation and the quest for equality with Euro American middle- and upper-class men has kept some feminist movements from truly fostering liberation. The type of liberation that many women of color seek encompasses freedom from oppressive economic, political, and social conditions for themselves and their communities (including their fathers, husbands, and sons). Women of color seek within the Scriptures stories that empower them to take control of their lives, bodies, and destiny, stories that show that their struggle is at times with women of the dominant culture. This approach to the Bible calls for women of color to collaborate with all oppressed groups to fundamentally change the economic, political, and social structures of society, and to cultivate a spiritual dimension of liberation through a reading of the Scriptures that challenges traditional biblical interpretations. Women of color reading the Bible from the margins can confront the prevalent sexism existing within their own ethnic and racial community, as well as the racial, ethnic, and class prejudice existing within the Euro American feminist community.

Crucial to women of color is the story of Hagar, the Egyptian slave girl of Sarah (Abraham's wife), recorded in Genesis 16:1–16 and 21:9–21. Hagar was marginalized by gender, ethnicity, and class. While most white women identify with Sarah, the matriarch in the story and the mother of the faith, most women of color resonate with the experiences of Hagar. Abraham and Sarah, who were wealthy, attributed their riches to God's blessings. Still, Sarah, like other women of her time, was considered property that could be sacrificed as needed. Remember, at least twice Abraham tried to pass her off as his sister in order to protect himself, meaning that she could have been accosted by the men of the towns through which they passed (Gen. 13:12–19; 20). Unfortunately, if the original structures of oppression are not dismantled, those who are oppressed can easily become oppressors. Sarah, the property of her husband, obtained her own property in the form of Hagar, a resident alien.

Sarah's inability to bear Abraham children led her to conclude that her barrenness was a curse by God, and so she took matters into her own hands. In keeping with the customs of her time, she offered her servant, a slave girl, as an instrument by which Abraham could sire an heir. Hagar, as womb, not person, was used to accomplish the goals of those who owned her body. Her body and labor existed to be exploited by those who had power over her. If a woman does not have control over her sexual organs and is forced to have sexual relationships with a man against her will, for whatever reason, the result is called rape. Hagar, as a slave, as property, was required to "perform" at the will of her owners, a familiar scenario for many black female slaves who, as possessions, had to satisfy their master's desires as well as face the dehumanizing practice of being "rented out" to other white men as concubines.

As the story proceeds, the unexpected happened. Sarah's property, a surrogate mother, experienced consciousness-raising and recognized her own dignity. Hagar became the first woman in the Bible to seek her own liberation by fleeing Sarah's cruelty (as well as sexual rivalry between barrenness and fertility). She thus chose death in the desert, if necessary, to challenge the power structures that oppressed her, even though she was pregnant by Abraham. While in the wilderness, Hagar was visited by a messenger of God, a God who accompanied the outcast in the midst of her unwarranted suffering. Yet the divine message for Hagar was to return to Sarah and "suffer affliction under her hand." Why would God require her to return to slavery? Perhaps it was crucial for the survival of her unborn son, who would then be born in the house of Abraham an heir to the promise of God. But is this liberation or a strategy for survival? Regardless, her child becomes an intruder to the covenant. It is to be noted that, breaking with biblical tradition, God's promise was made to a woman, with no reference to a man.

At this point, Hagar, the lowly marginalized woman, does the unexpected: she dares to give God a name, a privilege extended to no other person throughout the Bible. Ancient custom dictated that only a superior could name those who are lower in status, yet here a slave woman is the first biblically recorded person to give God a name. She calls God, *El Roi*, the God who sees, uniting the divine with her human experience of suffering.

The second time the Bible returns to Hagar, she has been cast out by those who own her. Sarah's jealousy got the better of her. Fearful that her son's inheritance could be jeopardized by Abraham's firstborn, Ishmael, she connived to have him and his mother Hagar, forced into exile. Again Hagar found herself in the desert facing death, thrown out as an old used object no longer needed by its owner, a familiar scenario for most domestic servants today. Homeless because of the unwillingness of the father of her child to shoulder his responsibility, she was abandoned, like so many women of color today. Alone in the desert, facing death, and questioning the promise God previously uttered about the multitude of her descendants, she must have wondered about the blindness of the God who sees. Yet, this time, God heard the cry of her son and rescued them.

Hagar suffered from classism (a slave), racism (an Egyptian foreigner), and sexism (a woman raped by Abraham). Because of her status, Hagar becomes a lens by which the biblical text can be read, a reading that focuses on the struggle for liberation and survival with dignity. The story of the used and abused woman is a motif that resonates with many women of color. Even natural allies, women of the dominant culture like Sarah, capitalize on her body. Nevertheless, God is found in the midst of the struggle of those relegated to the margins, even when these religious patriarchs of the faith have participated in their marginalization! Because God chooses to accompany those who are disenfranchised, Hagar and her child Ishmael complicated the history of salvation by becoming part of God's promise to make a nation by using Abraham's seed. Women of color continue to "complicate" how the dominant culture interprets God's promises.[5]

3

Orthoeros: A Biblically-Based Sexual Ethic[1]

Toe-curling, earth-shaking, climax-reaching sex is great! God may have declared all of creation to be good (Gen. 1:31), but when it comes to human physical intimacy, sex is beyond simply good. Sex is great because it can be a basis for healthy and just communities....And yet, while engaging in a conjugal relationship was recognized as a calling from God, historically Christianity developed a predominantly ascetic tradition, which idealized sexual abstinence and often associated it alone with godliness, purity and holiness. The concept of sexual sacredness leads many Christians to recoil. Many have come to conflate all sex outside of a monogamous heterosexual marriage with promiscuity, holding those in such lifestyles responsible for the moral degradation of our culture. Sex, for such Christians, is constructed as a powerful and dangerous desire whose lack of restraint and control has led to skyrocketing divorce rates and broken families.

Neither conservatives' sexual legalism nor liberals' permissiveness provides satisfactory approaches toward sexual ethics. A crusade against so-called "sexual immorality" is waged by conservatives who reduce sex to an act involving nothing more than the genitals, with emphasis placed on whom one engages in sex. A fear-driven discourse is created when the consequences of sex—for example, pregnancy, contracting a sexually transmitted disease, or condemnation for being lascivious—are used to define such activity as something dirty and unholy. Sex, as the epitome of sin, fosters control of bodies through guilt. Because of desire, sex is labeled as something good but too powerful, thus needing to be contained. Fear and coercion are used to ensure compliance with the sexual mores of the culture. In the minds of many past (and some contemporary) Christian leaders and believers, good Christians avoid sex, and if they participate, avoid pleasure. So to be a lesbian, gay, bisexual, or transgender person, to engage in premarital sexual relationships, or to become pregnant while unmarried becomes, in the eyes of many conservatives presently framing the Christian conversation on sexual morality, a blatant flaunting of hedonism. The job of the clergy is to rein in the sexual perversions of others, either through homilies within the church or legislation within the secular culture. The godly response to sex becomes celibacy when single, heterosexual coitus when married. Advocating public policies and legislative initiatives that socially reinforce these standards becomes the responsibility of the clergy, indeed all the faithful, who see themselves as safeguarding society from the destructive nature of unchecked sexuality.

For more liberal-minded individuals (including Christians), sex is reduced to a biological function, a private act between two consenting adults, resulting from a dopamine-elevated state. What occurs between two or more consenting adults is no one else's business. Because of the liberal's presupposed dichotomy between the public and private sphere, sex clearly falls under the category of the private. Sex, for the liberal, becomes depoliticized—reduced to a personal choice that has no impact on the overall society. For more liberal-minded individuals, sex is simply another bodily appetite, like eating or sleeping. It is simply what human mammals do—no more, no less. Therefore, as long as no one is being hurt by the sexual encounter, two or more consenting adults can participate in whatever sexual interaction they wish. When dealing with matters of sexuality, individual reason and experiences guide a utilitarian-type approach.

Neither the conservative nor the liberal view is adequate. Both sides overly emphasize sexual acts, debating and seeking answers to what is or is not sexually permitted. Both approaches are indicative of a dominant, Eurocentric, hyper-individualist culture, and as such, both share common problematic assumptions and presuppositions about sexuality. For example, they share a tendency to reduce the Christian faith to a personal piety that dictates which acts should be or should not be permissible. As such, sex is understood as something private rather than communal. Sex may indeed be a personal (for example, masturbation) or interpersonal act, but it is not private. It does have public, social, and cultural ramifications. What is required is a new way of approaching Christian sexuality. But how does one construct a sexual ethic within a conservative religious atmosphere that usually equates sex with sin or within a liberal secularized society in which sexual images run rampant on film and television, on our advertising billboards, and on the Internet? If the message of the New Testament is the fulfillment of the law with the commandment of love, then any sexual ethics constructed should concentrate on what it means to love my neighbor—more specifically, my sexually oppressed neighbor. The ethical act of unconditional love for the other—the neighbor—is what makes transformative relationships possible.

This chapter will attempt to construct biblically-based, ethical principles for enjoying sex (in spite of the Bible's patriarchal tendencies). Additionally, it can serve to present those engaged in the practices of ministry with a more holistic approach in providing guidance on how a sexual ethics should be implemented. Aware of how sexism, heterosexism, and even racism and classism have influenced past and current conversations on sexual ethics, this chapter will avoid predominant "conservative" or "liberal" approaches to sexual ethics. Instead, looking toward a "liberative" methodology that seriously considers liberation theology, this chapter will attempt to develop a sexual ethics influenced by those who reside on the margins of power and privilege.[2]

Orthodoxy, Orthopraxis, and Orthoeros

To implement a liberative methodology means that sexual ethics must: (1) listen to testimonies usually ignored, specifically the voices of those abused by the prevailing sexual norms; (2) pay close attention as to who benefits, either through power or privilege, from the present sexual norms of society; and (3) challenge sexual norms that prevent individuals from living the abundant life promised to them by Christ (Jn. 10:10). I argue that social injustices pervert human relationships and distort any definition or concept of love. Because justice-making (the fostering of non-oppressive structures) is an act done in obedience to unconditional love, any sexual ethics that ignores the communal ramification of sexual relationships will fall short of offering an alternative to either some stringent conservative purity code or some hyper-liberal view of "anything goes." For sex to be liberating, sexuality must be understood as relational and, hence, a justice issue. Great love-making is needed for justice-making to take place, and vice versa.

Those who ground their religious commitment on the insights provided by liberation theology participate in a liberative ethical framework that considers both "orthodoxy" (correct doctrine) and "orthopraxis" (correct action). Historically, Eurocentric Christian theological thought has predominately emphasized orthodoxy. What one believes in one's heart and professes through one's mouth becomes fundamental in defining whether one is truly Christian. Doctrine matters. And while believers may no doubt feel compelled to act upon their beliefs, in the final analysis, belief trumps action. In this view, it is more important to have correct doctrine than correct action.

In contrast, for historically disenfranchised Christian groups subsisting on the underside of the U.S. dominant culture, the emphasis is usually on orthopraxis, correct action. Orthopraxis is the cornerstone of living out liberation theology. The actions committed, specifically actions leading toward social justice, are what define one's Christian commitment. What then becomes the correct action of liberative sexual ethics? I suggest "orthoeros" (correct erotic sex).

The orthoeros that I'm calling for focuses its critical eye on the sexual prejudices of those in power. Those whom society empowers usually impose restrictions upon the powerless, so as to enhance and secure their privileged spaces. In an attempt to construct a proper "orthodoxy," a proper doctrine, many quickly move from saying sex is good (only in a monogamous heterosexual marriage) to developing a list of "dos" and "don'ts." But such lists have more often than not led to sexual repression and oppression. Those privileged by the prevailing sexual patterns remain complicit with oppressive structures, specifically structures that lead to domination of wives, partners, and/or their supposedly economic or racial "inferiors." From the underside of today's normative sexual patterns lie the seeds for producing a justice-based sexual ethics but only if we are willing to listen to the stories and testimonies of the disenfranchised, learning from their experiences, resisting the temptation of paternalistically fixing the problem, and standing in solidarity with those abused by the present social structures.

The goal of this chapter is, therefore, not to limit what makes sex great but to enhance sexual pleasure and spiritual intimacy through the process of unmasking those oppressive structures put in place to control the "flesh" so that the "spirit" could supposedly flourish. And here lies the paradox that prevents so many from experiencing great sex: total surrender, each to the other, can never be achieved as long as one of the two parties is holding on to power over his or her partner. If we can construct this liberative orthoeros, we might bring to fruition the words of the psalmist, "Steadfast love and faithfulness will embrace, justice and peace will kiss" (Ps. 85:10).

Basis of Mutual Giving and Vulnerability

To love and be loved is part of what defines our humanity. Correct erotic sex, orthoeros, occurs within a familial relationship that is based on love and commitment while remaining vigilant against the suffering of others due to that relationship. When I refer to familial relationships, I realize that this does not necessarily signify a marriage. Although church or civil weddings are rituals publicly proclaiming the existence of a familial relationship, these events do not create family; people do. A church wedding simply blesses the relationship. A familial relationship may occur absent of a religious ritual; likewise, a legally married couple where both spouses lack appropriate vulnerability or have not given freely of themselves would be the ones "living in sin." There may be a marriage because a ritual occurred in a church building, but if a sexual relationship fails to meet the deepest physical, emotional, spiritual, and intellectual needs of both partners, there is no family. Orthoeros promotes a familial relationship based on mutual giving and vulnerability.

Mutual Giving

A scriptural guiding principle for all human relationships is the placing of others first. Paul, in his letter to the Ephesians wrote, "Be subject to one another in the fear of the Lord" (5:21). Within an intimate familial relationship, the needs of one's partner before one's own needs become a biblical norm. Yes, this view is contested by many feminists—and for good reasons. No doubt, most Christian men have historically insisted that it be the women who must put male needs first. But this is a misreading, for patriarchy is the antithesis to mutual giving. Participating in mutual giving can never mean forfeiting personal autonomy. One can only give of oneself if one has authority over one's own personhood. Mutual giving (rather than taking) presupposes autonomy. Mutual giving means that the participants seek the best, each for the other. Sex must, therefore, occur in a safe environment, where the fear of abuse, abandonment, or domination can be eliminated. Giving of oneself to the drunkenness of love can only occur if it is mutual, and mutual giving can only be possible when both parties become totally vulnerable.

Vulnerability

Mutual giving is marked by vulnerability. I suggest that the ideal paradigm for a vulnerable relationship can be found in the Genesis creation story. We are told that "the man and woman were both naked, yet felt no shame" (Gen. 2:25). This supposedly was the pristine relationship that existed prior to the "fall," prior to the establishment of patriarchy. To the ancient Hebrew mind, "nakedness" was a metaphor for vulnerability. Picture this, if you will: both the man and woman were standing stark naked before each other, totally vulnerable, yet they were not ashamed of their bodies, of their personhood.

Only when two individuals are totally vulnerable with each other and are able to stand naked—warts and all—are they truly free to become one flesh, fully sharing themselves with each other in body, spirit, and soul. When I am with my beloved in the privacy of our home, I can stand before her, totally naked, and feel no shame whatsoever. Even though I am unable to hide my sagging excess weight, stretch marks, wrinkles, and grayness, I can stand totally vulnerable and exposed to her gaze without fear of ridicule or abandonment. I stand before her not just physically naked but also emotionally, intellectually, and psychologically naked. And here is the good news: she can do likewise. We are able to stand fully before each other because for years, during good times and bad, we have created a familial relationship based on mutual giving and vulnerability.

Five Principles

This orthoeros ethics that I call for, based on mutual giving and vulnerability, focuses upon strengthening, securing, and supporting familial relationship. Familial relationship is not so much a set of rules that are to be followed but a way of being. The focus is therefore not on the type of sex acts that occur between individuals. Rather, I argue, that for orthoeros to blossom, sex must be safe, consensual, faithful, mutually pleasing, and intimate.

Safe

For a relationship to be vulnerable, it must be safe—safe from harm, danger, and abuse. The apostle Paul reminds us that, "Nothing to me is forbidden, but not all things do good. All things to me are lawful, but not all things build up. Let no one seek their own advantage, but each that of the other" (1 Cor. 10:23–24). Sex is not forbidden, but not all sexual encounters are good or safe. No one should seek, through the use and abuse of others, mere gratification of their sexual desires. Instead, each should seek the sexual good of the other. Sex that brings no harm to self or others, but rather builds the other up, becomes safe.

Consensual

For sex to be mutually giving, it presupposes that both partners are mature and equal in power. By definition, it eliminates adults in full capacity of their faculties from engaging in sex with the mentally impaired, children, subordinates, or anyone for whom they have a role based on fiduciary responsibility (like clergy in relation to members of their congregation). Even when apparent consent is given, an uneven relationship between the parties denies the existence of true consent. A mentally impaired person may agree to sex with a person having "full" mental capacities, while not realizing all that is entailed in the encounter. A child may agree to have sex with an adult family member as a perverse understanding of love. A student or employee may agree to engage in sex with a teacher or employer in hopes of a better grade or job security, attraction to the power the holder has over him or her, transference, or simply out of a fear of the consequences the power holder might inflict if the subordinate does not acquiesce.

Faithful

Another important point to recognize is that nowhere within the biblical text is monogamy established as the standard for all forms of Christian marriages, except perhaps as found in Titus 1:6, which requires elders to be the husbands of one wife. Still, if our hope is for sex to be great, then both mutual giving and vulnerability must be present. Trust and safety from rejection or abandonment fosters the ability of both partners to feel vulnerable enough to mutually and fully give of each other, which in turn leads to a bonding that enhances the physical sexual experience. For this reason, any violation of this bond shatters fidelity.

Mutually Pleasing

To touch, to feel, to nibble, to fondle, to penetrate or be penetrated is more than simply sultry pleasure. It is trust—trust in a partner who will neither hurt you nor deny you pleasure. Improper sex occurs when conducted solely in search of self-serving pleasure, when love is absent from lovemaking. When the other is denied to share in pleasures; when the other is reduced to a commodity to be used and abused for self-gratification; or when the other, due to uneven power relationship, is forced to participate in sexual acts against her or his will, then orthoeros is absent

Intimate

For some, the act of sex with the same partner can become somewhat routine and predicable, if not repetitive. But what makes sex great is not the act of obtaining physical gratification with and through another body, but the intimacy that comes with vulnerability. Through the process of revealing our inner self to our beloved, an intimacy capable of bringing healing to our dysfunctionality is created, reassuring our deepest fears and satisfying our most intense yearnings. Even when sexual pleasure is unattainable, due to illness, old age, or forced separation (for example, war or imprisonment), sex can still remain great so long as it enhances intimacy.

Conclusion

Now that we know what constitutes orthoeros, we are left to consider an important question: Can relationships that are love-making prove to be justice-making? Consider the obverse. If our interpersonal, intimate relationships function in accordance to a hierarchical structure based on an active-passive oppressive model, why then are we surprised that this model is echoed within public sphere? Social structures mirror the patriarchal hierarchy existing within many households. The writer of 1 Peter clearly testifies to these connections. Believers are to be subject to the political structures of imperial Rome, even to the point of honoring the emperor (2:13–17), and they are to be subject to the economic structures imposed by their masters, even when masters are unfair (2:18–25). Similarly, women are to be subject to their "lords"—their husbands—even if their husbands are not believers (3:1–6). The same logic used to reinforce the obedience of women within the household is extended to the political sphere and the marketplace.

The basis for most unjust social structures is the denial of body rights—the right to clothe, feed, and shelter the body—through economic oppression. Denying the right of (any)body to participate in the fruits of society because of her gender, skin coloration, or sexual orientation is oppressive. Our society's obsession with the white, heterosexual male, idealized body leads to injustices that are usually manifested in the form of classism, sexism, racism, and heterosexism. The idealized bodies born of these systems are privileged and are often granted power and control over against poorer, darker, and/or female bodies. This power and control often finds expression in male-centered, female-passive patriarchal sex, while eroticizing domination. Pleasure is found perversely both in domination and in being dominated. Christianity has come to be interpreted so as to justify spiritually white, heterosexual, male supremacy both in the home and in the broader society. Consequently, sexual justice cannot be understood and/or achieved apart from seeking class, gender, and racial justice.

Orthoeros, by providing an ethical pattern for our most intimate human relationships, attempts to remedy these public injustices. To seek justice deepens love for the other. Training one's heart to love others more deeply impacts one's love for one's beloved. Reaching deeper levels of love can only enhance one's sexual encounters. Now, if the major goal for justice-seeking is an equitable sharing of resources and power, then dismantling power structures designed to privilege one group at the expense of another becomes the major task for those seeking a justice-based social order. Because oppressive patriarchal structures exist in the bedchamber, then seeking justice "between the sheets" becomes an ethical issue. In this intimate space, power-sharing becomes the paragon upon which other social relationships are based.

Pope Benedict XVI hints at this in his 2006 encyclical *Deus Caritas Est*, where he argues that a mature form of sex is unselfishly concerned with others, creating a type of love that leads to justice. He wrote, "Love looks to the eternal. Love is indeed 'ecstasy', not in the sense of a moment of intoxication, but rather as a journey, an ongoing exodus out of the closed inward-looking self towards its liberation through self-giving, and thus towards authentic self-discovery and indeed the discovery of God."[3]

What we do with our flesh in the privacy of our bedroom with our beloved can be a means of learning how to love selflessly in the public sphere. It can become a model for the generous extension of compassion for others. Sex can humanize its participants, providing a self-giving paragon by which to relate to others. Sexuality ceases to be a private matter as it moves to the public sphere as a moral imperative. Even though sex may occur in private, it has social ramifications. It can school us to attend with love to the needs of others. Sex provides the opportunity to move beyond the self toward the other. To desire sex, is foremost, a plea for communion, where the psychological and physiological needs of lovers are met. Sexual fulfillment within a vulnerable and mutually giving relationship validates our humanity, because to be human is to be in relationship with our beloved, with our God, and with our neighbor. Although physical sex may be limited to the beloved, still, the principles of putting the needs of others first become the foundation for creating justice-based relationships.

Sex can be a pleasurable experience, both physically and spiritually, designed to achieve wholeness with —*shalom* with *shlemut*. But let's be clear. Seeking a sexual liberationist ethics does not provide a pseudo-religious permission wherein "anything goes." To fully engage in a liberative sexual ethics is to rely fully on the power of God's grace while affirming *shalom* with *shlemut* for the self as well as for the beloved. From the get-go, liberative sexual ethics dismisses any sexual relationship that prohibits *shalom* with *shlemut* from being established. Sexual abuse and exploitation are unequivocally defined as wrong and therefore evil. Will mistakes and errors occur in our quest for great sex? Of course, for after all, we are humans. But if we recognize that failures and mistakes are themselves powerful learning devices that lead to personal growth, and understand grace as God's healing from wrong choices and painful experiences, then we can boldly move forward in our quest for great sex without fear or incrimination.

Nevertheless, fear of and incrimination from sex runs rampant in many of our churches. For conservatives, such a liberative approach to sexual ethics is considered antifamily. Family values becomes the battle-cry for reasserting, according to Christian ethicist Marvin Ellison, "white, affluent, male hegemony as the necessary social mechanism for preserving both the family (read: "male-dominated, affluent families") and the capitalist social order."[4] To establish orthoeros, the task is not to define the type of relationship (male-centered, patriarchal, heterosexual marriage) through which sex can occur but to establish biblically-based principles of justice within all relationships, sexual and nonsexual, so as to dismantle societal injustices.

PART TWO

Sex and the Divine

4

Physical Union
and Spiritual Rapture[1]

For most of early Christian church history, sex was viewed as something requiring forgiveness, rather than something that can lead to spirituality. It is difficult to remember that there is another side to this coin, and that the antipleasure and anti-body strains, although powerful and influential, do not tell the whole story. Consider several biblical passages that seem to celebrate sexual pleasure: Proverbs 5:19 advises "Let her [your wife] be the company you keep, hers the breasts that delight you every time, hers the love that ravishes you." Passages about Sarah the matriarch fondly recall her youth when her husband Abraham could sexually pleasure her (Gen. 18:12); or the biblical text's last words about Moses, prior his death, inform the reader that in spite of his advanced years, his sexual vigor was not impaired (Deut. 34:7). These passages illustrate the biblical witness to the importance of sexual pleasure. But sex is more than simply physical gratification. Sexual physical union, in a mystical way, reflects our spiritual union with God.

Singing the Song of Solomon

No other biblical book best exemplifies the celebration of sexual pleasure than the erotic poetry known as the Song of Songs. Contrary to the "pleasure as sin" mentality prevailing in the development of Christianity, the Song is unique because it vividly describes sexual yearning, debunking the prevalent fear of sexual desire. Here, sex is not reduced to the singular act of copulation, but encompasses the pleasure and passion that builds toward a final release. How did such a lustful book ever make it into the Bible? After all, the book contains no mention of God, no guidance for ethical living, and no historical account concerning the Jewish people. What it does contain is an erotic description of female orgasm, wet dreams, allusions to oral sex, and the sexual frustration of not satisfying physical urges. Could its inclusion in the Word of God confirm that God's Word, contrary to Pope Gregory the Great or St. Benedict, avows sexual pleasure?

Since it became part of the Bible, early Hebrew scholars have read the Song of Songs as a love story, an allegory to Israel's love for God. Although all biblical writings were considered holy, the Song was considered among the earliest rabbinic texts to be the "Holy of Holies."[2] Why would a biblical work celebrating desire and sexual intimacy be considered the "Holy of Holies"—the name for the special place in the ancient Temple where God's presence resided? According to the thirteenth century Torah commentator Rabbi Moshe ben Nahman, God is present among couples in the intimate moment of becoming one flesh. For example, the Sabbath, God's holy day of rest, was considered the ideal time for having sex, thus connecting a holy act with the holy day.[3] In effect, what these rabbinical commentators are insinuating is that the bedchamber becomes the Holy of Holies. To express the concept of sexual intimacy as the Holy of Holies in a Christian understanding is to depict sex as holy communion.

Although not denying the postmodern possibility that a text can contain multiple meanings, it is important to stress from the offset that the Song of Songs is first and foremost a desire for and affirmation of sexual pleasure. The text never mentions procreation, and no attempt is made on the part of the biblical book to reign in, suppress, legislate, control, shame, or punish sexual expression. Quite the contrary. The text subverts the assumption that sex can only occur within a marriage, as these two unmarried lovers (8:7b) play a coy cat-and-mouse game of searching for each other, describing their sexual arousal, lingering over past trysts, and anticipating the ultimate union. They burn for each other with a fire that comes from Yahweh, a fire that no flood can quench or drown (8:6–7). The text immediately starts with foreplay, demanding that the lover "kiss me with the kisses of your mouth" which taste "better than wine" (1:2). The sexual remembrances and desires of the lovers are celebrated throughout eight erotic chapters. As such, the book serves to correct the anti-body aspects that developed within Christianity.

In her book, *Exquisite Desire*, Carey Walsh illustrates the erotic and lustful sexual yearning laced throughout the Song of Songs by providing meaning to the ancient literary symbols used. For example, when the woman's breasts are described as "two fawns, twins of a gazelle" (4:5; 7:3), she explains that the ancient Hebrew mind would have instantly recognized what this description signified—that her breasts are "bouncy, dainty, and even in size (twins)." Elsewhere, her breasts are referred to as "clusters of vine" (7:8). While today a locker room description of women's breasts would more likely compare them to melons or grapefruits (depending on the size), to the ancient Hebrew mind, grapes were characterized as being hard, dark, smooth, ripe, and tart, probably signifying the oral pleasure of savoring, plucking, and nibbling upon the woman's hard, dark, smooth, ripe, and tart nipples.[4]

Fruits and their juices also become signifiers for body parts and the bodily fluids they distill. The constant enjoyment of "eating the choicest fruits" (4:16) becomes a double entendre for enjoying various sexual pleasures, specifically oral pleasures. Her garden (of paradise?) that she opens to her beloved to enter is a euphemism for her vagina. Her garden (vagina) is locked up (4:12) but his "fountain" can make her garden fertile as streams of living water flow down (4:15). The beloved comes into the garden and eats and drinks from it (5:1), he comes down to her garden to enjoy it (6:2). In her garden are clusters of grapes (7:12), triangular in shape, surrounded by foliage, and gorged with juices.[5]

These lovers (who are not married, for her brothers wonder what to do with her on the day she becomes engaged [8:7]), are obviously intimately familiar with each others' bodies. "The curves of your thighs are like jewels, the work from the hands of an artisan. Your navel is like a round goblet that never lacks mixed wine. Your belly is like a heap of wheat, hedged all around with lilies" (7:1–2). He obviously has seen and enjoyed the woman's thigh, belly, and whatever the lilies represent! Likewise, she is familiar with his "belly [which is like] an ivory plate overlaid with sapphires" (5:14), no doubt a reference to his abdominal muscles, which are as precious as sapphires and carved as ivory. She craves for the day when her beloved, like a bag of myrrh (a scent customarily to enhance the lovemaking experience, per Esth. 2:12; Prov. 7:16–18), lies on top of her, between her breasts (1:13). They have already been in the lovemaking "spoon" position, with his left hand under her head and his right hand embracing her (2:6; 8:3). They have fully drunk of each other's bodies to the point of recalling with fondness and desire the lasting pleasure of gazing upon the beloved.[6]

Such drinking is more than simple metaphors. "I would make you drink the spiced wine from the juice of my pomegranates" (8:2). Remember, the seed formation of a pomegranate that has been sliced in half, can resemble a clitoris. If so, the pomegranate, red and hard full of seeds, requires the dexterity of the tongue to retrieve its sweet and tart juice. Likewise, the woman's "juices" she so willingly wants to surrender can only be tasted through oral sex, leaving her with the expectancy of having her lover eat her "honeycomb with [her] honey" (5:1). These tasty treats of "honey and milk" can be found under the beloved's tongue (4:11). In an earlier passage the allusion to oral sex is more pronounced. "My beloved thrust his hand through the opening and I trembled to the core of my being for him. Then I rose to open myself to my beloved, my hands dripped with myrrh, pure myrrh off my fingers, on to the handle of the bolt" (5:4–5). In this passage, the hand of the beloved is found thrust into her "opening" causing her body to shudder in ecstasy. Opening herself to her beloved leads to fingers dripping with myrrh—the scent, as previously mentioned, employed for lovemaking. The same scent is found a few verses later on the lips of the beloved. "His lips are like lilies dropping flowering myrrh" (5:13), raising the question of how the wetness of the woman symbolized by myrrh is now dropping from the lips of her beloved. Later, in returning the favor, he is an apple tree and she gets to "taste his sweet fruit" (2:3).[7]

Subverting Patriarchy

But although she pines for her beloved to enter her garden, and opens it up for him to enjoy it ripened fruit, it remains "her" garden (8:12). His presence is by invitation only, thus subverting the prevalent patriarchal order evident throughout the rest of the biblical text. The Song of Songs not only celebrates sexual pleasure from a woman's perspective, but it achieves this pleasure because she maintains the autonomy of her garden. Reading the Song through a woman's eyes undermines an otherwise androcentric (male-centered) biblical text, overturning woman's supposedly subservient position within society. It is she, and not her brothers, to whom she is required to submit—who determines who will romp through her garden. Because of her autonomy, she seeks her lover on her terms, cautious not to stir up or arouse love until it delights (2:7; 3:5; 8:4). Through mutual giving and vulnerability she gives herself permission to become intoxicated with the sweet wine of lovemaking. But at the end of the day, even though her beloved has tasted her choicest fruits and drank in their juices, it still remains her garden—to be opened again for her beloved at a future time of her choosing.

The text reverses the normative patriarchal order of the day by making the woman's sexual desires and wants the center of the ethical discourse. In the Song of Songs, she is no longer an object, an extension of the male. Instead, she is her own subject who celebrates her sexuality without fear or shame. The woman of the Song seeks sexual intimacy with her beloved, quite apart from the patriarchal structures of her day. Besides desiring her lover's body, she also wants sex apart from a male dominant-female subordinate relationship. Love and sexual pleasure, for her, exist for their own sake! For this reason, the Song is more than simply an erotic psalm alluding to our love for God and/or Jesus. It is a protest song—protesting patriarchy.

The bold rebellion of taking control of her sexuality comes at a price. The city's watchmen, charged with maintaining the law and order of the patriarchal establishment (a law and order designed to justify and privilege male dominance), beat her (5:7). And although the Song does not end on a sad note to show moral consequence for her actions, it does reveal the reality faced by women who chose to rebel against the law and order established to protect patriarchal privilege. Those women who attempt to determine their own destiny could expect a certain degree of hostility from the dominant male-centered culture.

Becoming One with Your Lover

Despite the societal consequences that befall the woman in the Song of Songs, the psalm teaches that both partners in a relationship have a right to become one through sexual pleasure, fulfillment, and satisfaction. What the lovers crave, what they want, and what they ultimately desire, is to become one with each other. This process is possible when a familial relationship exists in a safe environment in which both lovers can be totally vulnerable, so that they can fully relinquish control over the partner and the self; in other words, they lose oneself in each other. The possibility of intimacy among lovers can at times be forfeited due to a fear of it or, more specifically, a fear of not being in control and instead being taken advantage of. The pain of possible betrayal prevents some from becoming vulnerable and totally abandoning themselves to the other.

A 2005 study conducted by the University of Groningen at Copenhagen, Denmark, confirms this. The study showed that women genuinely achieve orgasm when the area of the brain involved in fear is deactivated. Brain scans taken of women being sexually stimulated by their partners showed that those achieving orgasm were able to do so only when fear (and high anxiety) was absent.[8] The study seems to indicate that only when vulnerability exists without fear and anxiety can great sex occur. Only then can climaxing be experienced as an ephemeral yet awe-inspiring burst of intense overwhelming pleasure, creating an ethereal state of being. When two lovers become one with each other, not only is pleasure heightened, but they create *shalom* for the participants. The Hebrew concept of *shalom* is a complex word that denotes peace, solidarity, well-being, and wholeness. When *shalom* is connected to the Hebrew word *shlemut* (which connotes a concept of completeness), the highest level of peace becomes attainable. *Shalom* without *shlemut* simply imply the absence of hostilities, but *shalom* with *shlemut* moves further, toward harmonious completeness. *Shalom* with *shlemut* can be achieved both in sexual union with one's beloved and spiritual union with one's God. As sociologist Meredith McGuire reminds us, "important parallels exist between spiritual and sexual ecstasy."[9] Sex as a cause of *shalom* unites opposites. In the process of uniting opposites—spirit and flesh (matter), life and death, light and darkness, subject and object—wholeness, completeness, and solidarity can be achieved, as this rapture of sexual ecstasy dissolves the boundaries between the lovers. Entwined lover's limbs make it difficult to ascertain where one person begins and the other ends. At the moment of mutual orgasm, lover's subjectivity dissolves as they lose themselves, each in the other. A transcendent alter state results. For lovers, this transcendent *shalom* with *shlemut* is achievable as they lose control of themselves in a safe environment of mutual giving and vulnerability and as they become one flesh.

Ultimately, becoming one is not limited to the lovers, for there is a divine nature in sexual intimacy. We can get to know God as well as we know our beloved. Jesus stated in his prayer to God, "That they [my disciples] all be one. As you Father are in me, and I am in you, may they also be one in us so that world can believe that you sent me" (John 17:21). As God the Father and Son are one in the Trinity (along with the Holy Spirit), so we too can become part of the Trinity, becoming one with God in similar fashion. The possibility of mystical union becomes possible through a Trinitarian awareness—that is, as three Gods in one is a mystery beyond reason, so too is the union of the human soul with God.

Becoming One with God

Saint Bernard of Clairvaux (c. 1090–1153), founder and leader of the monastery at Clairvaux that housed over seven hundred monks, delivered a series of eighty-six sermons on the Song of Songs from 1136 until the time of his death in 1153. He got only as far as the chapter three, verse one. For seventeen years, Saint Bernard preached the erotic Song of Songs to celibate monks, many of whom had enjoyed worldly pleasures before renouncing them to join the order. Much time was spent on the allegorical kisses of Christ, seen as the union of two natures. Saint Bernard was not alone in his allegorical interpretation. As mentioned above, early Hebrew scholars have read the Song of Songs as a symbolic representation of Israel's love for God, while later Christians interpreted the text to symbolize Christ's love for the church.

The casual reader of the biblical text will soon discover the recurring theme of God (or Jesus') relationship to believers described as marriage, complete with sexual metaphors and the emotions sex produces—specifically tenderness, jealousy, and betrayal. The prophets of old would constantly describe God as the husband of Israel. "For your husband is your Maker and Yahweh of hosts is his name" (Isa. 54:5). The prophet Ezekiel provides a more erotic example: "You developed and grew, reaching marriageable age. Your breasts are formed and your hair is grown, but you were naked and bare. I passed by you, gazed upon you, and behold, your time had come, the time for love. I spread my skirt over you and covered your nakedness. I swore to you and entered a covenant with you, declares the Lord Yahweh. You became mine" (16:7–8). In similar fashion, Jesus is portrayed as the bridegroom, and the church as his bride (Mt. 9:15; 25:1–13). And remember, "to the bridegroom belongs the bride [the church]" (Jn. 3:15).

But God's gentle wooing, offers of unconditional love, and the intimacy that comes with union, can quickly turn violently jealous. When God's people worshiped other gods, their unfaithfulness was likened to adultery. "As a woman betrays her lovers, so have you, O House of Israel, have betrayed me" (Jer. 3:20). They were whores for rejecting God's love, deserving to be humiliated, crushed, and cast out, even to the point of being set up for gang rape (Ezek. 23). In an allegorical tale, Jerusalem is described as Oholibah, whoring after Egypt even to the point of bestiality, becoming "infatuated by profligates big-membered as donkeys, ejaculating as violently as stallions" (Ezek. 23:20). To symbolize God's marriage to a whore, he commands the prophet Hosea to do likewise. "Go and take for yourself a whore for a wife, and have children with a whore. For [Israel] has gone whoring away from Yahweh" (Hos. 1:2). So Hosea marries Gomer, paying fifteen silver shekels for her fidelity (Hos. 3:2).

Whether referring to God or Jesus, the paradigm used to describe experiencing the Divine is through a personal relational model, specifically a marriage. But this is not some platonic asexual relationship. Contrary to the dualism of body and soul that was prevalent in the early development of Christianity, God is found in our sensuality. God is love, love understood as agape (unconditional) and eros (erotic), absent of any imposed human dichotomy. Divine-human relationships are biblically understood as being rooted in the ultimate intimacy between partners, with violation of fidelity described in the sexual terms of unfaithfulness.

So if God can be found in our sensuality, where is God while a couple is engaging in sex? If it is true that God is present when two or more gather in God's name, and if it is true that God in Jesus lives in us, then is it also true that when a couple united in God have sex, God is also present? Is this an active presence? Does God's presence allow the couple to become co-creators with God? In the creation of one body? In the possible creation of new life? Such questions move us beyond reducing sex to simply a gift from God. Such questions ponder God's omnipresence (God is everywhere at all times) even at moments of extreme intimacy.

The concept of sex with God does not mean God is physical, for all Christian groups confirm and understand God as spirit. Rather, sexuality symbolizes ultimate communion. Sexuality becomes the means by which to understand the mystery of our oneness with God. If God's defining characteristic is love, then profound passionate love is the only foundation for any relationship between God and humans. Jesus who answered the question "Which is the greatest commandment?" by stating: "You shall love Yahweh your God with all your heart, and with all your soul, and with all your mind" (Mt. 22:37). The love we are commanded to have for God imitates the love I hold for my beloved wife, because I love her with all my heart, all my soul, and all my mind. The spiritual rapture in which oneness with God is achieved, and the sexual union in which oneness with one's beloved is reached, produces similar effects. Sexual intercourse with my beloved becomes sacred because it is the ultimate celebration of love, and thus a precursor to the type of spiritual relationship and love celebration we can expect to have with our Lord! As great as sex is between humans, it is still but a pale reflection, a shadow, a poor substitute, compared with the ultimate intimate relationship we can expect to have with our God.

But how do mortals become one with God? In the same way we become one with the beloved—through mutual giving of each other in an atmosphere of total vulnerability. The Gospel of Mark expresses this paradox: "For whoever desires to save their soul shall lose it but whoever loses their soul for my sake and the gospel, this one shall be saved" (8:35). By losing control of one's life, a life in God is gained. But not only does the human become vulnerable, so too does the Divine. Vulnerable unto death! Life is achieved through self-negation, the giving up of control before a God also willing to become vulnerable and mutually give of Godself. The self and the Absolute find union in the self-negation of each.

The negation of the self means the emptying of one's appetites that hinder union with one's beloved, both the temporal lover and the eternal Beloved. Self-negation demands a death to self through a renunciation and rejection of possessions: the possession of power over the Other, the possession of "rights" over the Other, the possession of privilege before the Other. When the self dies in the Absolute (as expressed in Galatians 2:20: "With Christ I have been crucified, and I live, but no longer I, rather Christ in me"), the Absolute dies in the self. Union with God is the simultaneous self-negation of the Divine on the cross and the self-negation of the individual before that cross. At the foot of the cross, the dichotomy between sacred and secular ends as the Trinity makes room for humanity. Two spaces become one. The self becomes more than just "dust and ashes." The self, through its self-negation, becomes one with the Absolute.

For Juan de la Cruz (1542–1591), the Discalced Carmelite friar, becoming one with the Absolute is "the prayer of union," the indwelling of the Spirit of God in the soul. This *mystagogy* (the gradual initiation of the believer's soul into the mysteries of the indwelling Spirit by one's experience in this mysticism) is described metaphorically as a spiritual marriage between Christ and the soul, the soul possessing and being possessed by Christ. Juan de la Cruz wrote:

> The Bridegroom [Christ]: "Beneath the apple tree [the cross]: There I took you for my own, There I offered you my hand, And restored you, Where your mother was corrupted."...

> The Bride [soul]: "There he gave me his breast; There he taught me a sweet and living knowledge; And I gave myself to him, Keeping nothing back; There I promised to be his bride."[10]

Both Juan de la Cruz and Teresa de Ávila (1515–82), a Carmelite nun, described the mystical union with God as a spiritual marriage in which the human soul's relationship with God is the mutual relationship existing within the Trinity between Father and Son. Not only does the soul get to know God, but through this relationship the soul gets to know itself. Love that leads to ultimate union creates the effect of a likeness between lover and object loved. For the soul to know anything, it must become like the object of its knowledge. This "union of likeness" of God and the human soul is what makes possible both self-revelation and a purely spiritual knowledge with God. God ceases to be an object and becomes instead another self spiritually present in the lover.[11] Mystical union with the Divine can best be understood as touches of "mutuality" in "accord with the intensity of the yearning and ardors of love."[12] This mutuality and equality existing between God and soul is expressed in love terms—love as eros where God is "touched, felt, and tasted,"[13] and as such becomes the paradigm for relationships between earthly lovers.

The biblical word used to refer to the union of God with the human soul is *yada*, translated as "know," the same word used to describe sexual intimacy between a man and a woman, as in "Adam *knew* Eve his wife, and she conceived" (Gen. 4:1). Of the 949 times that *yada* appears in the Hebrew Bible, 22 times are direct references to sexual intercourse. This suggests *yada* can be used as a double entendre. To "know" is be vulnerable and exposed in more ways than one. Does the mutual self-negation of the Absolute and of the self imply such an intimate union? Yes, in a mystical or spiritual sense. Thus St. Paul, who can only see but a "dim reflection in a mirror," would pine for the day when he would "know as fully as [he] is known" (1 Cor. 13:12).

The writings of Teresa de Avila reveal this type of intimate union, in which the soul becomes immersed in God, whose transcendence is understood as relational. For her, these mystical contemplations on being fully known by God lead to a burning desire for union manifested as ecstasy. Gianlorenzo Bernini's masterpiece, *The Ecstasy of St. Teresa* captures in marble the moment of Teresa's spiritual penetration, when the Divine and the human meet, embrace, and become one. The erotic sculpture, located at the Cornaro Chapel in Rome, reveals a swooning, toe-curled Teresa at the instant of rapture beneath the figure of an angel ready to impale her by thrusting his spear (a traditional phallic symbol) into her exposed breast. In her own words, she describes how she abandons herself to God with obvious sexual overtures:

> In [the angel's] hand I saw a great golden spear, and at the iron tip there appeared to be a point of fire. This he plunged into my heart several times so that it penetrated to my entrails. When he pulled it out, I felt he took them with it, and left me utterly consumed by the great love of God. The pain was so severe that it made me utter several moans. The sweetness caused by this intense pain is so extreme that one cannot possibly wish it to cease, nor is one's soul then content with anything but God… So gentle is this wooing which takes place between God and the soul.[14]

Teresa encounters God, described in sexually symbolic language signifying a higher reality, one achieved through the vulnerable state of the self dying to itself. The use of sexually charged terms to describe her role as the "bride of Christ" obviously does not signify a physical encounter communicated to the intellect through corporeal senses, but a spiritual love that craves oneness in the same way passionate lovers do. Through self-negation, a mutual encounter based on a relationship between two subjects, as opposed to two objects, occurs. This act, which we call an encounter with the Divine, is the saving faith mortal humans crave—a new life in God that transcends the physical and the grave. The core of union that occurs in the "center of the soul" becomes the *dolor sabroso* (the delicious pain) of St. Teresa, the ecstasy of God's oneness with each individual soul.

But the "delightful union" of rapture vividly described by Teresa falls short of what she also calls the "true union," a union attained with a great deal of effort. Like any deep relationship between two lovers, it is a union of intimacy that takes place over time as two become one in more ways than simply physical. For example, my wife and I have been one for so long that a simple glance, sigh, posture, or facial expression by one is fully understood by the other. No words are needed to convey what the other is thinking or feeling, such as how one partner begins a sentence and the other finishes it. Teresa described this true union with God in similar terms: "two persons of reasonable intelligence, who love each other dearly, seem able to understand each other without making any signs, merely by their looks." Similarly, God and the soul glance at each other, "as these two lovers do: the Spouse in the Song [of Songs], I believe, says this to the Bride."[15]

Spiritual Ecstasy for the Everyday

The mystic union with God, like any healthy sexual relationship, moves from a delightful union, characterized as a short lived passionate rapture occurring at the moment of climax, toward a true union of daily intimacy, characterized by the constant presence of the beloved. True union with God occurs in the everyday. Among many Hispanic theologians and believers, God, who takes on human flesh, still continues to enflesh Godself in the everyday lives and experiences of those who resides on the underside of society—those who live on the margins of power and privilege. An important element in ethical and theological reflection is what has come to be referred to as *lo cotidiano*, the literal Spanish word for "the everyday." The everyday experience of the world's oppressed people becomes the starting point in how God's presence is understood. The salvific experience of God—in the here and now, not just in some ethereal hereafter—is experienced by the marginalized in their daily struggle for dignity, justice, and civil rights. The spirituality of disenfranchised groups is contextual, making their everyday experiences the subject and source of religious thought.[16] Of course, God's presence cannot be limited to the trials and tribulations of those who suffer. Although it is true that God comforts those who mourn, God also dances with those who, in spite of hardship, rejoice! God is not just present in the struggle for life, but also in the passion for life's pleasure!

Like a beloved who shares in both the struggles and joys of life, God's presence testifies God's love for us. The love God calls us to reciprocate becomes the standard by which all other human relationships are measured. This love becomes a moral imperative toward creating justice—the doing of love—toward our neighbors. This concept of connecting justice to love leads to the second part of 'the greatest commandment,' "You shall love your neighbor as yourself" (Mt. 22:39).

5

Jesús: Androgynous?[1]

Part of the Latino/a *ajiaco* [mix] identity, which is all too often masked, is our gender diversity. We know Jesús was born as a male. There is no question that he was physically male, a fact proven when we consider that the Roman custom was to strip the condemned and crucify them naked to increase their humiliation, shame and vulnerability.[2] But if Jesús is the ultimate reflection of the Divine, does this imply that God is also male? Such an assumption has led to centuries of patriarchy. And yet, if Jesús is a liberator, then how does the materiality of his body engender liberation for nonmales?

We are told that God dispatched a messenger named Gabriel, whose name means, "God is my strength," to the town of Nazareth, an insignificant barrio located in Galilee. There he approached a young teenaged virgin, a nobody, a "lowly servant girl" who was betrothed to a man named José, a distant descendant of Israel's famed King David. The messenger went to her and said, "Rejoice, O blessed one, for the Lord is with you. Blessed are you among women." His words greatly troubled María and she wondered what this messenger's words might mean. "Do not be afraid María," Gabriel continued, "for you have found favor in the eyes of God. You will conceive and give birth to a child, and you will call him Jesús. He will be great and will be called the son of the Most High. The Lord your God will give him the throne of his father David, and he will forever rule over Jacob's descendants, his reign will know no end." "But how could this be," María asked the messenger, "since I am still a virgin, unknown and untouched by man?" The messenger responded, "The Spirit of God will come on top of you, and the potency of the Most High will overshadow you. Thus, the holy one who is begotten will be called the Son of God" (Lk. 1:26–35, 48).

Central to Christian thought is the immaculate conception of Jesús who was born of a virgin. This assertion has lead biologist Edward Kessel to draw very interesting conclusions concerning Christ's androgynous identity due to his parthenogenetic birth. We are taught by biology that males have XY chromosomes. Women, on the other hand have XX chromosomes. Upon conception, each parent contributes one of their chromosomes to the fetus. Women only have an X chromosome to contribute while the male can contribute either an X or a Y chromosome. If the man contributes his X chromosome, then the fetus will develop into a girl because it has the combined XX chromosomes. If, however, the man contributes his Y chromosome, then the fetus will develop into a boy because it has the XY chromosomes.

Further complicating Jesucristo's conception is the understanding that the Spirit who came on top of María has consistently been viewed throughout the biblical text as feminine. Both the Hebrew word (*ruah*) and the Greek word (*pneuma*) for Spirit are female gendered. So, if there is no human male figure with a XY chromosome involved in María's pregnancy (remembering she is unknown and untouched by man) then Jesús cannot contain a Y chromosome required to determine male physical identity. The literal acceptance of Jesús' virgin birth would conclude that he cannot be biologically a male, although he obviously was physically a male as attested to by his crucifixion, and much earlier, his circumcision.[3] When we consider that Scripture and centuries of Christian theology has taught us that Jesús is the exact imprint of God's very being (Heb. 1:3); we can begin to better appreciate the inclusiveness of Genesis 1:27, where: "God created humanity in God's image, in God's image God created them, male and female God created them." Both male and female and everything in between and beyond find their worth and dignity in the image of God fully revealed in the intersexuality of Jesús. To say that Jesucristo exists in the in-between spaces of male/female, human/divine, Jew/Gentile is to say that Jesús is a *bilingüe*, a bilingual.

6

Why Does God Need a Penis?[1]

Close your eyes and imagine what God looks like. More than likely, most pictured a male body. Maybe the image is something similar to Michelangelo's renowned mural *The Creation of Adam* (1512) in the Sistine Chapel, in which God is illustrated as an old but well-built white man with a flowing white beard. Eurocentric art has taught, normalized, and legitimized a white male image of God. And it is this image of God that justifies patriarchy and influences a sexual ethics detrimental to women. No discussion concerning sexual ethics can take place until we first debunk God's purported male gender.

Most of us refer to God as a "He" without giving it a second thought because we construct "Him" in our minds as male. Yet the biblical text teaches us that when humans were created, they were formed in the very image of God. According to the first creation story found in Genesis 1:27: "God created *adam* in God's image, in God's image God created him, male and female God created them." Most Bibles read by Americans have translated the Hebrew word *adam* as "man." The verse is hence rendered: "God created man in God's image."

But is rendering *adam* as "man" the proper translation? In Hebrew, *adam* can be used to refer to a proper name, as in Adam, the husband of Eve. *Adam* can also be translated to refer to a male-gender individual, as opposed to the Hebrew word *issah* for "woman." And finally, *adam* can be used to refer to mankind, as in all of humanity. Now the text tells us that when God created *adam*, *adam* was created as male and female by God. So, if we translate *adam* to mean the person Adam, or render *adam* as "man" as opposed to a woman, does this mean that Adam the person or generic man was created with both male and female genitalia? If so, was Plato correct in imaging a primordial split? But what if we were to translate *adam* to mean humanity? Is humanity male and female? Yes, both males and females make up humanity. For this reason, when reading Genesis 1:27, "humanity" is a better translation for the word *adam*.

The fact remains, however, that for the vast majority of Judeo-Christian history, God has been thought of as a male, just as Michelangelo painted him on the ceiling of the Sistine Chapel. But what does it mean that we conceive of God as male, complete with a penis? If the functions of a penis are to urinate and to copulate, why would Yahweh need a penis? Or does the penis have a spiritual meaning? If men conceive of women as castrated by the Almighty Himself and as envious of what only God and men possess, then, the reasoning goes, should it not be natural for woman to submit to men—who, unlike women, are created like God? In the nineteenth century, Sigmund Freud (1856–1939) came to the conclusion, from a purely secular standpoint, that women are envious of men's penises. If man, like God, has a penis, does it not stand to reason that all who have penises are closer to the perfect image of God? Following this line of thinking, the penis itself becomes a sacred object shared by God and males.

With this view in mind, it should not appear strange that in biblical times the great patriarchs of the faith, such as Abraham and Israel, placed great spiritual value on their penises by swearing oaths upon their genitals (Gen. 24:2–3; 47:29–31). More disturbing are biblical accounts concerning penises, such as the time God tried to kill Moses but was prevented by Zipporah, Moses' quick-thinking wife, who cut off the foreskin of her son's penis and rubbed it on Moses' penis, thus appeasing God (Ex. 4:24–26). Or King David's winning of his wife Michal through the gift of the foreskins of a hundred Philistine penises (2 Sam. 3:14).

What is important to note is that the sign of the covenant between God and man begins with the penis—specifically, cutting off its foreskin through the ritual of circumcision (Gen. 17:10–14). How then do women enter into a covenant with God if there is no penis to circumcise? Reserving that covenant for men only, the privilege of having a penis must therefore be protected at all costs from the threat of women. Hence the biblical enjoinment that if during a brawl, a woman "puts out her hand and lay hold of [a man's] genitals, then you shall cut off her hand and your eyes shall not pity her" (Deut. 25:11–12).

It is true that the Bible refers to God as a "He," but God is also said to have eyes, ears, a strong arm, and so on. God is anthropomorphized and given human features so that humans' temporal minds can attempt to conceive the eternal. The biblical text is not trying to tell us what color God's eyes are; rather, it is meant to convey the concept that God sees, so the act of seeing is understood by humans through the symbolical language of giving God eyes. The same concept is in play when the biblical text says God is a burning bush (Ex. 3:2) or a consuming fire (Heb. 12:29). Does this mean God is combustive? No, the symbol of burning fire helps us to better comprehend that which is beyond comprehension. And when the Bible refers to God as a mother who would not forget the child from her womb suckling her breast (Isa. 49:15) or as birthing Israel (Deut. 32:18), this isn't intended to mean that God lactates and has a vagina; these too are symbols to aid our comprehension.

Contemporary scholars Paul Tillich (1886–1965) and Paul Ricoeur (1913–2005) were correct in asserting that one can only speak of or describe God through the use of symbols, connecting the meaning of one thing recognized by a given community that is comprehensible (such as *father*) with another thing that is beyond our ability to fully understand (that is, God). As important as symbols are to help us better grasp the incomprehensible essence of the Divine, they are incapable of exhausting the reality of God. To take symbolic language literally (for example, God is exclusively male or female) leads to the absurd (for example, God has a penis or a vagina) and borders on idolatry (the creation of hierarchies in relationships according to who is closer to the Divine ideal). To speak of God as male, as fire, or as mother is to speak of God in symbols that, through analogies, convey limited knowledge for understanding what God is like.

The radical nature of the Hebrew God, as described in Genesis, is that unlike the gods of the surrounding Canaanite neighbors, Yahweh has no genitalia. The gods of the people surrounding the Hebrews were depicted in small statuettes about the size of a hand. If these gods were female they were manifested with large, pendulous breasts, broad hips, and prominently featured vaginas. The male god statuettes usually were depicted with large, protruding and erect penises. Even though this was the norm for fertility gods, the god of the Hebrews, who was also responsible for creating and sustaining all that has life, had neither breasts nor a penis. The revolutionary concept of the Hebrew god is that this God was neither male nor female and thus was male *and* female. In short, this God named Yahweh was beyond gender. For this reason it was considered blasphemy to make any graven image of the true God (Ex. 20:4), for such a God was beyond the imagination of finite minds.

To give God a penis is to subjugate women to all those who also have penises. As feminist theologian Mary Daly wrote, "If God is male, then the male is God."[2] If men are gods, then women, because they lack a penis, fall short of divinity. Being less than men, women, as understood via the biblical text, were reduced to the status of property, incubators, the weaker sex, and the fallen Eve.

PART THREE

———

Engaging In Sex

7

Fifty Shades toward Ethical Christian-Based Sadomasochism[1]

Much ado has been made about the blockbuster *Fifty Shades of Grey*, a disappointing screen adaptation of E. L. James's poorly written bestseller. And yet, the film's opening weekend box office take was $81.7 million! The allure of titillating forbidden desire sells. By now we are all familiar with Christian Grey, the young, good-looking kinky billionaire bachelor who seduces the innocent Anastasia Steele to participate in sadomasochism (S&M). Although the film could have proven to be groundbreaking, exploring enriching ways to express our sexuality; the film instead seems to have reinforced traditional gender roles with a certain glorification of the sexual abuse of women.

That said—I am left wondering if an ethical S&M ethics that celebrates our sexuality can be constructed. The problem in pursuing this loathly goal is overcoming 2,000 years of sexual baggage based on a Christianity that has gotten sex wrong. Rather than celebrating human sexuality, Christianity's disdain for the body infused a form of S&M in our relationship with a domineering God bent on our humiliation whenever we choose to explore our bodies.

We see this at play when, for example, Pope Gregory the Great (540? to 604 C.E.) recounts an episode experienced by St. Benedict (480–543 C.E.) on how he conquered sexual desire. The Pope wrote:

> The moment [the Tempter] left, [St. Benedict] was seized with an unusually violent temptation. The evil spirit recalled to his mind a woman he had once seen, and before he realized it his emotions were carrying him away. Almost overcome in the struggle, he was on the point of abandoning the lonely wilderness, when suddenly with the help of God's grace he came to himself. He then noticed a thick patch of nettles and briers next to him. Throwing his garments aside he flung himself into the sharp thorns and stinging nettles. There he rolled and tossed until his

46

whole body was in pain and covered with blood. Yet, once he had *conquered pleasure through suffering,* his torn and bleeding skin served to drain the poison of temptation from his body [author's emphasis]. Before long, the pain that was burning his whole body had put out the fires of evil in his heart. It was by exchanging these two fires that he gained the victory over sin. So complete was his triumph that from then on, as he later told his disciples, he never experienced another temptation of this kind.[2]

As I read the ascetic life of saints like Benedict, I cannot help but wonder about the existing relationship between seeking submission to God and S&M. Does the quest to be dominated, or in the case of Benedict for physical pain, become a form of sexual pleasure? The concept of S&M, a composite of both sadism and masochism that developed several centuries after the ascetic life of saints, might help us better understand the ambivalent relationship between agonizing sexual pleasure and agonizing physical pain.

Sadism, named after the Marquis de Sade (1740–1814 C.E.), is the practice of inflicting violence on the other person to stimulate one's own sexual pleasure. Masochism, named after Leopold von Sacher-Masoch (1836–95 C.E.), is the practice of deriving sexual satisfaction and pleasure from receiving pain and being violently dominated. The underlying assumption of S&M is that constant exposure to pain eventually become pleasurable. The cultivation of this stimulus slowly replaces the ability to become sexually aroused by any other means, such as genital stimulation. The infliction or receiving of painful stimulus becomes necessary to experience intense and extreme sexual arousal. And yet, the pleasure received from S&M is not so much the pain received or inflicted, but rather the knowledge of control over another.

Are the extreme cases of self-denial and self-mutilation practiced by the early Christian ascetics in their desire to pursue heavenly pleasure a sanctified form of S&M? Was pleasure achieved through self-flagellation? If so, did we develop a type of Christianity where the ultimate desire to please God is satisfied through the prolongation of human pain?

No doubt the Christianity that developed found pleasure in the state of being dominated by God. In the early Christian ascetics' renunciation of sexual pleasure, did they turn God into a dominatrix? If so, this creates an image of a God who erotically desires humans to self-inflict pain, as though God would take pleasure from humans' repression of pleasure. The idea of God as dominatrix would then seem to justify the repression of those who fall short of the ascetic ideal. Furthermore, because of the intertwining of religion and politics, the sexual repression that developed in Christianity also became manifested in the political arena. Political repression that brought pain to commoners in this world was offset with the promise of heavenly bliss in the next.

Benedict illustrates how S&M exists in the religious antipleasure views of the early Christian believers who linked pain—specifically, the self-deprivation of sexual pleasure—with salvation. Self-denial of the flesh's desires was deemed essential for achieving an elevated spiritual plateau. We can even detect an element of S&M in the theology of atonement, developed by Anselm of Canterbury (1033–1109 c.e.). According to his theology, God's honor was offended by the sins of humans (specifically original sin), so he had to respond: either by punishing humans (because God is all holy) or by demanding a substitute—a sacrifice to take the place of the offending humans (because God, after all, is merciful). Hence the need for Jesus to violently die on the cross, shedding his blood to compensate for the iniquity of humans. In other words, God, to satisfy God's vanity, must humiliate, torture, and brutally kill God's child, Jesus, rather than the true object of God's wrath, so that God can be placated. The problem with Anselm's theory is that it casts God as the ultimate child abuser who is satisfied by the domination, humiliation, and pain of God's child.

So what is it about S&M in human relationships, in which bondage, humiliation, and physical pain serve as the ultimate aphrodisiac and arousal comes from an overt dominant-subordinate power relationship? Because of the abuse many women face in relationships marked by domestic violence, there is much concern about whether S&M should be considered an acceptable sexual practice. I suggest that if we employ orthoeros (a term I coined to signify correct erotic love), guidelines rather than rigid rules can make S&M an acceptable form of sexual gratification.

Sexual pleasure is God-given. This doesn't mean that sex should be our ultimate goal in life, or it becomes an idol. But this also means that sex isn't wrong. Sex is part of the human experience to be enjoyed, and that pleasure should not be limited to men. According to the Talmud, men are expected to meet and satisfy the sexual needs of their wives.[3] In the privacy of the bedchamber, couples can participate in whatever kind of sexually satisfying activity they choose. Their sexual activity, according to the Mishnah Torah, can be "natural or unnatural."[4]

Based on this healthier understanding of sexuality, I have argued for a sexual ethics based on 1 Corinthians 10:23–24 that states: "All things are permissible to me, but not all things are beneficial. All things are lawful to be, but not all things are edifying. Let no one seek their own good, but instead what is good for others." While all sex is permissible to me, not all sexual encounters are beneficial, especially if it ignores the well being of my partner. In practice, all sexual acts "natural or unnatural" are permissible as long as they at least remain (1) safe, (2) consensual, (3) based on a trusting vulnerability, and (4) mutually pleasing.

If consenting adults in a familial relationship in the privacy of their bedchamber mutually choose to engage in S&M, then, like any other sexual activity, it should occur only in the context of orthoeros code; that is, in a context in which unconditional love is linked to a justice-based relationship. S&M sexual acts can only be entered into with an uncoerced agreement to remain safe, sane, and consensual. If S&M becomes a form of role-playing, then clear signals and open communication are required to delineate the boundaries between, on the one hand, play and pleasure, and on the other, violation and pain. Fantasy role-playing can only be acceptable if both parties remain in full and complete control of what is occurring. There is a fine line between mock sexual games and the terrifying feeling of having no control over what is happening to you. When either party loses this type of control, their vulnerability and trust are betrayed.

Mr. Grey will see you now, or maybe not.[5]

8

The Private Sin[1]

For many who are single, either by choice or circumstance, masturbation provides a way of stimulating sexual gratification and reducing sexual tension. According to the all-too-familiar joke, 90 percent of all individuals admit to having masturbated and the other 10 percent are lying. Most studies show that for the vast majority, masturbation starts around the age of ten and continues until death.[2] Despite the fact that almost every human being over that age has masturbated at some time, and even though there is no biblical justification for the prohibition of masturbation, it has long been considered a sin among Christians, even today.

The original belief behind this view was that the woman, as an incubator, only provided nutrition to the creation of life. The woman's womb was like a field waiting for the insemination of the male seed, which contained all the necessary substance required for human life. Within the male sperm existed the entire potential child. The womb, by contrast, was neutral, adding nothing to the child's genetic makeup. Therefore, to waste male sperm, as in the case of masturbation, was to literally destroy the potential for human life. For these same reasons contraceptive devices, while preventing pregnancy, still spilled the male seed, so by the same reasoning they are akin to murder. Religious leaders like Martin Luther saw onanism as a sin more hideous than heterosexual rape, because at least rape was in accordance with nature, whereas masturbation was considered to be unnatural.[3]

Historically, medical authorities equated masturbation and sexual promiscuity with insanity. During the late fifteenth century, syphilis made its appearance in Europe. Untreated, syphilis could lead to insanity. Early observation of this disease found a correlation between those who succumbed to the disease with those who were sexually active, specifically those who patronized brothels. The primitive medical establishment, unaware that syphilis was a sexually transmitted disease (a discovery that would not be made until the nineteenth century), concluded that those who engaged in excessive sexual activity, including masturbation, would become feebleminded, if not insane.

During Victorian England, cages were constructed that fitted over the boy's genitals during sleeping hours to avoid masturbation. This cage was locked, and some were even spiked to prevent the boy from sexually stimulating himself. To "cure" those girls who wished to sexually stimulate themselves, a clitoridectomy (the partial or total removal of the external part of the clitoris) was an acceptable medical practice. Throughout the nineteenth and twentieth centuries, this medical procedure was common in English-speaking nations (until 1946 in the United States) as a means of stopping masturbation. The girl was "cured" because the procedure reduced the possibility of obtaining sexual arousal.[4] Although penis cages for boys are no longer used, the mutilation of women's genitalia continues to be practiced in a number of cultures. It is quite common in Indonesia and many countries of sub-Saharan Africa, east-Africa, Egypt, Sudan, and the Arabian Peninsula. As of 2005, Amnesty International estimates that 135 million of the world's girls and women have undergone genital mutilation, and two million girls a year are at risk of mutilation—approximately six thousand per day. The practice is so common that it has reemerged in Europe and the United States among immigrants.[5]

Another reason why masturbation was frowned upon by the church was the belief that male sperm was a fluid that contained male energy, so that wasting this energy would also lead to feebleness. For this reason, an ascetic life, even within marriage, supposedly secured a long and healthy life. To constantly be losing one's seed was judged akin to Samson's getting a haircut, putting male strength and virility in jeopardy. Even today the common advice persists that boxers and other athletes should abstain from ejaculating, so as not to risk impairing their athletic performance in the boxing ring or on the field.

Early in the twentieth century, the scientific community began to study and test the effects of masturbation. Even though masturbation has historically been taught to have negative physical and emotional consequences, the medical health community has found no negative correlation between masturbation and a person's physical or emotional health. In fact, recently researchers have suggested that men who regularly masturbate can reduce their risk of developing prostate cancer.[6] And there is no evidence of a cause and effect between masturbation and mental disturbance, with the possible exception of those who feel guilty because they believe masturbation to be a sin.

Despite these findings by the medical community, masturbation is still taboo among many modern-day Christians, leading many to struggle with a culturally imposed guilt. Some Christians who wish to refrain from masturbation will wear a masturband, a black plastic bracelet worn on the wrist. You continue to wear the band as long as you restrain from masturbating, but if you succumb, then you must remove the bracelet, making your hidden shame public. This prohibition is unnecessary when one considers that the Bible is silent on the topic of masturbation with the exception of a few verses.... The Song of Songs (5:2–6) vividly describes a woman dreaming of her beloved "thrust[ing] his hand into the hole," only to awaken with her "fingers dripped with myrrh," in other words, with her own wetness, the product of a wet dream.

The biblical story that has historically been used to condemn masturbation is the story of Onan, found in Genesis 38:1–11. According to the biblical text, Tamar married Judah's oldest son Er. However, Er offended God (his offense is unknown) and died as a result. Unfortunately he died childless. Following tradition, Onan, Er's brother, took Tamar to perform his duty of impregnating her so that a child could be born in his brother's name. But whenever Onan copulated with Tamar he would pull out before climaxing and thus spill his seed on the ground. God found this offensive, so he slew Onan. Christian commentators have historically understood Onan's sin to be masturbation, because he "spilled his seed on the ground"; *onanism,* a synonym for masturbation, is derived from his name. But Onan's sin was not masturbation. According to the text, he spilled his seed on the ground because he deliberately abdicated his duty of ensuring that his brother's name would continue. To be specific, his sin was avoiding his levirate obligation to his dead brother by performing *coitus interruptus.*

Many claim Jesus spoke indirectly about masturbation during the Sermon on the Mount. He states, "You have heard that it was said to the ancients, 'Do not commit adultery.' But I say to you, that anyone looking at a woman to lust after her has already committed adultery with her in his heart" (Mt. 5:27–28). . . .[T]he emphasis of this passage may have more to do with debunking the predominant male view that adultery only applied to women, by suggesting that even gazing upon a women with intent was enough to find a man guilty. Still, because a certain degree of lusting is required to achieve climax during masturbation (especially for men), is Jesus stating that masturbation is akin to adultery? This question finds traction when we consider that in the verse that follows, Jesus stated that if our eye (by which we see the woman that we lust after) causes offense, it should be plucked out. Jesus then states, "And if your right hand causes you to offend, cut it off and throw it away" (Mt. 5:30). Could this be a reference to masturbation, for what we do with our hand completes the lust begun with the eye? Rabbinical literature seems to think so. According to the *Niddah* (a treatise found in rabbinical texts—the Mishnah, Tosefta, and both Talmuds—about the state of uncleanness), masturbation is referred to as "adultery by the hand"[7]—praiseworthy among women, but for men, the hand should be "cut off."[8]

The physical purity code of the Hebrew Bible also labels those who experience wet dreams (whether or not they masturbate during their waking hours) as unclean and defiled, needing purification (Deut. 23:11–12). Remember, according to the Jewish mind-set, unconsciously violating a purity law was not understood as a sin in the more modern Christian sense. It meant avoiding dirt—that is, becoming unclean—a concept that has shaped moral discourse. The individual experiencing a wet dream is not morally depraved, but dirtied by the body fluids.

We can conclude, however, that Jesus' focus during his Sermon on the Mount was not masturbation. He was replacing the traditional physical purity code with an insistence of maintaining a purity of the heart—a purity of intent. As Paul would write, "I know and am persuaded in the Lord Jesus that nothing is unclean by itself, except to the one who regards anything as unclean it is" (Rom. 14:14). The issue of purity ceases to be the actual sexual act (masturbation) and instead becomes the intent of maintaining unjust sexual or social relationships (males, unlike women, engaging in adultery without penalty). If the act has the intent of continuing the objectification of the Other, or of retarding a familial relationship, then for that person, that particular act (whether it be sexual or not) may be wrong. In Jesus' example he places the emphasis on the intent of married men, who traditionally could never be guilty of adultery unless they had sex with another man's property. For such men, if even thinking of violating their familial relationship was enough to pronounce them guilty, how much [guiltier] would they be if they were to act on those thoughts?

Even without specific biblical censure to back them up, many claim that masturbation is detrimental because it is self-centered, due to its solitary nature aimed at self pleasuring. This focus inward was believed to eventually cause separation between the individual and their beloved. But if we remember the church's antipleasure views… it should not be surprising that it was prohibited, even though most people masturbate in this solitary way in their youth and still grow up to be involved in loving and healthy partnered relationships. Although a dimension of intimacy may be lacking in masturbation when compared to intercourse, masturbation can still create bonds between loving partners in many situations. Masturbation can enhance coupling, as in the case of injury, disability, or old age in which the use of one's sexual organs is difficult if not impossible. Masturbation can serve to bring people together emotionally, as in the case of couples separated due to travel, work, or war. Masturbating can help to heal grief, as in the case of a widow or widower. Mutual masturbation during foreplay, especially as a means of increasing the possibility of orgasm, brings lovers closer, both physically and emotionally. Those who are not in a familial relationship may masturbate to relieve sexual energy along with the stress and tension it creates. Those who masturbate are often able to share with their partners suggestions on what leads them to an organism. The biblical text is silent on the use of masturbation in situations like these. We don't have to be. Because of its potential of enhancing great sex, masturbation can play a role in the sexuality of Christians.

9

Testimonies of the First Man and Woman[1]

Genesis 2:24–25:

Born to mutuality and harmony, a man and a woman live in a garden where nature and history unite to celebrate the one flesh of sexuality. Naked without shame or fear, this couple treats each other with tenderness and respect. Neither escaping nor exploiting sex, they embrace and enjoy it. . . In this setting, there is no male dominance, no female subordination, and no stereotyping of either sex.

—Phyllis Trible[2]

For this reason, a man will leave his father and mother, from whom his own bone and flesh was formed, cleave to his wife, and the two will become one flesh. Genesis provides a definition for the ideal marriage before it becomes institutionalized and before the first human rebellion (or fall) occurs. This ideal marriage is presented not as a covenant, which is more apropos for business contractual transactions, but as a familial relationship rooted in the action "clings to," or "cleaves to" (NRSV, KJV, RSV), that is, sexual intercourse. This union, this oneness, is even evident in the word play used: 'îš for man is found inside 'iššâ for woman. We are told that this familial bond created between the two is to be stronger than the previous relationship existing between parents and child. It is interesting to note that the man leaves a father and mother, even though Adam as the first man supposedly had no father or mother. No mention of the woman's parents is made, thus reinforcing the concept of her independence from patriarchal structures, which unfortunately, will soon radically change with the first rebellion.

Although the passage may provide a paradigm for an ideal marriage, we must use caution in assuming that the "cleaving" that took place between the first man and the first woman was a marriage as we understand it today. Marriage was neither required in the biblical text nor universally accepted throughout early Western Christendom as a prerequisite for sex. Before marriage was elevated to a sacrament during the Council of Trent (1563), it was not regarded as sacred. The ideas that marriage had to be licensed by the state or sanctioned by the church are modern innovations. Marriage was mainly a civil arrangement void of clergy officiated ceremonies. The definition of marriage has always been evolving, from an understanding of marriage along the lines of property rights, to marriage as a means for procreation, to a family-dominated arrangement designed to protect wealth, to more recently as a response to attraction, love, and mutual respect. In fact, what we call the traditional marriage is quite a modern invention (since about the seventeenth century). Our modern definition of the traditional marriage based on love, trust, vulnerability, and commitment are really not traditional; it is also not biblical. However, in this verse in Genesis we do find the seed of mutuality and vulnerability upon which our present ideal understanding of the concept of marriage can be based.

Ironically, what has come to be called "the biblical definition of a traditional marriage" is not rooted in the biblical text. Biblical marriage, as it came to be defined after the first rebellion, meant male ownership of women who existed for sexual pleasure. Upon marriage, a woman's property and her body became the possession of her new husband. As the head of the household, men (usually between the ages of eighteen to twenty-four years old) had nearly unlimited rights over wives and children. A woman became available for men's possession soon after she reached puberty (usually eleven to thirteen years old), that is, when she became physically able to produce children. The familial relationship based on mutuality and vulnerability as described in verses 2:24 and 25 differs significantly from how the Bible came to define marriage.

Furthermore, the biblical understanding of the purpose of marriage has been reproduction, even to the point that a man could dissolve his marriage if his wife failed to bear him heirs. Besides reproduction, marriage within a patriarchal social order also served political and economic means. Marriages during antiquity mainly focused on codifying economic responsibilities and obligations. Wives were chosen from good families not only to secure the legitimacy of a man's children, but to strengthen political and economic alliances between families, clans, tribes, and kingdoms. To ensure that any offspring were the legitimate heirs, the woman was restricted to just one sex partner, her husband. Meanwhile, the husband maintained the right to have multiple sex partners—wives, concubines, war booty, sexual slaves, even prostitutes.

This concept where a man would leave his father and mother and cleave to a woman can inform how our modern society might define a healthy marriage, but it should not be limited to the civil institution of marriage. It becomes a biblical pattern for all who cleave to each other to become one for the purposes of establishing a familial relationship. "Familial," that which is of or common to a family, is relation-centered. At its very core, a familial relationship is based on mutual commitment and vulnerability. It serves as a corrective measure to the hyper-individuality salient within Euro American Western culture by reinforcing the family, not the individual, as the basic social unit of society. Generally speaking, the familial relationship is not limited to two individuals forming a bond to become one flesh; it can also encompass children, siblings, elders, and all others whom we term extended family. Thus, not all familial relationships are sexual, nor should they be.

But through the cleaving that took place between the first man and the first woman, sex bonded such relationships. Sex is so great that it occurs within humanity's innocence, within the garden of Eden, before the first rebellion and the "fall." When two choose to become one flesh within a familial-based relationship, where mutual sexual pleasure can be epitomized, the opportunity to create intimacy exists. This sexual pleasure is not only abundantly satisfying, it also opens us up to the possibility of communing with God: at its best, sex creates a feeling of security, fulfillment, and ultimate love due to the process of two becoming one mind, one flesh, and one spirit.

As important as becoming one flesh may be, creating a familial relationship does not necessarily signify marriage. Although church weddings are religious rituals and celebrations that publicly proclaim the existence of a familial relationship, these events do not create family—people do. Church weddings serve to bless a relationship. If a sexual relationship fails to meet the deepest physical, emotional, spiritual, and intellectual needs of both partners, there may be a marriage, because a ritual occurred in a church building, but there is no family.

Man and woman are called to become "one flesh." The word used for "one" in Hebrew is *'echad*. In this passage, *'echad* connotes a union of separate entities, even though this sense is not endemic to *'echad*. Nevertheless, it is curious that this is the same word used in the Shema, "Hear O Israel: The Lord is our God, the Lord is [*'echad*"] (Deut. 6:4 author trans.). The union of two individuals in marriage patterns itself after the essence, the oneness of God. For Christians, the theological concept of Trinity, developed in the late second century by Tertullian,[3] creates a model that can be emulated with familial relationships. According to this particular doctrine, God is one and yet has been revealed to humanity as Yahweh, Jesus Christ, and the Holy Spirit. The doctrine maintains that these manifestations of God are coequal in the sharing of substance, power, and importance. In spite of the fact that many Christians attempt to view Divinity in hierarchical terms—placing the Father first, followed by the Son, and finally the Holy Ghost—the actual doctrine insists that Trinity exists within a nonhierarchical model.

Regardless of whether one accepts or rejects this doctrine, what it represents can be useful in understanding the proper healthy relationship between two individuals. While many have tried to explain the Trinity, trying to solve it as if it was some cosmic puzzle, marginalized communities of color have instead emphasized the Trinity along the terms of communal relationships. Whatever we wish to say about God, God's character is relational, based on the act of sharing. Trinity symbolizes the sharing of authority. This paradigm of being one can become the model for humans, specifically the two who become one flesh. Although there was no marriage ceremony or ritual recorded taking place for the first man and woman, the relationship between the first man and woman can nevertheless inform modern-day marriages or any other relationship where the two, cleaving to each other, become one flesh. For two to be one means that the ideal familial relationship or marriage must exist absent of any hierarchical structures.

In other words, the relationship of oneness was originally intended to be non-patriarchal. It is with divine judgment, after the human's first rebellion, that this relationship becomes perverted and patriarchal.

Can this one flesh ever be dissolved? When the Pharisees attempted to trap Jesus on the question of divorce, he answered them by first quoting Genesis 2:24, and then stating, "what God has joined together, let no one separate" (Mt. 19:6). For Jesus, this verse brings God into the equation of marriage, and expands the importance of the union by prohibiting divorce. The oneness between couples becomes the same oneness we are called to share with God. Elsewhere, Jesus reminds us that not only do we have the capacity to become one with each other but also one with God (Jn. 17:21–23). In a sense, the familial relationship between two individuals is based on the oneness we can experience with our God.

This is why Jesus states that anyone who divorces his wife or marries a divorced woman commits adultery (Mt. 5:32). Divorce is painful because it tears apart the flesh that was made one in God. While it is hard to imagine the admonition against divorce being liberating in modern days, Jesus' pronouncement against divorce was liberating for women who, trapped within a patriarchal social order, were financially vulnerable when their husbands easily divorced them for the most trivial of matters. Still, circumstances exist where divorce may be the more liberating recourse. As injurious as divorce can be to the soul and body, it can also at times be the means by which the soul and body might be saved. The destruction of a human, created in the image of God, is a sin that can be manifested through spousal abuse, whether it is physical, emotional, or psychological. For some, their alternatives are choosing to stay within an abusive relationship or divorce, neither one being ideal. But when divorce leads to saving and/or restoring a person's worth and dignity, then divorce might very well be the better of the two alternatives.

The text gives the example of a male and female becoming one flesh, but is this example normative for everyone? The early rabbinical writers seem to have thought so. Rabbi Akiba wrote, "*And he shall cleave, but not to a male; to his wife.*" [4] This leads us to wonder if two males or two females can cleave to each other and become one flesh. Maybe this is the wrong question to ponder. The question may not be if two same-gender loving partners can cleave to each other and become one flesh, for they have always done so, and continue to do so. Maybe the question is how we might understand this verse in light of the reality of what is occurring more openly today with several states legalizing same-sex marriages. True, the story is about Adam and Eve, not Adam and Steve, as opponents to same-sex marriage want to remind us, although Augustine, due to his misogynist views, thought it would have been better for God to place another man, instead of a woman, in the garden with Adam.[5] Still, the story exists to answer important human questions, including what should be the bases for developing a familial sexual relationship, not whom that relationship should be based with. Because same gender loving people have created familial relationships by cleaving to each other and becoming one flesh, it might be better to ponder why a portion of the faith community opposes this.

Historically, the purpose of marriage was to procreate, to be fruitful and multiply. Hence, religious leaders saw any act that prevented procreation from occurring to be contrary to the will of God and the purpose of marriage. Not surprisingly, certain sexual acts that did not inseminate a woman (i.e., oral, anal, masturbation, sex during a woman's menstrual cycle, use of contraception, or sex with a woman past menopause) were considered an abomination. Indeed, if a woman was unable to produce a child, preferably a male child, the husband had an obligation to divorce her and procure a more fertile replacement. Not surprisingly, same-gender sexual relationships, because they do not lead to pregnancy, were also considered an abomination. If we define the purpose of marriage to be procreation, then, yes, same-sex marriage should not be allowed. But if marriage is more than simply having children, if marriage is to become one flesh by creating a familial relationship, then the race, faith, ethnicity, or gender of the participants ceases to be of importance.

Both the man and the woman were naked, and yet, they felt no shame. For the ancient Hebrew mind, nakedness was a metaphor for vulnerability (as it is for many today). That they were able to stand stark naked before each other, totally vulnerable, and yet not be ashamed goes beyond their innocence concerning sexuality. After all, if they "cleaved" to each other in the previous verse, they were no longer all that innocent. The beauty of this verse is the affirmation that after cleaving to each other, after becoming totally vulnerable in each other's presence, they still felt no shame.

PART FOUR

Sexism

10

War on Women[1]

Step 1. Observing

In 2012 the House Oversight and Government Reform Committee were debating if insurance plans should contain a mandate for covering the cost of contraceptives. One of the scheduled speakers, Sandra Fluke, a Georgetown University law student, was not allowed to testify by the Republicans on the committee. She instead later testified before Democrat members. Rather than debating her assertions, radio personality Rush Limbaugh labeled her a promiscuous "anti-Catholic plant," and called her a "prostitute." According to Limbaugh, Fluke is a "slut" who "wants to be paid for sex." Fluke, Limbaugh said, is "having so much sex, it's amazing she can still walk." Confusing contraceptives with Viagra (which is covered by most insurance policies), Limbaugh accused Fluke of "having sex so frequently that she can't afford all the birth-control pills that she needs."[2] It seems that whenever so-called uppity women refuse to stay in their places, men attempt to shame them into silence, at times by using misinformation as though it was fact.

During the 2012 election, we learn from Missourian senatorial candidate Todd Akin that "legitimate" rape does not result in pregnancy because "the female body has a way to try to shut that whole thing down." And while many conservatives from Akin's own party rejected and rebuffed his understanding of rape, still it was disturbing that some supported him, specifically the Family Research Council (FRC)—the political arm of Focus on the Family. Connie Mackey, the president of FRC Action PAC, released a statement stating, "We support [Akin] fully and completely."[3]

Akin was not the only politician during the 2012 election cycle holding views most women and many men found offensive. Richard Mourdock, candidate for a U.S. Senate seat in Indiana, while discussing why he opposed abortion, even in case of rape or incest, said, "I think even if life begins in that horrible situation of rape, that it is something that God intended to happen."[4] Another U.S. senate candidate, Tom Smith of Pennsylvania, compared pregnancy due to rape with "having a baby out of wedlock."[5] The insensitive gaffes made about issues that primarily concern women (although these issues should concern all people) were prevalent during the 2012 election. But the end of the election did not end the ignorance and misconceptions on the part of some male and even female politicians as to how a woman's body operates.

Celeste Greig, president of the conservative California Republican Assembly, told the *San Jose Mercury News* that pregnancies by rape are rare "because it's an act of violence, because the body is traumatized."[6] Another example came from Arizona representative Trent Franks (R-AZ), who during a July 2013 House Judiciary Committee meeting that was considering banning abortions after twenty weeks of pregnancy, argued against a Democratic amendment to make exceptions for rape and incest. According to Franks, pregnancy from rape is rare. He said, "Before, when my friends on the left side of the aisle here tried to make rape and incest the subject—because, you know, the incidences of rape resulting in pregnancy are very low."[7]

It is important to note and make abundantly clear that there exists no scientific evidence whatsoever that those who are victims of rape or incest are less likely to become pregnant—quite the contrary. A St. Lawrence University study published in 2003 concluded that because women do not plan on being sexually assaulted, pregnancy resulting from rape occurs at significantly higher levels than it does in other cases.[8] A 2011 San Francisco State University study in Columbia confirmed that young women who experienced sexual violence resulted in significantly higher levels of unintended pregnancies.[9]

As troublesome as misogynist comments made by politicians and pundits against women are, more damning is the legislation that is proposed based on politicians' beliefs (in most cases their religious beliefs). This war on women can easily be mapped out by the political, economic, social, and traditional acts taken in multiple areas of daily life; however, due to limited space, this chapter will concentrate only on: (1) U.S. workplace opportunities (equal pay), (2) violence toward women (rape) within the United States, (3) control over American women's bodies (reproduction rights), and (4) the global manifestation of this war on women.

Workplace Opportunities

Sexism has historically been the norm in the workplace. "Sexism" is the name given to social structures and systems in which the "actions, practices, and use of laws, rules and customs limit certain activities of one sex, but do not limit those same activities of other people of the other sex."[10] This becomes obvious when we compare the wages of women to men. Women (5.52 million) are twice as likely as men (2.3 million) to work in occupations that pay poverty wages. Even though women represented almost half (47 percent) of the U.S. labor force, in every work category and at every education level they were paid less than men.[11] On June 10, 2013, fifty years to the day since the Equal Pay Act was signed into law, women still earned an average wage ratio of 77 cents for every dollar earned by a man.[12] At our present rate of progress pay parity eventually will be achieved in the year 2057, almost a century after the law was originally passed.[13] Not surprisingly, women of color fared worse with African American women making 55 cents.[14] According to 2012 data from the U.S. Census Bureau, nearly 40 percent of all households headed by African American and Latina women live below the poverty level.[15]

Although the situation has improved for white women since the law was signed in 1963, at which time women earned 60 cents for every dollar a man made, the narrowing of the gap over the past half-century, according to the Council on Contemporary Families, had more to do with wage losses among men rather than wage gains among women. This continuing disparity, according to economist Stephanie Seguino, means that women must work for fifty-two years to earn what a man will make in forty years.[16] Another way to calculate this disparity is: if the wage gap was eliminated, a full-time working woman would have enough for approximately (1) eighty-nine more weeks of food, (2) more than seven months of mortgage and utilities payments, (3) more than a year of rent, or (4) more than three thousand additional gallons of gasoline.[17]

Most of the progress made in income parity occurred among single women, making a woman with children the greatest predictor of wage inequality. Mothers earn 5 percent less per hour per child then comparable childless women and are less likely to be hired.[18] This becomes especially problematic when we consider that 40 percent of all households in 2013 with children under the age of eighteen include mothers who are either the primary source or the sole source of income for the family, an increase from 11 percent in 1960. While 5.1 million (37 percent) of these mothers are married with higher incomes than their husband, the vast majority, 8.6 million (63 percent), are single mothers with an annual median family income of $23,000. These single moms are more likely to be Latina or black and less likely to have a college degree.[19]

When we solely consider white-collar employment, women do not fare better. The median wages of female managers in 2012 was 73 percent of what male managers earned. A Catalyst surveyed revealed

that female MBAs received on average $4,600 less in wages than male
MBAs' starting salaries, a trend that continues throughout their career
as they witness men outpace them in salary and rank growth even if the
women remained childless. Among the one thousand top Fortune 500
companies, only 4 percent of CEOs are women. The highest paid female
CEO is Marissa Mayer of Yahoo, who in 2012 earned $36.6 million.
Compare this to the highest paying male CEO, Lawrence J. Ellison of
Oracle, who made $96.2 million.[20]

Studies also indicate that as an occupation becomes more dominated
by women (e.g., social workers and primary school teachers), wages
for those jobs begin to decline when compared with similar job skills
associated with occupations dominated by men.[21] Women can also
expect to be among the last hired. According to John Challenger, CEO
of a Chicago-based global outplacement firm, men snagged three out of
every four of the 2.4 million new jobs created between 2009 and 2012,
leading him to nickname the recovery from the 2008 Great Recession as
the "he-covery" or "mancovery." The threat of a continuing mancovery
is that gains women made in the workplace could be reversed, as
occurred in the 1940s, when men returning from war pushed women
out of jobs.[22]

Disparity does not solely exist with wages and recovery hires.
When it comes to health insurance, women can expect to continue
paying more for the same health coverage as men, even though the
new health care laws known as Obamacare prohibit such "gender
rating" starting in 2014. The gap will persist in most states, with no
indication that insurance companies will take action to reduce the gap.
For example, in 2012 a thirty-year-old woman in Chicago can expect to
pay 31 percent more than a man of similar age for the same coverage
($375 a month vs. $258.75). A forty-year-old nonsmoking woman in
Louisville, Kentucky, can expect to pay 53 percent more for the same
coverage as a nonsmoking man of the same age ($196 a month versus
$128). In Arkansas a twenty-five-year-old woman can expect to pay 81
percent more than a man, even though a similar plan in the same state,
but with a different company, charges women only 10 percent more.
Maternity cost does not explain the rate differential, because it seldom
is included as part of the standard package; rather, it is covered as an
optional benefit with a hefty additional premium, also known as an
insurance rider.[23]

Discrimination against women, especially in the workplace, has
been based on the popular adage that women could not be fulfilled
wives and successful mothers while pursuing a career. In 1962,
psychiatrists maintained that "normal" women renounced aspirations
outside the home so as to meet their feminine need for dependence—a

view that two-thirds of Americans agree with, according to a University of Michigan survey at the time. The survey revealed that the most important family decisions "should be made by the man of the house."[24]

Since then, a revolution of attitudes concerning women in the home and workplace took place. Consider that in 1977 two-thirds of Americans believed it was "better for everyone involved if the man is the achiever outside the home and the woman takes care of the home and family"; but by 1994, two-thirds of Americans rejected this notion. And yet this 1994 trend of thinking began to reverse. From 1994 to 2004, the model of male breadwinner and female homemaker rose in popularity among Americans from 34 percent to 40 percent. From 1997 to 2007, the number of full-time working mothers who would have preferred to stay at home increased to 60 percent from 48 percent.[25]

The historical patriarchal assumption that the woman's domain is within the domestic sphere while men are charged with being the primary breadwinners continues to be challenged in today's age. And yet 28 percent of Americans believe that it is worse for marriages if wives earn more than husbands. Economists discovered that wives with higher education and possible better earning potential are less likely to work.[26] The economic challenges that women face in the workplace (e.g., lack of paid paternity leave and minimal maternity leave) are forms of institutional violence. Unfortunately, they also face physical violence.

Violence toward Women

On average, more than four women a day are murdered by their husbands or boyfriends in the United States,[27] with one out of every four women experiencing violence at the hands of their boyfriend or spouse (current or former)—some two million injuries from intimate partners each year,[28] and one in fifty experiencing stalking victimizations.[29] Black women were four times more likely than white women to die at the hands of a boyfriend.[30] Homicide is the second leading cause of traumatic death for pregnant women, accounting for 31 percent of maternal injury death, with black women experiencing seven times more fatalities when pregnant than white women..[31]

According to one statistic, about five hundred rapes occur per day in the United States.[32] One in six U.S. women have, at some time, experienced an attempted or completed rape, with more than 300,000 women being "forcibly"[33] raped and more than 4 million being assaulted.[34] All women are at risk of abuse, those with the highest rate of rape or sexual abuse are women between the ages of twenty and twenty-four.[35] Native American women experience the highest rates of violence at the hands of their partners.[36] Violence, specifically sexual violence, all too often occurs early, before adulthood is reached. The second-highest age range for women who experience sexual assault or rape are those between sixteen and nineteen years old.[37] In the graduating U.S. high school class of 2013, 28 percent of the graduating students have survived some sort of sexual assault, 10 percent are survivors of dating violence in the past year, and 10 percent are survivors of rape.[38] And yet, according to the U.S. Department of Justice, only three out of every one hundred rapists ever serve prison time.[39]

Violence is the means by which control is maintained over the conduct, thoughts, beliefs, and actions of the Other, specifically women. The possibility of violence is sufficient for the one abused to docilely obey. The internalization of power teaches those who are abused to police themselves. As a form of survival or self-preservation, the one on the receiving end of the violence (more often than not women, but also includes girls and boys) learns to behave in the appropriate matter— a matter that reinforces her status of imposed inferiority. Self-disciplining leads to justifying one's oppression ("I deserved to be punished"), thus undermining one's sense of self-worth and dignity, which is crucial for the development of well-adjusted personhood.

One common form of violence that is usually categorized as benign by men is sexual harassment. Sexual harassment occurs whenever sexual favors are demanded to ensure professional and/ or economic gain or when refusing to provide sexual favors threatens one's professional and/or economic security. Sexual harassment is not limited to physical violence; it also encompasses economic deprivation, intentional degradation, public humiliation, spiritual manipulation, and verbal intimidation. While the abuse of women, whether it is manifested physically, sexually, spiritually, or psychologically, and whether committed by a family member, acquaintance, or total stranger, is first and foremost about power. Sexual harassment and/or violence (even in the case of rape), has nothing to do with sex, even though sex becomes the means by which power is enhanced.

We should recognize that sexual abuse encompasses more than harassment carried out by economically powerful men against women in their employ. Sexual abuse is also a threat to wives and young children, prostitutes and prison inmates, college students, the elderly and young teenagers, and it crosses all economic, gender, orientation, and racial lines. And while all men are not sexual predators, almost all women have experienced sexual harassment at least once. Although a thorough and comprehensive analysis of violence toward women in the workplace could prove productive, for purposes of this chapter we will focus on just one institution, the armed forces of the United States.

The acceptance of women within the military has been resisted by many means, perhaps most disturbingly sexual assault. That warriors rape women is nothing new. The U.S. liberators (known as the greatest generation) who landed in Normandy on D-Day to oust the Nazis instituted their own "regime of terror." According to historian Mary Louise Roberts's archival research, soldiers were "sold" on the invasion by its portrayal of an erotic adventure among oversexed Frenchwomen. But the so-called adventure was an excuse to unleash a "tsunami of male lust."[40] According to Roberts,

> Rape posed an even greater threat to the myth of the American mission as sexual romance. In the summer of 1944, Norman women launched a wave of rape accusations against American soldiers, threatening to destroy the erotic fantasy at the heart of the operation. The specter of rape transformed the GI from rescue-warrior to violent intruder. Forced to confront the sexual excess incited by its own propaganda, the army responded not by admitting the full range of the problem, but by scapegoating African American soldiers as the primary perpetrators of the rapes.[41]

Sexual assaults remains part of military culture of sexual violence; only now, female military personnel are the targets.[42] According to a Pentagon report, some twenty-six thousand service members were sexually assaulted in 2012, a 35 percent increase since 2010.

The climate of fear reigning in the military branches led then defense secretary Leon Panetta to acknowledge that the number of sexual assaults probably is far higher in the military than what official statistics show. The Defense Department believes one in three women in the military has been sexually assaulted, compared to one in six civilian women. About 20 percent of female soldiers who served in Iraq and Afghanistan experienced a sexual assault. And yet, only 3,374 in 2012 reported their abuse, likely due to the fact that less than one in ten sexual assault reports results in court-martial convictions.[43] For a woman to come forward with an accusation can be a career-ender; worse yet the victim could face administrative retribution and reprisals, especially given that reports are handled within the military chain of command. A woman choosing to report an assault or abuse within the military is very often forced to continue to serve under the command of her assailant. Not surprisingly, many refuse to report their abuse. And if they do report their rape, as did Sergeant Kimberly Davis, it usually is covered up, at times by the officer assigned to the case, leading her to conclude: "The sexual assault program in the Air Force is a joke."[44]

Tragically, two days after the 2012 Pentagon report on sexual violence was released, Lieutenant Colonel Jeffrey Keusinski, the officer responsible for the Air Force's sexual assault prevention programs, was arrested and charged with sexual battery. A couple of weeks later, Sergeant Michael McClendon of the U.S. Military Academy at West

Point was accused of videotaping female cadets, without their consent, as they showered or undressed in the bathroom.[45] Senator Susan Collins (R-ME) probably said it best, "If I were a parent with a daughter who is thinking of going into the military today, I would think twice about whether the environment is safe for her, not from the enemy, but from sexual assault from her fellow military members."[46]

Sexual assault is not restricted to the military. According to the U.S. Department of Justice, 8 percent of all rapes occur at workplace.[47] But a violent attack at work is not the only way a woman suffers while on the job; many times she is held responsible for what occurs during her off hours. At times society, especially religious institutions, tends to "blame the victim" who suffers physical abuse. Take the example of Carie Charlesworth, a second-grade teacher in El Cajo, California. Following a domestic-violence incident involving her ex-husband, Holy Trinity School, where she worked, fired her. Although she did nothing wrong in the classroom, her school district viewed her as a liability and thus, due to the domestic-violence dispute, too unsafe to have around. Diocese officials are concerned about her ex-husband's "threatening and menacing behavior," and as a result will not allow her to teach. Ms. Charlesworth, the one that was abused, is punished with loss of employment by the religious institution for which she worked.[48]

Other times, a woman is punished for whom she loves. Take the example of Carla Hale, who was fired as a teacher from Bishop Watterson High School. When her mother passed away, the obituary noted that the survivors included Hale and her partner. As a result, the Roman Catholic Diocese of Columbus fired her for being in a committed, loving, same-gender relationship. Although, according to Bishop Frederick Campbell, Hale was fired on "moral issues," she maintained, "I've never thought my sexual orientation is a sin."[49] Women who leave their relegated domestic space of the household have faced, and continue to experience, all form of abuse solely because they are seen as invading the male public domain.

Control over Women's Bodies

A study conducted by the Guttmacher Institute reveals that issues related to reproductive health and rights received unprecedented attention in 2011 at the state level. State legislators in all fifty states introduced more than 1,100 reproductive health- and rights-related provisions, a sharp increase from the 950 in 2010. By year's end, 135 of these provisions had been enacted in thirty-six states, an increase from the 89 enacted in 2010 and the 77 enacted in 2009.[50] By 2012, and additional 43 provisions were enacted in nineteen states.[51] When can heartfelt opposition to abortion on moral and ethical grounds be separated from a larger campaign to assert control over women's sexual lives?

For many politicians, the present strategy seems to be to incrementally narrow abortion rights on the state level (where Republicans gained control of the legislatures) until a sympathetic Supreme Court is in place that can overturn *Roe v. Wade*. For example, as of 2012 twenty-six states require a waiting period for a woman seeking an abortion; thirty-five states require mandatory counseling; three states established stringent regulations that only affects abortion providers, but not other providers of outpatient surgical and medical care;[52] three states require abortion providers to have hospital admitting privileges, but not other providers of outpatient surgical and medical care;[53] and eight states mandate invasive ultrasound prior to having an abortion.[54] Attempts have been made in several states to either declare legally that life begins at conception or to grant human rights to embryos as a pathway to legally overturn abortion.

By 2012, ten states had banned abortion at or beyond twenty weeks' gestation. In 2013 Texas joined these states by also banning abortions after twenty weeks. Furthermore, Texas now holds abortion clinics to the same standards as hospital-style surgical centers. Although supporters claimed that the new regulations on abortion clinics were put in place to provide better health protection for women, opponents argued that the stringent restrictions were designed to place an exorbitant financial burden on these clinics in the hopes of shutting them down.[55]

The most restricted bans, and strongest challenge to *Roe v. Wade*, was passed in North Dakota, calling for a ban on abortions after six weeks, when a fetal heartbeat can first be detected using a transvaginal probe, and in Arkansas, calling for a ban at twelve weeks, when the fetal heartbeat can be detected with an abdominal ultrasound.[56] By May 21, 2013, a federal appellate court panel struck down Arizona's abortion ban, claiming that it was unconstitutional "under a long line of invariant Supreme Court precedents" that guarantee a woman's right to end a pregnancy any time before a fetus is deemed viable outside her womb, generally at twenty-four weeks.[57] By July 22, 2013, a federal judge blocked the enforcement of North Dakota's band calling it "invalid and unconstitutional."

Within twenty-four hours, Congressional House Republicans proposed federal legislation that would ban all abortions after twenty weeks' gestation (the twenty-second week of pregnancy).[58] After the bill, the Pain-Capable Unborn Child Protection Act was approved by the House Judiciary Committee in June 2013 along party lines (20–12); it was passed by the House that same month, mainly along party lines (228–196).[59] In an attempt to frame the conversation, bill supporter Kristi Noem (R-SD) proclaimed "I'm not waging a war on anyone."[60]

Of course, not all opponents of abortion are engaged in a war on women, but this is not the first time that the House has tried to pass legislation that abortion rights supporters argue would endanger the lives of women.[61] In 2011, the House attempted to allow hospitals receiving federal funds from refusing to perform emergency abortions even when the life of the mother was at stake.[62] Regardless of one's view on abortion, the political system seems to be moving toward a stance that the reproductive organs of women must be regulated by the government (if not state, then federal), whose majority of legislators are comprised of men.

Similar struggles have taken place around sex education and the availability of birth control. A woman who is sexually active but is not using contraception has an 85 percent chance of becoming pregnant within a year.[63] Nearly one in five female teenagers who are at risk for an unintended pregnancy were not using any method of contraception during their last intercourse.[64] Eighty-two percent of teen pregnancies were unplanned, accounting for one-fifth of all unintended annual pregnancies.[65] Of all these teen pregnancies, 17.8 percent ended with an abortion, the lowest since abortion was legalized.[66]

The 2008 rate of 68 per 1,000 teens represented a 42 percent decline from 117 per 1,000 since 1990.[67] The main reason for this decline (86 percent) was due to improved contraceptive use among teenagers; the rest was due to teenagers deciding to delay sexual activity.[68] Despite this decline, the United States continues to have one of the highest rates of teen pregnancy among industrial nations.[69] And yet opponents of abortion are usually opposed to the availability of contraceptives and sex education.

Title X, the main federal family planning program created in 1970 with the support of Republican President Richard Nixon and Congressman George H. W. Bush, does not pay for abortions. A 2009 Congressional Research Service report cited Title X with preventing nearly a million annual unintended pregnancies. Experts also estimate that Title X helps prevent about four hundred thousand abortions a year. The majority of Title X's funds also provide about five million women, especially poor women, with lifesaving cervical and breast cancer screening, HIV and STD testing, adolescent abstinence counseling, and infertility counseling. Some of its funds cover birth control. About a quarter of Title X's $300 million budget went to Planned Parenthood, which serviced about a third of Title X's patients in 2011.[70]

For example, the poor women of San Carlos, an improvised town in southern Texas, have relied on Planned Parenthood to obtain breast cancer screenings, free birth control pills, and pap smears for cervical cancer. Maria Romero, a housecleaner with four children, is one of those women. Before the clinic closed in the fall of 2011, a lump was discovered in her breast. The San Carlos clinic closed, along with over a dozen others throughout the state, when financing for women's health was slashed by the state's Republican-controlled legislature by about two-thirds. Some four hundred thousand women, including Maria Romero, were left without services. The next-closest clinic to Romero is in Edinburg, sixteen miles away. She has no means by which to get there, and even if she did, the wait time for an appointment is four weeks. To make matters worse, she cannot afford the $20 for a monthly supply of birth control tablets, which she previously obtained for free. Ironically, even though none of these clinics performed abortions, the supporters of the cutbacks were mainly motivated by their opposition to abortions. Governor Rick Perry rejected receipt of $35 million in federal funds that would have financed women's health programs in order to ensure that Planned Parenthood received none of those funds. Other states are following Texas's lead in some way or another.[71] But these tactics are not limited to the state level. Since 2011 the Republican-controlled House of Representatives has attempted to pass legislation that would have eliminated all funding for Title X, mainly because of its connection to Planned Parenthood.[72]

Additionally, seven states moved to disqualify family planning providers from eligibility for funding.[73] Only two states in 2012 added new restrictions,[74] effectively barring family planning clinics not operated by health departments from being eligible for grant funds. Even though new private health plans that are written on or after August 1, 2012, are mandated to cover contraceptive counseling and services with no out-of-pocket costs to patients, twenty states allow certain employers and insurers to refuse compliance with the mandate. Finally, five states since 2010 enacted legislation concerning sex education; all but one supported abstinence-only education. By 2013, twenty-six states stressed abstinence in sex education.[75]

The opposition to contraceptives by religious organizations can be noted by the 2012 actions of thirteen Roman Catholic dioceses, evangelicals, Mennonites, several related religious groups, and some private corporations (i.e., Hobby Lobby) who filed more than forty-five lawsuits across a dozen federal courts claiming that the inclusion of contraceptives in basic health-care coverage was a violation of their religious freedoms, even though the contraception-coverage mandate exempts houses of worship.[76] But should religiously affiliated organizations (hospitals, schools, charities) that believe the usage of contraceptives is a sin be forced to provide them via their insurance coverage to their female employees? A study conducted by the *American Journal of Obstetrics and Gynecology* discovered that besides abortion restrictions, the most frequent issues associated with religiously affiliated hospitals revolve around the lack of birth control and sterilization for women seeking it after giving birth.[77] This raises some interesting questions. Are religious hospitals imposing their religion upon women's bodies, or are they simply being faithful to their convictions? Can a pharmacy refuse to fill contraceptive medication because the pharmacist's personal convictions consider its usage to be a sin?

David Green, founder of Hobby Lobby, who pays his employees almost twice the minimum wage, forsakes profits on the Sabbath, and provides comprehensive health insurance, has no objection to covering contraception, but he considers the "morning-after pill" to be an abortion-inducing procedure. Green, who considers himself a conscientious Christian capitalist, believes that the morning-after pill is irreconcilable with the Christian principles upon which he operates his company. If Green adheres to his conscious and does not cover the morning-after pill, he could eventually face a fine of $1.3 million a day.[78] But can a corporation have a soul? If the Supreme Court ruled in the *Citizens United* case that corporations are protected by the First Amendment's freedom of speech clause, then does the First Amendment's freedom-of-religion clause also protects the corporation's conscious? After all, the First Amendment allows churches and religious organizations to preach and speak against the usage of contraceptives, declaring its usage to be a sin. Still, in a 1990 decision, Justice Scalia wrote that to make "the professed doctrines of religious beliefs superior to the law of the land [would allow] every citizen to become a law unto himself. Government [w]ould exist only in name under such circumstances."[79]

When the Obama administration declined to renew the contract with the U.S. Conference of Catholic Bishops to aid victims of human sex trafficking, the administration was charged for being anti-Catholic. The contract, however, was not renewed because the bishops required its subcontractors not to use federal monies to pay for contraceptives and abortion referrals and services, thus failing in the government's eyes to meet the needs of those who were sexually abused.[80] Furthermore, according to federal district court Judge Richard Stearns, the bishops' requirements violate the First Amendment because they impose religion-based restrictions on the use of taxpayer dollars.[81]

Global Sexism

The phenomenon of the oppression of women, which is based on male supremacy, is a problem not only to the United States, but also globally. The danger when making comparisons between the United States and other cultures is the tendency to conclude that "our" sexism is not a bad as "theirs" and that "our" women are treated better then "theirs." Although the concern of making the racial or ethnic Other more misogynist exists, the fact still remains that other cultures and societies engage in their own wars on women. Although sexism may appear differently with varying degrees of oppression, we must avoid the temptation of ranking sexist acts in such a way that redeems Eurocentric expressions as not being so bad in comparison to Others. To the oppressed and repressed victims of the war on women, all forms of marginalization are damning.

Many may look in horror at the case of a twenty-three-year-old student in India who was so viciously gang raped in 2013 on a bus ride home from the movies that it led to her death two weeks later. Such stories reinforce some latent belief that those people "over there" are somewhat uncivilized and barbaric, all the while ignoring our own form of uncivilized and barbaric behavior. Consider another case, that of the Steubenville, Ohio, high school football players who on August 11, 2012, repeatedly raped an unconscious sixteen-year-old girl as they lugged her from party to party. In both cases, the "victims were blamed." In a poll conducted in India, 68 percent of judges listed "provocative attire" as an "invitation to rape." Probably the most barbaric act of all is the failure of Congress, as of this writing, to pass the International Violence against Women Act,[82] which would name and shame those countries that tolerate acts of violence toward women. Congress has also failed to pass the Trafficking Victims Protection Act.[83] As we turn our attention to the war on women overseas, it is important to remember that we here in the United States are not necessarily on the side of women during the global war on women.[84]

That being said, we begin by recognizing that women around the world face life-threatening situations simply because they were born as women. Millions of women and girls worldwide suffer from some form of violence on a daily basis. Violence can manifest itself as rape, as sexual abuse, as a tool of repression in war-ravaged regions, as early arranged marriages, as dowry-related murder, as honor killing, as sex trafficking, as female infanticide, as female genital circumcision and as acid attacks. The violence can be physical, but it also can be manifested verbally, economically, spiritually, and psychologically. Women from all cultures, all religious faiths, all economic strata, and all racial and ethnic groups are at risk of experiencing violence.

Violence against women is a common phenomenon. According to a 2013 briefing paper from the United Nation, one in five women throughout the world will become a victim of rape or attempted rape as some point in her lifetime; as many as 70 percent will experience violence sometime during their lives. Women subjected to sexual violence (according to the World Health Organization) ranges from 6 percent in Japan to 59 percent in Ethiopia. Half of all women worldwide who are victims of homicide are killed by their current partner or husband. For example, in Australia, Canada, Israel, South Africa, and the United States, it is estimated that 40 to 70 percent of female deaths by homicide were at the hands of their partner.[85] Fear of stigma prevents many women from reporting the violence they face; hence, we can expect current data to be underrepresentative of the situation. Rather than concentrating on the men who perpetuate this violence, the historical trend has been to "blame the victim."

Women, in the minds of some, are to blame for their victimization because of the way they dress (showing off too much skin by wearing revealing clothes), because they drink alcoholic beverages, because they work outside the home, or because they entice men by flirtation (flirtation as perceived and defined by men). When women who participated in public protests in Tahrir Square spoke out in Cairo, Egypt about their rapes, the police general and lawmaker, Adel Abdel Maqsoud Afifi responded by stating, "Sometimes a girl contributes 100 percent to her own raping when she puts herself in these conditions." Sheik Abu Islam, a television cleric who is a political powerbroker responded, "You see those women speaking like ogres, without shame, politeness, fear or even femininity. . . [Such a woman] is like a demon. . . [They] went there to get raped."[86]

Women have always faced abuse at the hands of the military, as rape is used as an instrument of war. For example, during the military conflict in the Democratic Republic of Congo, some 1,100 rapes were reported each and every month. It is estimated that over 200,000 women suffered from sexual assault since the start of military conflict. The region of Darfur has also seen rape used as a military tactic. The Rwanda conflict of 1994 witnessed 250,000 to 500,000 rapes, while the Bosnia conflicts of the 90s reported between 20,000 and 50,000 rapes.[87] In addition to rape as a tactic, women are also forced into sex slavery. According to Toru Hashimoto, leader of a populist political party in Japan, sex slavery during the war is a necessary evil. Referring to the usage of "comfort women" during World War II, he upheld the popular belief among many Japanese (including Prime Minister Shinzo Abe) that no evidence exists that women were forced to serve in brothels, thus ignoring the voices and testimonies of women from many countries who claimed to have been sexual slaves. Historians estimate that two hundred thousand women were rounded up to serve as "comfort women" by the Japanese imperial forces.[88]

Rape is not confined to war. The custom of early marriage (male adults marrying girls) is a common practice worldwide, especially in African and South Asian countries. Rape of children in these cases is masked under the term "marriage." Arranged marriages that are against the wishes of the bride are also a form of rape. More problematic is when such marriages end in the death of the wife. For example, dowry murder predominantly occurs in South Asia. In India a woman harassed for years by her husband and his relatives was finally kidnapped, raped, strangled, and tossed into a ditch. Her father, Subedar Akhileshar Kumar Singh, an army officer, has tried for over a year to have her husband arrested, but to no avail. He believes that she was killed by her in-laws, who were unsatisfied with her dowry. In India alone it is estimated that 25,000 to 100,000 women a year are killed over dowry disputes, many of whom are burned alive. One way to avoid paying a dowry is to have no daughters, accomplished by aborting female fetuses.[89]

Honor killing of women (as many as five hundred thousand in 2012) occur when a family's honor has been damaged by premarital sex, the accusation of adultery of a woman or girl, or rape.[90] For a woman in Afghanistan to be alone with a man who is not her relative constitute sufficient grounds for arrest on the charge of attempted adultery. Among those jailed for "moral crimes," based on the testimonies of their abusers, are Asma, who ran away from her husband after he beat her, threw boiling water on her, gave her a sexually transmitted disease, and announced his engagement to his mistress; fifteen-year-old Fawzia, who took refuge with a family that drugged her and forced her into prostitution; sixteen-year-old Farah, who eloped with her brother's friend; and Gulpari, who is also sixteen, who was kidnapped by a stalker who wanted to marry her.[91]

For a woman to choose her own spouse can be, in some regions, sufficient grounds for a death penalty. Take the example of Nusrat Mochi of Karachi, Pakistan. She ran away from home to marry a man of her own choosing, rather than the husband, who is fifteen years her senior, selected by her parents. For four years her parents' wrath has trailed her, forcing Mochi and her husband to flee towns where they settled after receiving threats. Mochi's parents are willing to call off the feud if her husband pays them $2,110 (he earns $2.11 a day).[92] Such threats are real when we consider what recently occurred to another couple, Almas Khan and Shamim Akhtar, who defied their parents and married. They were killed over the Id al-Fitr weekend marking the end of Ramadan. They were lured back home with promises of forgiveness, then shot, and their bodies strung from trees.

Only through the death of these women can honor be restored to the family. Honor can be maintained by keeping women ignorant. In some places the desire of women to become educated (the first step toward any hope of liberation) is met with violence. Take the example of Malala Yousafzai, the fifteen-year-old Pakistani pupil who in October 2012 was shot point-blank in the head and neck by the Taliban in in order to silence her. Her crime? Not only did she dare to defy the Taliban's ban against girls going to school, but also she was vocal about the rights of girls to an education. According to UNESCO, there are 66 million girls out of school worldwide, much more than boys, who do not face the same discrimination and obstacles.[93] Six months after attack on Malala Yousafzai, in June 2013, eleven students were killed and twenty wounded in a bomb blast on a Sardar Bahadur Khan Women's University bus in the city of Quetta, in western Pakistan. As the victims were taken to the hospital, gunman showed up and continued the assault. The region has been experiencing a surge of militant violence by Islamist groups who oppose women's education.[94]

It is estimated that as many as 27 million men, women and children around the world are the victims of human trafficking, of which 4.5 million are sexually exploited, an estimated 98 percent of whom are women and girls.[95] One of those women forced into prostitution is Valentina, from Romania. She was promised a job in La Jonquera, Spain, working at a hotel. When she arrived, she was instead forced into prostitution. If she refused, the man who made the travel arrangements, whom she thought was her boyfriend, threatened to beat her and kill her children. She now spends her life, standing by a roundabout, charging $40 for intercourse and $27 for oral sex. Valentina is one of the 200,000 to 400,000 trafficked women forced to work as prostitutes just in Spain.[96]

On the other side of the world, in China's Yunnan Province, women become a major export, shipped off by their families to the thriving sex businesses of Thailand or Malaysia to work in the brothels. Previously, these women were kidnapped and forced into sex slavery, but since 2005, the trade has become largely voluntary, motivated mainly by the poverty of Yunnan Province. If they stay at home, they become a liability, another mouth to feed; if they leave, they can provide their family with a relatively affluent lifestyle.[97]

In the United States, we have the case of thirteen-year-old Maria Elena, from a small village in Mexico. A family acquaintance assured her family that she could make ten times more money waiting tables in the United States. Maria Elena, along with other girls, was smuggled across the border, walking for four days through the desert. They finally arrived at a run-down trailer in Texas where they were forced into prostitution. Maria Elena was compelled to have sex with up to thirty men a day. When she got pregnant, she was forced to have an abortion and sent back to work the next day.[98]

Violence against females occurs early in the form of female infanticide, prenatal sex selection, and the systematic neglect of girls, a problem in South and East Asia, North Africa, and the Middle East. For some three million girls a year who survive infancy, the horror of genital mutilation awaits them. It is estimated that 100 to 140 million girls and women alive in 2013, mainly in Africa and some Middle Eastern countries, have undergone genital circumcision.[99] As these girls mature, they still face grave dangers if they rebuff the advances of a potential suitor or become the imaginary cause of a husband, lover, or boyfriend's jealousy. Afghanistan, Bangladesh, India, Pakistan and more recently Columbia, report acid attacks (throwing sulfuric or nitric acids into a woman's face to disfigure her) as a cheap and quick way of destroying a woman's life.[100]

As horrific as these global situations are, we would expect some worldwide outcry, some attempt by international institutions to band together in solidarity with the half of the world's population that faces life-threatening situations in the conduct of their daily activities. In March 2013 the work of the U.N. Commission on the Status of Women was hampered by delegates from Iran, Russia, and the Vatican who attempted to eliminate from the final communiqué and admonition to states to refrain from invoking custom, tradition, and religious considerations as a way of avoiding their obligations to condemn all forms of violence against women.[101] Delegates from Poland, Egypt, several Muslim states, and conservative Christian groups in the United States objected to other parts of the document, including, but not limited to, references to abortion rights and references to the term "rape" when used to describe forcible sexual behavior by a woman's husband or partner.[102] It appears that as long as women are kept from participating in education, society, and the political arena, men who dominate in these spheres of human life will continue to define what is abuse and liberation for women.

Step 2. Reflecting

Since ancient times, the woman's domain was the home, while the man's domain was the public sphere. Even in 2013 half of Americans believed that children are better off if their mothers stay at home without employment, while only 8 percent say the same thing concerning the father.[103] The roots of these modern-day assumptions are found in the ancient honor-shame code. The family's place and reputation within any given society was based on either acquiring honor or inducing shame. Honor is male-centered activity. It was the responsibility of men to maintain or improve the honor of their family while simultaneously avoiding anything that might bring shame upon their family name. Through the man's participation in the public sphere, honor can be increased or decreased through his interactions with other men. While honor is achieved in the public sphere, the domain of men, shame is created within the private sphere, the domain of women.

Because of patriarchy, a woman who belonged to one man yet was used by another brought shame to the "owner" of her body. So to protect one's honor, man confined women to the household, where they can remain secure and protected from enemies wishing to bring shame upon the good name of the one who owned their bodies. This honor-shame code helps explain the binding of feet in some Asian countries, the societal pressure to wear a burka in some Islamic countries, the forced medical procedure of female circumcision in some African countries, or simply the required custom of chaperoning unattended women.

The residue of this ancient honor-shame value system can be seen throughout the development of Christianity. Eve's association with the fall makes her the counterpoint to Mary, the mother of Jesus and the perpetual virgin. Eve represents the ultimate temptress who leads men, and by extension all of humanity astray. Mary, on the other hand, signifies the ideal model for all Christian women to emulate. Christian women have historically been given a choice between the purity that comes with motherhood or the wantonness that comes with independence from benevolent male authority—in short, between the virgin and the whore, and thus between the pivotal values of the ancient world: honor or shame.

Not surprisingly, merchants and soldiers during the fifteenth and sixteenth centuries who left for business or crusades to liberate the Holy Land would protect the family's honor by fashioning chastity belts on their wives. A man could leave in peace knowing that his sexual property was locked and protected from trespassers (with the possible exception of the local locksmith). Remaining tied to her domestic habitation forestalled shame. "As the snail carries its house with it," Martin Luther reminds us, "so the wife should stay at home and look after the affairs of the household, as one who has been deprived of the ability of administering those affairs that are outside and that concern the state."[104] Women's redemption from Eve's influence, and from the shame she herself could bring upon the honor of her man's name, was to seek virtue, either through chastity, which becomes solely her responsibility, or by becoming a prolific mother. If she is a mother, her worth and respect increase proportionately to the number of males she births.

Yet, regardless as how much honor the woman brings to her husband's name, she remains inferior, someone who is less than a male. But women are not the only ones that can be designated as feminine; seeing Others as feminine (whether they be female or male) justifies their subjugation, helping us to better understand the underpinnings of both colonialism and imperialism. Sexism also serves as a paradigm for the subjugation of all people groups that fall short of the white male ideal. Because inferiority has historically been defined as feminine, all who are oppressed, be they females or males, are feminized. While this is not an attempt to minimize oppressive and violent structures toward women in communities of color, it is an attempt to stress that all forms of oppression are identical in their attempt to domesticate the feminine (i.e. inferior) Other, to place the Other in a subordinate position.[105]

The danger that sexist comments made by politicians and pundits poses to society goes beyond some ignorant misogynist remark; they provide us with a blueprint for maintaining and sustaining the racist, elitist, classist, and imperialist structures of society through sexist paradigms these structures advocate. Theologian Mary Daily quipped, "If God is male, then the male is God."[106] And probably this truth is what undergirds the historical war on women. Because God is male—in other words, because God, like males, has a penis—then the male is a god lording over all who lacks a penis. Women, as well as nonwhites (females and males) and the poor (regardless of skin pigmentation) are subordinated to those who possess a penis.

Throughout Judeo-Christian history, God has been thought of as a male, consistently referred to as a "he." But if the function of a penis is to urinate and/or copulate, why would God need a penis? Or does the penis have societal meaning? If women were castrated by the Almighty He, envious of what only God and men possess, should it not be natural, then, for woman to submit to men who, unlike women, are created in the very image of God? Is Sigmund Freud's theory of "penis envy" therefore accurate?

With this in mind, we can understand why Abraham and Israel placed great spiritual value on their penises, swearing oaths upon their genitals (Gen. 24:2–3; 47:29–31); or why King David wins Michal as his wife through the gift of a hundred foreskins from Philistine penises (2 Sam. 3:14). More importantly the very sign of the covenant between God and man begins with the penis, specifically cutting off its foreskin through the ritual of circumcision (Gen. 17:10–14).[107] How then do women enter into a covenant with God if there is no penis to circumcise?[108]

To use a psychological analysis, when "the Man" looks into Lacan's mirror, he constructs his male identity through a distancing process of negative, defining himself through the archetype of "I am what I am not." For example, because women are emotional, when the man looks into a mirror, he does not see a woman, and therefore he is not emotional. Because women are inferior and weak, when he looks into a mirror, he does not see a woman, therefore he is not inferior or weak. In the formation of the subject's ego, an illusory self-representation is constructed through the negation of a penis, which is projected upon Others, those who would be identified as non-men.

Ascribing femininity to the Other, regardless of gender, forces feminine identity construction to originate with the domesticating man. In fact, the feminine Object, in and of itself, is seen as nothing apart from a masculine Subject, which provides unifying purpose.[109] The resulting gaze of the white, elite male inscribes effeminacy upon Others who are not man enough to "make" history, or "provide" for their family, or "resist" their subjugation. Ironically, no one really has a penis. The man lives, always threatened by possible loss, while the non-man is forcibly deprived. The potent symbolic power invested in the penis both signals and veils heterosexual male domination, as well as white supremacy and socioeconomic power. Constructing those oppressed as feminine allows men with penises to assert their privilege by constructing oppressed Others as inhabitants of the castrated realm of the exotic and primitive. Lacking a penis, the Other does not exist, except as designated by the desire of the one with a penis. While non-men are forced to flee from their individuality, the white man must constantly attempt to live up to a false construction.[110]

When Sandra Fluke attempted to speak for herself, Rush Limbaugh attempted to define her as an oversexed slut while defining himself through the self-negation of his construction of her. Publicly discrediting women is not a new strategy; historically, whenever women have attempted to declare their own agency, they have historically been shamed into silence. Consider Mary of Magdala, who, for many within the church, was believed to be a prostitute. Yet nowhere in the biblical text is Mary of Magdala referred to as a prostitute. All three Synoptic Gospels (Mt. 27:55–56; Mk. 15:40–41; Lk. 24:10), instead refer to Mary of Magdala as first among Jesus' female disciples. Contrary to tradition, which credits Peter as the first to witness the Resurrection (1 Cor. 15:4-6); it was Mary of Magdala who first saw the risen Lord and the first to proclaim the good news of the resurrection (Mk. 16:9–10; Jn. 20:1–18). The biblical text and the early writings of the first church[111] testify to the leadership position she held. Nonetheless, as the early Christian church reverted to patriarchal structures, Mary of Magdala had to be discredited so as to disqualify her position of authority within the church. Hence, the church tradition constructed by men, protecting male privilege, arose that she was a prostitute, an attempt to question her contribution in the establishment of Christianity.

Step 3. Praying

The biblical text has historically been interpreted within Christianity in such a way that it has contributed to the creation and prorogation of abuses toward women that remain not so well masked within many churches today. Probably the best biblical way to maintain control over women is through the construction of the traditional biblical marriage, as defined by most religious conservatives; even though such a concept is foreign to the biblical text. In fact, it would be hard to find a modern-day Christian who would actually abide by a biblical marriage in practice, for the biblical understanding of marriage meant that (1) women are property to be owned by men, (2) women are human incubators, (3) women are the weaker sex, and (4) women are the cause of evil.

Male ownership of women meant that women, as the property of men, existed for male desires. Early in the biblical text, we are told that the woman's desire would be for her husband, while he would rule over her (Gen. 3:16).[112] Upon marriage, a woman's property and her body became the possession of her new husband. Women became available for male possession soon after they reached puberty (usually eleven to thirteen years old)—that is, when a woman became physically able to produce children.

Throughout the Hebrew Bible, it is taken for granted that women (as well as children) are the possessions of men. The focus of the text does not seriously consider or concentrate upon the women's status, but constructs their identity by their sexual relationship to the man: virgin daughter, betrothal bride, married woman, mother, barren wife, or widow. A woman's dignity and worth as one created in the image of God is subordinated to the needs and desires of men.

As chattel, women became the extension of a man, thus any trespass against the man's possession becomes a direct violation of the man. Not surprisingly, women are often equated with a house or livestock (e.g., Deut. 20:5–7), which is demonstrated in the last commandment, "You shalt not covet thy neighbor's house, wife, slave, ox or donkey" (Ex. 20:17). Because women are excluded from being the subject of this commandment, the woman, like a house, slave, ox or donkey, is reduced to an object, just another possession, another piece of property that belongs to the man, and thus should not be coveted by another man. This is why regulations concerning sexual activities appear in the biblical text under the category of property law. If a daughter was raped, the perpetrator had to either pay her father (who own her virginity) three times the original marriage price for the lost in value of his property or marry the young girl (Ex. 22:15–16, 23–29).

A man could have as many sexual partners as he could afford. Patriarchs of the faith, Abraham, Jacob, and Judah, had multiple wives and/or concubines, and delighted themselves with the occasional prostitute (Gen. 38:15). King Solomon alone was reported to have had over seven hundred wives of royal birth and three hundred concubines (1 Kings 11:3). The book of Leviticus, in giving instructions to men wishing to own a harem, provides only one prohibition, which is not to "own" sisters (Lev. 18:18). The Hebrew Bible is clear that men could have multiple sex partners. Wives ensured legitimate heirs; all other sex partners existed for the pleasures of the flesh. A woman, on the other hand, was limited to just one sex partner who ruled over her, unless of course, she was a prostitute. Sins like adultery never applied to men, but only applied to women, which explains why the man involved with the woman "caught in the act of adultery" (Jn. 8:3) did not need to be brought to Jesus, but she did. After all, if she was caught in the very act, was there not also a man present?[113]

Second, the biblical understanding for the purpose for marriage has historically been reproduction; women were understood to be human incubators. A barren Sarai offers her slave girl Hagar to Abram for rape so that she, Sarai, can give him an heir (Gen. 16:2). Rachel, Jacob's wife, demands that her husband "Give me children, or I shall die" (Gen. 30:1). If the woman was unable to bring forth a child, the marriage could be dissolved by the man. Besides reproduction, marriage within a patriarchal order also served political and economic means. To ensure that any offspring were the legitimate heirs, the woman was restricted to just one sex partner, her husband. Biblical marriages were endogamous, that is, they occurred within the same extended family or clan, unlike the modern Western concept of exogamous, where unions occur between outsiders.

The early shapers of Christian thought believed that the only purpose for a woman's existence was her ability to procreate. Only through childbearing could a woman be saved, a disturbing understanding of salvation as reiterated by Paul: "It was not Adam who was led astray, but the woman who was led astray and fell into sin. Nevertheless, she will be saved by childbearing" (1 Tim. 2:14–15). Paul, the promoter of salvation solely through grace, not works, implied that unlike men, women are saved through childbearing, a concept rooted in patriarchy. Birthing children took precedence over the life of the mother. Or as Martin Luther instructed women, "Bring that child forth, and do it with all your might! If you die in the process, so pass on over, good for you! For you actually die in a noble work and in obedience to God."[114]

On a side note, if the only natural reason for participating in sex is procreation, then all sexual activities that do not lead to children are, by definition, unnatural. Hence, for a man to engage in intercourse with a barren woman, a menopausal woman, or menstruating woman becomes an abomination because of her inability to conceive (Lev. 15:24). Any sexual act that does not directly lead to human conception automatically becomes defined as "unnatural," be it oral sex, anal sex, homosexual sex, using condoms during sex, or sex for the pure sake of pleasure.[115] Hence the admonition from the first century Christian thinker Clement of Alexandria (ca. 150–215): "To indulge in intercourse without intending children is to outrage nature."[116]

Third, an underlying assumption found throughout the biblical text is that men are physically and morally superior to women, the weaker sex. According to 1 Peter, "Husbands must treat their wives with consideration, bestowing honor on her as one who, though she may be the weaker vessel, is truly a co-heir to the grace of life" (1 Pet. 3:7). Although equal in grace, still the purpose for the woman as the "weaker vessel" is to be ruled by the man. In his first letter to the Corinthians, Paul insisted that women cover their heads because the woman is the "glory of man." Specifically, he writes: "For man...is the image and glory of God. But the woman is the glory of man. For man did not come from woman, but woman from man. And man was not created for woman, but woman for man" (1 Cor. 11:7–9).

Because man is closer to the spirit, he is a rational subject ordained to rule; and because woman is closer to the flesh, she is an emotional object ordained to be ruled. Thus, subjecting woman to man becomes the natural manifestation of subjecting passion to reason. Paul makes this view obvious when he writes: "But as the church is subject to Christ, so also are wives to be subject to their husbands in everything" (Eph. 5:24). Just as the body must submit to the spirit, which is superior, and the church must submit to Christ, so too must the wife submit to her husband. Ephesians (along with Col. 3:18–19) sets up the marriage relationship in which husbands are commanded to love their wives, while wives are commanded not to love, but submit to their husbands.[117] This makes women, according to Thomas Aquinas, a "defective and misbegotten male"—probably due to "some external influence, such as that of a south wind, which is moist."[118]

Fourth and finally, another assumption of the biblical tradition can be summed up as the following: because women are responsible for the evil in the world, they must be controlled for their own good. Their shapely curves incite passion among holy men. Thus, they are the cause of man's disgrace and downfall. One of the major Christian themes is that women, represented by Eve, are the cause of sin and consequently the reason *man*kind was led astray from God's perfect will. She was first to be deceived and was responsible for deceiving the man. Like their mother Eve, all women today are the incarnation of temptation.[119] Connecting Eve with all women, the early Christian thinker Tertullian (ca. 165–220) proclaimed: "You [woman] are the one who opened the door to the devil...you are the one who persuaded [Adam] whom the devil was not strong enough to attack. All too easily you destroyed the image of God, man. Because of your desert, that is, death, even the Son of God had to die."[120] In conclusion, the use of the biblical text in the war on women becomes somewhat problematic in the quest for liberation.

Step 4. Case Studies

1. Since 1979, China has a one-child policy, an attempt to deal with a growing population that is placing a strain on national and global resources and on the environment. Village officials are charged with charting the menstrual cycle of every childbearing woman and providing pelvic-exams within their rural region. Women who are impregnated without government permission must pay an exorbitant fine or risk a forced abortion. Feng Jianmei, who was carrying a second child in violation of the national policy, was forced by local officials to abort a seven month-old fetus. Until she ceded to official demands, peasants in her village of Yuping were led in a march that denounced family members as "traitors." Her husband was even beaten. She could have kept the second child if she would have paid the $6,300 fine (anywhere from three to ten times a household income, depending on the province).[121] Compare her plight with that of Zhang Yimou, the celebrated film director and arranger of the Beijing 2008 Summer Olympics' opening ceremony. He also violated the one-child policy by fathering seven children with four different women.[122] But unlike Feng, Zhang is wealthy and thus can easily afford the penalty. What is a ferocious tiger for Feng is but a paper tiger for Zhang.

- Are mandatory abortions ever ethical? Even for the common good? State officials argue that without the one-child policy, the economy would falter and the population would explode. Do the needs of the State trump the rights of the individual? Does the one-child policy reduce women to a means of production? Could this be why China has the highest rate of female suicide in the world?
- Should family planning be determined by the ability to pay? Should those who are successful be allowed to have more children, that will have the economic means of also succeeding?
- What if it is determined that the fetus is female, do parents have a right to abort in hopes that the next pregnancy might produce a boy? Sex-selection abortions have skewed China's sex ratio to 118 boys for every 100 girls. Is this problematic? Why or why not? In the United States, the House rejected a measure that would have imposed fines and prison terms on doctors who performed sex-selection abortions.[123] Was the rejection of this legislation moral? Why or why not?
- In the western state of Rakhine, Myanmar, which has the highest Islamic population within a Buddhist-majority country, local authorities have imposed a two-child limit for Muslim families.[124] How problematic is this regulation? Although Muslims represent

4 percent of the country's population; the state argues this policy will reduce sectarian violence. In 2012, Buddhists armed with machetes razed thousands of Muslims homes leaving hundreds dead and forcing 125,000 to flee. Is securing future peace by controlling Muslim women bodies worth considering such regulations? Why or why not?

2. Melissa Nelson, a ten-year dental assistant for Dr. James Knight, was fired from her job because he found her attractive. Both he and his wife were concerned that the women might become a threat to their marriage, so he fired her to save his marriage. Nelson sued and lost. The all-male Iowa Supreme Court ruled that employers could fire whom they found to be an "irresistible attraction," even if the employee did nothing warranting termination. Justice Edward M. Mansfield wrote that such firings are lawful under state law because they were not motivated by gender, rather by feelings and emotions. Knight's attorney interpreted the decision as a victory for family values. Nelson's attorney, Paige Fiedler, on the other hand, said the courts failed to recognize the discrimination women consistently experience in the workplace. She went on to say, "These judges sent a message to Iowa women that they don't think men can be held responsible for their sexual desires and that Iowa women are the ones who have to monitor and control their bosses' sexual desires."[125]

- Should Knight be praised for his fidelity to his wife in going to extreme lengths to save his marriage? Is it better for men to admit their "irresistible attraction" for certain beautiful female employees rather than to subject them to unwanted attention or sexual harassment? What responsibility, if any, does Ms. Nelson hold in her dismissal? Was the ruling fair and just? Why or why not?
- Can a married female employer fire an attractive man whom she finds attractive? What about an employer who finds an employee of the same gender attractive, even if the employee is a heterosexual? Does the ruling objectify bodies based on desirability? Can the argument of sexual desire be used as an excuse to dismiss unwanted employees?

3. Taj Mohammad, who lives in a sprawling refugee camp in Kabul, Afghanistan, is unable to repay a debt to a fellow camp resident and elder. He makes $6 a day, when he can find work as an unskilled laborer. He borrowed the money to pay for his wife's hospital treatment and medical care for some of his nine children. If the debt is not paid, he is at risk of losing what he put up as collateral, his six-year old daughter Naghma. Unless he repays the $2,500 loan, Naghma will be forced to leave her home and marry the creditor's seventeen-year-old son.

Unfortunately, Mohammad does not have the money. He is so poor that his three-year-old daughter, Janan, froze to death during the bitter winter because he could not afford enough firewood.[126]

- Afghan tradition allows the groom's family to pay a "bride price," in this case, the forgiveness of the $2,500 debt. If this is an acceptable traditional practice, are Westerners imposing their sense of morality when they say it is wrong? Is a "bride price" fine as long as it does not involve children? If Westerners become involved in denouncing bride price, are they being paternalistic toward Afghan women?
- Is the use of woman as property universally wrong under all circumstances regardless of traditions and cultures? Is ethics and morality a construct of specific people groups, or do they transcend cultures and traditions regardless of time periods? If certain moral truths apply to everyone, everywhere, always, who then gets to determine what is universally right or wrong?
- Before Naghma was handed off to her husband to repay a debt, an anonymous donor stepped forward and paid the loan.[127] This story has a happy ending, but how many unknown Naghmas are being sold as property, and what can be done about it? Even though her trade was considered illegal under Afghanistan's Elimination of Violence against Women law, the law can only be enforced if the one abused or her relative files a complaint. How can the Naghmas of the world be safeguarded without the end product appearing paternalistic or seem as an imposition of a Western sense of morality? Or maybe Western morality is superior? Why or why not?

4. Beatriz of El Salvador, already a mother of a toddler who believes abortions are almost always wrong, is experiencing a high-risk pregnancy that could ultimately kill her. The fetus she is carrying is not viable, suffering from anencephaly, with almost no chance of surviving. Although the doctors are urging her to abort the fetus, El Salvador prohibits abortions under any circumstances.[128] She and her doctor could face up to eight years in prison if he performs the abortion. She awaits the decision of the Salvadoran Supreme Court to determine her case. The Salvadoran Roman Catholic Church has argued that the fetus' malformation should not be met with a death sentence. "This case," according to the Episcopal Conference of El Salvador, "should not be used to legislate against human life."[129]

- Is the church right? Does the life of the unborn trump the life of the mother? Should the matter of life and death remain only in the hands of God? Or is the church imposing its religious views upon the people, some of whom may not believe in a God? Still, if abortion is indeed murder, as the church claims, should the church then do everything in their power to uphold this universal claim?

- On May 29, 2013, El Salvador's highest court in a 4-to-1 ruling denied Beatriz's request for an abortion. Beatriz's lawyer described the ruling as "misogynistic," claiming, "Justice here does not respect the rights of women."[130] Is her lawyer correct in her assessment? Why or why not? Travel abroad is not possible because the trip could kill her. So what other options are available to her?

- Although abortion is not an option because of the court's decision, Salvadoran health Minister, María Isabel Rodríguez stated that at the point Beatriz's life is in danger, doctors can "induce birth" via an abdominal or vaginal birth. Less than a week after the court decision, a caesarean section ended her high-risk pregnancy.[131] Did doctors unable to perform abortions terminate a pregnancy without technically violating the law? The fetus was placed in an incubator and provided fluids, expiring within five hours. Is this a creative way around the law, or is it a result of decisions concerning women's bodies being beyond the control of women? Is this a victory for women rights, or a quick fix on one particular case?

11

Book Review of Pope Francis's *Open Mind, Faithful Heart*

Open Mind, Faithful Heart, which reads as a devotional, provides the reader with insight into the mind and heart of Pope Francis. This is the last book he wrote as cardinal, originally published under the title *Mente abierta, corazon creyente* (2013). Jorge Bergoglio gathered his most significant writings concerning Christian life in preparation for his seventy-fifth birthday, at which time he planned to present his resignation to Pope Benedict XVI in accordance with canonical norms. His election to sit on St. Peter's throne, however, has made this book required reading for any student of the Vatican. The book provides insight to the public pronouncements and praxis performed as Pope Francis; revealing also the ideological foundation of his recent apostolic exhortation.

The thesis of *Open Mind, Faithful Heart*—like the thesis of *Evangelii Gaudium* (EG)—can be summed up as his joyful evangelical call for a renewed encounter with Jesus Christ and Christ's covenant with humanity. Bergoglio's down-to-earth and accessible essays reveal the depths of his spirituality, exposing the heart of a pastor. If ever I were depressed, hurt, or doubtful, I would want Bergoglio to be my priest, someone who can comfort and humbly pray with me. But if I'm oppressed, I am not so sure I want him to lead me toward liberation.

There is no question Bergoglio makes a preferential option for the least among us (28). He states, "without mincing words, that there is an inseparable bond between...faith and the poor" (EG 1:V:48). While the inclusion of the poor is evident, there appears silence on how to dismantle the very structures responsible for causing poverty. Emphasis seems to be on salvation by ministering in the midst of struggle; rather than liberation from these struggles as synonymous with salvation. Opposition to economic oppression a liberationist does not make. Readers of this book must be careful not to fall into the common U.S. ideological dualism, which neatly separates capitalist from socialist (taken to be synonymous with communist). Rather than being a liberationist thinker, he simply continues to operate within the century-old social teachings of the Church, which also makes a preferential option for the poor.

Although I would want Bergoglio to be my spiritual pastor, I remain ambiguous about his ability to lead the oppressed toward liberation. The most disturbing pronouncements in his book are based on his medieval understanding of women. Throughout the book, whenever he references a woman (with the exception of Lois and Eunice of 2 Tim 1:5 [on page 132]), she is either portrayed as faithful—mainly as virgin—or as adulterous (4, 44–51, 89, 108, 122, 147, 154–5, 161–2, 188, 193, 272, 280). He subscribes to the Christianization of the ancient honor-shame tradition manifested as the choice between the virgin or the whore, Mary or Eve. He writes, "The Church's holiness [whom the Church Fathers called the 'chaste prostitute'] is reflected in the face of Mary, the sinless one, pure and spotless one, but she does not forget that she gathers in her bosom the children of Eve, mother of all us sinners" (45). Women as temptation is best captured when he claims that "the ire of a lustful woman, the swaying of a flirtatious dancer, and a whimsical request" made to the "corrupt and feeble heart of Herod" led to John the Baptist's decapitation (122).

Pope Francis dualist understanding of women leads to the paternalism found in *Evangelii Gaudium* where he speaks of the "icon of womenhood" (EG 5:II:284); essentializing women when he "acknowledges the indispensable contribution which women make to society through sensitivity, intuition and other distinctive skill set which they, more than men, tend to possess" (EG 2:II:103). Women may be "indispensable" due to their feminine characteristics; nevertheless, they cannot fully participate as man's equal. Bergoglio maintains centuries of institutionalized violence by reaffirming the biblical mandate (Eph. 5:22–23) of husbands being the head of wives (148). He strengthens patriarchy by rejecting the ability of women to be "builders of bridges." Women cannot be priests (*pontifex* or builders of bridges) not so much because the Church prohibits it, but because Jesus Christ, who does the choosing, doesn't seem to choose women (8–9). If "the image of the Lord is the priest" (171); then can the image of the Lord be found in women? Pope Francis may claim that "Mary is more important than the bishop;" nevertheless, he insists that "the reservation of the priesthood to males, as a sign of Christ the spouse… is not a question open to discussion" (EC 2:II:104). Neither Pope nor Church can ever be a symbol of liberation as long as it remains complicit with the oppression of half of the global population, regardless of the flowery compliments about indispensability expressed.

Also troubling is Pope Francis's response to a question concerning homosexuality: "If someone is gay and he searches for the Lord and has good will, who am I to judge?" (7/28/13). Although a novel and encouraging approach toward a Vatican taboo, it is not as revolutionary as most have hailed it to be. When discussing in his book the adulterous women caught in the very act as recorded in John 8, Bergoglio does not raise the patriarchal structures that may have caused this women to participate in this act; rather, he concentrates on how Jesus addressed those willing to trap him while still encouraging the woman to live responsibly (4). But asking the obvious, where was the man if she was caught in the act, he concentrates instead on the pastoral response to a sinner. Likewise, his approach to homosexuals—who am I to judge—may appear refreshing, yet he still understands homosexuality to be a sin to which the church's response should be pastoral aimed at restoring the "sinner's" fullness of life. For him, Sodom and Gomorrah remains "a sin of the flesh" (220). Hence, his approach to homosexuality is not that different than other conservative churches who encourage "hating the sin while loving the sinner." Pope Francis best expresses his views on homosexuality when he writes: "Marriage now tends to be viewed as a form of mere emotional satisfaction that can be constructed in anyway or modified at will" (EG 2:I:66).

Also troubling is Bergoglio's romanticization of missionary conquest. He writes "The first evangelizers [of South America] gave Native Americans knowledge of why they should engage in struggle… we should help people to learn the real reason for their struggle" (31). Yet several Indian scholars have responded that Christianity is the real reason for their struggle, a struggle against the physical and cultural genocide implemented by the evangelizers. Nevertheless, Bergoglio credits symbols of the Virgin for the spiritual unity of Latin American nations, bringing as one "Spaniards and Indians, missionary and conquistador, Spanish colonization and racial assimilation" (102). Problematic is the lack of nuance in his view of the Church that he describes as "glorious precisely because it is a history of sacrifices, of hopes, of daily struggles" (96); a history unrecognizable to many on the underside of Christendom, specifically the Indian, the conquered, and the assimilated.

It is appropriate to end this review of Bergoglio's book by first repeating his quote of St. Loyola. "For the enemy moves people who have good intentions but bad information to reject that which they do not understand" (66). And secondly, encouraging him "as the Bishop of Rome, to be open to suggestions which can help make the exercise of [his] ministry more faithful to the meaning which Jesus Christ wished to give it and to the present needs of evangelization" (EG 1:II:32).

12

Lot's Wife: Vain? Materialistic? Or Just Human?[1]

The Sodom and Gomorrah story reaches its climax when Lot's nameless wife is turned into a pillar of salt. This nameless biblical woman has been dismissed throughout history as a vain and materialistic woman who, because of her character, deserved her punishment. The rabbinical text blames the destruction of Sodom on their wickedness, and the transformation of Lot's wife on her unbelief. When people leave wickedness behind, some still pine for their previous evil ways symbolized by glancing reminiscently toward the past. As Jesus would eventually warn: "No one placing their hand on the plow and looking at the things behind, is worthy for the reign of God" (Lk. 9:62).

Her sinfulness has become normative in modern biblical hermeneutics. For example, *The Interpreter's Bible* notes that Lot's wife was "the woman caught in the whirlwind of fire from doomed Sodom because she was still too reluctant to leave the wicked city... she was representative of all those in every time who are caught in the consequences of the evil they cannot quite let go." Lot's wife's condemnation even comes from the mouth of Jesus, the only other place in the Bible where she is mentioned. When discussing the urgency by which the last days approach those accustomed to luxurious living, Jesus provides us with a warning to "Remember Lot's wife" (Lk. 17:31). The assumption is that Lot's wife was narcissistic, seeking the pleasures of this world. This theology is read back into the text, even though the Genesis account is silent about the character of Lot's wife.

All that the text tells us about her is summed up in six Hebrew words that translate to: "And his wife looked back from behind him and she became a pillar of salt." Based on this solitary mention, elaborate character portraits of Lot's wife are constructed. Why? To justify her demise. If she is not portrayed as a foolish woman with a self-indulging heart, then her punishment would appear capricious, especially if, because she's a woman, Lot did not bother discussing the options facing them as he did with his prospective sons-in-law. After all, the text fails to note any discussion with Lot's wife concerning what could befall them. Verse 19:15 simply has the angels stating, "Take your wife and your two young daughters...lest you [masculine singular] be consumed." For most of us, our sense of justice is offended that the God of second-chances, the God of love, mercy, and forgiveness would act so harshly, especially when we consider that the text is ambiguous about who was informed concerning the danger of looking back. In order to justify Lot's wife's punishment, she must either be vilified, or simply ignored.

Even though her presence is implied throughout the Sodom and Gomorrah story, she remains invisible. For example, when we are told that Lot prepared the two angels a meal of unleavened bread (Gen. 19:3), more than likely it was his wife, under a patriarchal rule, that did the preparing, serving, and cleaning-up. Yet, for a brief moment, Lot's wife takes center stage in the story. Lot's wife becomes visible when she looks back and is turned into a pillar of salt. This becomes a disturbing tale of a person who is punished for attempting to see the destruction of the city. And yet, when Abram also looked toward Sodom's demise, he is not turned into a pillar of salt (Gen. 19:27–28).

Rather than depicting Lot's wife as either the totality of worldliness or the other extreme of virtuousness, maybe we should see her like we see the rest of us: a human who falls short of the glory of God. As an invisible member within a patriarchal society, she probably did the wash with her neighbors—also nameless women. They might have been present when she twice gave birth, as she might have been when they gave birth to their own children. She shared gossip and stories with them as she tended her garden, prepared meals or simply rested under the stars after a long day of heavy, menial work. The men of the city may all have been wicked, but these women with whom she shared a similar fate of patriarchal oppression, more than likely, were her friends.

Sodom, with all its imperfections, was her home—just like many of us have made our homes in the entrails of the empire. She might have looked back to see the life that would no longer follow the well-established rhythms of the everyday. She might have looked back to mourn friends swallowed up in God's wrath who were now no more. She might have looked back to say adieu to all the daily rituals and routines that marked her life and provided meaning to her existence. Who among us would not have also taken a peek, along with Lot's wife and Abram? Those of us who have known exile, being cast from the land that witnessed our birth, are always in a quest to see the cause of our estrangement. Only then can we hope to find healing and create healthy, well-adjusted lives. We look back, lest we forget our identity.

It does not really matter why she looked back. The reality is that we will never ascertain the motives of her heart. The fact is that she looked and was swiftly punished by God. If she did know of the consequences and still looked back, then she committed suicide. But if patriarchal rule meant Lot did not need to inform her of what was occurring, then her looking back was an accident, making her a victim of homicide. Lot's wife is killed because she is prohibited from remembering. There are no opportunities for absolution or redemption offered to her. This is one of those verses in Scripture that is profoundly disturbing, for it seems as if the God of Lot is not the merciful and forgiving God to whom we have become accustomed.

PART FIVE

Sexual Abuse

13

Testimony of Sarah[1]
Genesis 20:1–20:18; 21:1–7:

I want sex. One or two times. That's all. You get your green card. You won't have to see me anymore.
—ISAAC R. BAICHU, U.S. FEDERAL IMMIGRATION OFFICER [2]

Woman's true sphere is within the family circle. He who would substitute anything else, frustrates her true nature, disrupts the providential plan of God and creates serious problems for society at large, which becomes filled with neurotic unhappy, useless and very often, and worst of all, disruptive women!
—MONSIGNOR JAMES ALBERIONE [3]

Abraham apparently learned nothing from his first earlier encounter with Pharaoh. Once again, he is pawning off his wife by claiming that she is his sister. Even though Sarah may very well be in her nineties, she is supposedly such a gorgeous woman that royalty lust over her, desiring to possess her. Some scholars insist that the events that unfolded at Gerar are simply another version of the earlier events that occurred when Abraham journeyed to Egypt (Gen. 12:10–20), with the earlier account being a product of the J source, while the Gerar events being a product of E. Although that may be true, both stories can also be viewed separately, even though obvious connections and divergences exist. For example, unlike the earlier version that claimed that Pharaoh took Sarah as his wife, thus implying a sexual relationship, the Gerar version takes great lengths to insist no inappropriate physical activity took place between the king and the matriarch of the faith, possibly because soon after this encounter, Sarah is with child. The Gerar account could very well be one event among many where Abraham pimps his wife to secure security and possessions. Telling inhabitants of the towns they encounter that Sarah is his sister appears to be his modus operandi. Abraham specifically instructed Sarah that *everywhere* they travel she is to say that he is but her brother. This might explain why, unlike the earlier Egyptian episode (which could very well be the first time this form of deception was implemented) there is no indication that this time Abraham consulted with his wife. They each simply played the part of siblings. There was no need to remind Sarah of the deception because she already knew her "place."

In the previous chapter, we are told that Abraham has made his home at the oak of Mamre, near Hebron. The story opens with him traveling south to the land of Negeb, near the border of Egypt, the same region where Hagar had earlier run away from her master and named the God who sees. There Abraham settled between Kadesh and Shur in an area called Gerar, a city whose exact location remains undetermined. When Abraham met the king of Gerar, Abimelech (either a personal name or a title translated as "my father is king"), he told the king that Sarah was his sister. Gazing upon this elderly beauty, Abimelech took possession of her.

But that night the king had a dream in which God appeared to Abimelech, warning that he will die for taking another man's wife. Although not always the case, God can prevent sin from occurring. The king professes his innocence, truthfully claiming he was deceived; nevertheless, God still hold him accountable for sin he almost committed....

When confronted by Abimelech, Abraham finds lame excuses, excuses similar to the ones he earlier voiced to the Pharaoh. According to Abraham, he feared for his life, believing that the inhabitants of Gerar had no knowledge of God. Besides, he technically was not lying. Sarah was his sister, half sister to be exact, sharing the same father. But Abraham was wrong; Abimelech did fear God, as demonstrated by his actions. It was Abraham who feared humans more than he feared God, willing to sin by handing over his wife. Or maybe the real issue was not fear but greed. The story ends similarly to the Egyptian account, with Abimelech showering Abraham with sheep, cattle, slaves, and a thousand pieces of silver, along with permission to settle anywhere within his domain that Abraham chooses. Abraham's deception has proven to be very profitable, thus possibly explaining why he continues to reemploy the scam.

While the focus remains on Abraham and Abimelech, this is truly a testimony about Sarah and the many women who have historically found themselves in similar situations. Like the earlier Egyptian narrative, migrant women are the ones who are usually placed in the most vulnerable positions for the sake of their families. All too often, migrant women like Sarah are forced to participate in unwanted sexual activities in order to obtain or keep employment so as to feed their families. Millions of noncitizen women live in a kind of legal no-man's land, at the mercy of employers and federal immigration agents for their livelihoods, increasingly fearful of approaching law enforcement agencies for protection from abuse, specifically sexual blackmail. Take the example of Isaac R. Baichu, a federal immigration officer in New York City, who pleaded guilty in April, 2010 for demanding sex from a twenty-two-year old Colombian wife of an American citizen in December 2007 in exchange for a green card.

It is impossible to tell how widespread sexual blackmail is, but Baichu's case is not an isolated instance. For example, immigration agent Lloyd W. Miner of Hyattsville, Maryland, induced a twenty-one-year-old Mongolian woman to stay in the country illegally, harboring her in his home. A sixty-year-old immigration adjudicator in Santa Ana, California, was charged with demanding sex from a twenty-nine-year-old Vietnamese woman in exchange for approving her citizenship application. Immigration agent Eddie Romualdo Miranda was acquitted of sexual battery in August 2007, although he did plead guilty to misdemeanor battery and was sentenced to probation. In Atlanta another adjudicator, Kelvin R. Owens, was convicted in 2005 of sexually assaulting a forty-five-year-old woman during her citizenship interview in the federal building. And in Miami, an agent of Immigration and Customs Enforcement responsible for transporting a Haitian woman to detention instead took her to his home and raped her. According to congressional testimony given in 2006 by Michael Maxwell, former director of Homeland Security's internal investigations, more than three thousand backlogged complaints of employee misconduct had gone uninvestigated for lack of staff, including 528 involving criminal allegations.[4] The New York City Colombian woman, like so many vulnerable migrant women, was forced to engage in oral sex with a representative of the "king" in order to stay in the country with her family. Unfortunately, when her husband found out, he left her. In addition, as of 2010, she still lives in limbo, at the mercy of other unscrupulous Abimelech officials waiting for her green card.

Although the text reassures the reader that nothing sexual transpired between Abimelech and the migrant woman Sarah, it probably still raised eyebrows to discover a few verses later, at the start of chapter 21, that Sarah is with child. We have no way of knowing if Isaac is born nine months after the Abimelech affair. To complicate the situation, if she was already pregnant when she was at Gerar and entered the king's harem, she surely would have been executed for carrying another man's child once the king found out. While the text assures us that Abimelech is not Isaac's father, we are still left wondering if the father is Abraham. It is after God "did for Sarah as he had promised" (21:1) that she conceives. Did Abraham (as will be the case with a future Joseph,

Jesus' supposed father) have anything to do with conception? Is Sarah, like the future Mary, impregnated after God's visit?

Regardless, the biblical lesson being revealed is that God is author of all life, with the power to open and close wombs. As the Gerar episode concludes, we are told that God, on account of Sarah, closed the wombs of all the women (wife and slave girls) in Abimelech's household. It is only after Abraham intercedes for the king that their wombs are opened. According to the scriptures, a healing occurs in verse 17, uncomfortably implying that barrenness is some sort of disease visited on women by God.

God's promise to Abraham comes to fruition. Sarah gives birth. She recognizes the humor of nursing children in her advanced years, and thus laughs in joy with all who hear of her predicament. Having the elusive child is what finally completes her as a woman, a problematic proposition proposed by male church leaders to limit woman's fulfillment solely to the sphere of the family.

After eight days, we are told that Abraham circumcises the child, thus bringing the promised child into covenant. But while the birth of Isaac indicates God's faithfulness to the covenant made with Abraham, we are left wondering if the covenant should have instead been made with Sarah. After all, none of the other descendants of Abraham, (Ishmael by Hagar or the six sons bore to him by Keturah, the woman he married after Sarah dies) is the promised child of the covenant. Not all of the children Abraham sired are of the covenant, but Sarah's only begotten son is.

14

Testimony of Dinah[1]
Genesis 33:18—34:31

In moral reading of the text, Dinah represents the curious, wandering soul who brings destruction upon herself by abandoning the safety of the father's house. As exemplum, the fate of Dinah warns nuns and daughters to stay indoors, in the cloister or under their father's protection. Most interpreters tacitly or explicitly accepted cultural stereotypes that assumed that women provoke rape and find pleasure in it.

—JOY A. SCHROEDER[2]

Some scholars agree that he [Shechem] raped me [Dinah]. Others stand on their learned heads in order to prove, to their own satisfaction, that he in fact practiced pre-nuptial kidnapping, nothing more sinister than that, and that the terminology used—within the customs of the ancient Near East, as the sociologists will tell you— supports the notion that no rape was involved.

—ATHALYA BRENNER[3]

We know that Jacob was not just the father of boys. After the list of all the sons born to Leah, as an afterthought the birth of Dinah is mentioned (30:21). It is no wonder she goes out seeking the companionship of the other women of the land. An afterthought at home, she must have craved attention and relationships, not wanting to end up like her unloved mother, Leah, always desiring the elusive love of her husband. We can only wonder how many other daughters were born to Jacob that have remained invisible, only to be mentioned in passing (46:15). Dinah's birth is barely noticed because she was not male, and even now her appearance in the text is due to the sway it will have on her brothers Simeon and Levi. Throughout the entire story, Dinah remains the object;

she is never granted subjectivity. Her voice, her concerns, her pain, her emotions, her frustrations are never voiced. She never says a word! In effect, her testimony remains unheard. All that matters, and all we hear about, is how her abused body as object prompts the men in the story to act.

Dinah transgresses boundaries and ventures outside her father's home to visit the women of the region. This is the tale of a woman who leaves the safety of her domestic domain for the wider public domain of men. From the start, it seems as though Dinah is being set up to share in the blame for what is about to befall her, for venturing outside the home without a proper chaperone. The victim of rape, then as now, is somewhat held culpable. Death before dishonor becomes part of the acceptable collective consciousness still held by many men. Unescorted, Dinah catches the eye of one of Hamor's sons, Shechem, who carries the same name as the town. We are left wondering if Shechem refers to an individual or an entire clan, a similar concern that will later be raised with Simeon and Levi.

Regardless, Shechem gazed upon Dinah and fell in lust with her, carrying her off and raping her. He saw, he carried off, he raped. In the words of the biblical text, he "defiled" her. If we were to accept the biblical chronology concerning Jacob's life (30:21; 31:41), then Dinah would be prepubescent, and her older brothers but teenagers during this time. If true, then the crime committed is even graver, the rape of a child. It is interesting to note that several scholars, like Lyn Bechtel,[4] argue that no rape occurred, that this was simply a case of a mutual sexual encounter. Disturbingly, as the story develops, we discover that the one truly dishonored was not Dinah who was physically abused, but her two brothers whose reputations were challenged.

Within the ancient social order, a person's ranking within society was determined by either acquiring honor or inducing shame. It was crucial for men (like Simeon and Levi) to maintain or improve the honor of their family, while simultaneously avoiding anything that might bring shame upon the family name. Generally speaking, honor is male-centered, for through the man's participation in the public sphere honor can be increased or decreased through his bold and aggressive actions when interacting with other men. While honor is achieved in the public sphere, shame is created within the private sphere. Because of patriarchy, a woman who belonged to one man yet was used by another brought shame to the "owner" of her body. So to protect one's honor, the man must confine the woman to the household, where she can remain secure. Even though Dinah was not at fault for the lascivious action of Shechem, she was still guilty of bringing shame to her family. Dinah might have been physically raped by Shechem, but she was emotionally and spiritually raped by the males within her own family, as well as today's scholars and ministers who continue to either ignore her story or perpetuate her as the object of the story.

Shechem's lust soon turned to love as he began to speak tenderly to his victim's heart. Can the rapist have such a rapid change of heart, from violence to love? We know that a rapist (whether stranger or family[5]) is usually motivated by strong negative emotions like hate, anger, or revenge, not sexual libido. The rapist has a desire to demonstrate power over the victim, a power achieved through the victim's humiliation and domination. When reading this conversion from sexual violence to love, it is important to remember that rape has little to do with sex, even though sex becomes the means by which power is enhanced....

Shechem begs that his father, king Hamor, obtain the girl for him, so the father approached Jacob to barter for Dinah. If a young virgin was seduced (raped), the rapist had but two options; he either married her or he paid her father a fixed sum. If the father refused to give his daughter in marriage, the seducer was still liable for three times the original marriage price (Deut. 22:23–29). Rape was not an issue of sexual immorality; rather, it was a violation of property rights. The rapist was guilty of trespassing, sowing his seeds in another man's field. This was a crime punishable by death. If the woman failed to cry out for help, then she too must be put to death, unless the attack occurred in the countryside far from hearing. According to the biblical text, the true victim of rape was not the virgin girl but her father. Her despoiling made her unsuitable for marriage, resulting in a financial hardship for her father (her owner). The importance of marrying off one's daughters was in many cases a political decision, in order to create profitable alliances with other families. Virginity was such a profitable commodity that a father had to be compensated for damages (Ex. 22:15–16).

Hamor thus offered Jacob anything he wanted. He further proposed that they become allies and make all the land available to him to travel through or own. "Give us your daughters [Dinah's sisters] to us, and take our daughters for yourselves" Hamor proposed. Together, Jacob and Hamor tried to peacefully resolve the situation. From the unpleasant circumstance started by rape, the men saw an opportunity to create an ethnic, political, and economic merger. But try as they might, for Israel, miscegenation would continue to undergird the fear of assimilation. Regardless of what agreement would be reached with the men of Shechem, we know that the sons of Israel would never agree to merge with another people.

So when Jacob's son's returned from tending the livestock in the countryside, they were outraged and infuriated, for the rape of Jacob's daughter had insulted Israel. It was not the ordeal Dinah underwent that bothered them; rather, it was the insult to Israel's honor that enraged them. They provided a crafty reply to King Hamor. Because Jacob's family was unable to give their daughters in marriage to uncircumcised men, they would agree to an alliance under one condition: that all the men in the town had to be circumcised. Only then, through marriage, would they be able to become one kinfolk. Because Shechem was an important person within the king's household, and he was supposedly madly in love with Dinah, the king agreed to the condition of the alliance. Shechem set out to convince his compatriots to undertake circumcision for the sake of this new alliance. If the townsmen agreed, they would have not only the daughters of Israel at their disposal for marriage, but also their livestock and riches. The townsmen agreed, not knowing that by the end of the story it would be the sons of Israel who would make off with the townsfolk's women and riches.

Until now, all of the patriarchs have been depicted as men of peace, with the possible exception of Abraham's campaign against the four kings (14:1–16). Because they were small in number and vulnerable to their more powerful neighbors, an effort to avoid conflict has permeated the narrative as the patriarchs walked a fine line between being exterminated or assimilated. Here, for the first time, the sons of Israel resort to violent means in dealing with their neighbors. Sexual violence becomes the preamble for war.

On the third day of the procedure, considered the most painful time, when fever usually rises in the case of adults, the townsmen were still recuperating. At this most critical time for recently circumcised men, Dinah's full brothers, Simeon and Levi, took their swords and marched into the unsuspecting town. There they unleashed an uncontrolled and bloody orgy of vengeance. Taking advantage of the men's incapacitation, the two brothers killed them all. They took back their sister, along with all the flocks, cattle, donkeys, riches, and whatever other goods were in the town. They also carried off all the wives and little children. Vengeance can be profitable.

As sexual property, women could be claimed as war booty. The actions of Simeon and Levi became common practice in war. The "armies of Yahweh" were to kill all the men (Deut. 20:10–18), disperse the spoils of war, and kidnap the virgin women to serve in servitude or provide sexual pleasure. If a soldier was captivated by a captured woman, he was allowed to bring her into his home and make her his wife, as long as she was a virgin and was from some distant land so as not to snare their captors into religious cults (Deut. 21:10–14). She was permitted a month to mourn her parents, but after the time of grief the marriage was to be consummated. But with the passage of time, if he tired of her, he could allow her to leave. However, he could not sell her, for as the Bible states, "he had the use of her" (Deut. 21:14 author trans.).

War turned women into spoils of war that, along with other valuable possessions, go to the victors.

If the taking of women is a violation of property rights, then the plunder unleashed by the two brothers had more to do with avenging the property thief of Shechem than any emotions, pain, or feeling experienced by their sister. Not only did the perpetrator and his family pay for the crime committed against Dinah, but so did all the innocent inhabitants of the city. The massacre at Shechem leaves us wondering if it was carried out by just Simeon and Levi, or the warlike clans of Simeon and Levi. If the latter, then the taking of the all the wives and little children of the men they killed becomes mathematically sensible.

When Jacob heard of the sin his two sons had committed, he was upset, but not so much with the vengeful act itself. The text tells us he feared that once the other people in the area, the Canaanites and the Perizzites, hearing of what they had done, might join forces to annihilate him and his family. Being fearfully preoccupied with his more powerful neighbors might indicate why no comfort was apparently given to the abused Dinah. But his two sons indignantly responded to Jacob's timid rebuke by retorting, "Should our sister be treated like a whore?" No doubt, in a culture steep in the tradition of protecting and defending one's women lest shame befalls the family, the brothers are seen by the readers as the heroes. It is Jacob who comes off as "not manning up," of appearing weak, passive, and indecisive.

Nevertheless, these actions were not forgotten by Jacob. In his farewell address prior to dying, he angrily recalls the treachery. Reuben, the eldest, who should have been the head of the twelve tribes, lost that position of power when he climbed onto the bed of his father's concubine. Privileges of being the eldest would have passed to the next eldest, Simeon, followed by Levi. However, because of their duplicity and violence, they too lose the privileges of elder due them. That privilege now passed on to Judah, the fourth born.

So, what happens to Dinah? According to some rabbinical writings, Jacob's daughter becomes the unnamed wife of Job, who was possibly non-Jewish but was converted by his wife. Because the biblical book of Job lacks any indicators to historical setting, some rabbis have made him a contemporary of Jacob.[6] The identification of Dinah as Job's wife is based on the similarity in vocabulary between the description of Dinah's rape as a folly or outrage (*nebalah*) committed in Israel (34:7), and Job's rebuke of his wife as speaking as any foolish (*nabal*) woman might talk (Job 2:10).[7] Dinah, as Job's wife, counsels him, "Curse God, and die" (Job 2:9), a response that is possibly influenced by her own dramatic experiences at the hands of Shechem. Job counters, "Shall we receive the good at the hand of God, and not receive the bad?" This elicited response from Job would then have been referencing as much to his own misfortunes as to the traumatic unresolved tragedy Dinah experienced. Yet even such sage advice falls short.

Regardless of whether Dinah was Job's wife, to suggest that the evil she endured came from the hand of God is highly troubling. Such a God is not the father figure that Jesus would eventually teach about. But more troubling is not having answers for the questions: Where was God while Dinah and so many others after her were being raped? Why is God silent in the face of such terror? God is quick to lay down the law on what God finds pleasing and not pleasing. What is most troubling about Dinah's testimony, or its silencing, is God's own silence. Nowhere in the text do we find confirmation that God is angered, upset, concerned, or incensed about the violence Dinah faced. Nowhere does God shed a tear over her fate.

The inclusion of Dinah's story in the biblical narrative raises disturbing questions about God. Are the authors of these texts so steeped in patriarchy that their misogynic views are simply projected upon the deity? Because men don't care about Dinah's ordeal, then God also doesn't care. To find redemption, one is forced to read into the narrative one's own theology of hope and liberation. But doesn't the reading of one's theology into the text do violence to the text? Maybe so, but it is still necessary in order to save the text from itself. To leave Dinah with no recourse to God, hope, peace, love, and healing undermines the very purpose of faith.

Thus, boldly cognizant that the text itself is silent during the sexual violence faced by Dinah (and by extension millions of women today), we are forced to reread the text with an eye toward solidarity. Even though Dinah predates the Christ event, so that the promise of some future Messiah is fifteen hundred years away, which would have provided little comfort to her in the midst and aftermath of her abuse, still, the message of the gospel is that all the victims of sexual predators—present and future—are Christ crucified. For Christians, Christ's crucifixion is not an act of substitution due to our sins, as per Anselm of Canterbury; rather, it is an act of solidarity during unjust suffering. The victims of sexual abuse are among today's crucified people. They can find solidarity in a Christ who was also abused, beaten, broken, tortured, and humiliated. God was as silent during Christ's abuse, leading him to cry out why God had abandoned him (Mark 15:34), as God was silent during the sexual abuse of Dinah, and as God appears to be silent during the abuse of so many today. The responsibility that is given, as insurmountable as it might appear, is that patriarchal structures that foster sexual abuse must be dismantled. The hope that is given, as fleeting as it might appear, is that there is a resurrection after crucifixion. But even then, we should be patient if this is not enough.

15

Medieval Witches[1]

During the reign of Pope Nicolas (assuming it was Pope Nicolas V who reigned from 1447–1455) some unnamed bishop from Germany was visiting Rome on business. While there, "he fell in love with a girl, and sent her to his diocese" along with other acquired possessions, specifically some rich jewels. On her way to the bishop's diocese, this girl "with the usual greed of women" grew covetous of the jewels, so she placed a curse on the bishop. If the bishop was to die, she concluded, she could then take possession of the jewels. The next night, the bishop became gravely ill. On the third day, when all hope was gone, an old woman came to him and stated that she could heal him. She told the bishop: "Your illness has been caused by a spell of witchcraft, and you can only be healed by another spell, which will transfer the illness from you to the witch who caused it, so that she will die." After consulting with the Pope, the bishop agreed. The narrator explains what happened next:

> It is to be understood that at the very same hour and moment the illness left the Bishop and afflicted the girl witch, through the agency of the old witch; and so the evil spirit, by ceasing to plague the Bishop, appeared to restore him to health by chance, whereas it was not he but God Who permitted him to afflict him, and it was God Who properly speaking restored him; and the devil, by reason of his compact with the second witch, who envied the fortune of the girl, had to afflict the Bishop's mistress. And it must be thought that those two evil spells were not worked by one devil serving two persons, but by two devils serving two separate witches. For the devils do not work against themselves, but work as much as possible in agreement for the perdition of souls.

The bishop eventually visits the dying girl offering forgiveness; in response, "I have no hope of pardon, but commend my soul to all the devils in hell." After uttering these words, she died miserably.[2]

This fifteenth-century tale provides a glimpse into a worldview wherein Satan totally occupied the imagination of European humanity. It is a world were bishops take on young girls as mistresses without concern for improprieties, where the misogyny is a given, where illnesses are assumed to be caused by the Devil, and where nobody flinches when the Pope agrees to allow a witch, who made a pact with the devil, heal his bishop. For modern readers, this is a strange world where the boundary separating evil spirits from humans is porous. It is also a world whose religious views and masculine extremism would eventually bring great misery and death to countless women created in the image of God.

By the late Middle Ages, demons were everywhere. It was believed that one-third of the angels of Heaven were casted out with Satan. That means, according to the thirteenth-century bishop-cardinal of Tusculum, Peter of Spain (who in 1273 became Pope John XXI), of the estimated 399,920,004 angels that existed, 133,306,668 became demons. Of course, not all medieval doctors of the church agreed on this number. The estimates ranged from a low of 7,405,926 to a high of 2,665,866,746,664.[3] Regardless as to which number is ultimately used, let alone how one arrived at such numbers, in the mind of the general Christian population of that era, they lived in a world infested with demons. They were everywhere creating mischief, hoping to lead humans away from God. In the earlier medieval period, non-Christians were mainly seen as ignorant or misguided idolaters, led astray by the master deceiver and tempter, Satan. Yet with the church's consolidation of power in the High Middle Ages, these idolaters began to be seen as willful followers of Satan, if not demonically possessed. For those in power, specifically the official church, the institutionalization of Satan and the increasing social and religious discourse on the problem of evil created a means by which the populace can be controlled.[4]

As the Christian church expanded its power over Europe, fear of evil—then and now—proved to be a powerful tool by those demigods wishing to exercise and maintain control. Not only was the church interested in control, but it also sought the eradication of any residue of indigenous pre-Christian European spirituality. In this battle for the fidelity of the populace, the church's opponents were not only portrayed as evil but nonhuman—a shift in thinking that would have dire consequences upon humanity. The witch came to be linked to Satan, a move no doubt caused by the social conditions and attitudes that arose during the Middle Ages. But just as important are the historical origins of the witch. Although difficult and complex to delineate, witches can partly be understood as the reinterpretation of the pre-Christian cults (that is, the cult of Diana that flourished in the fifth and sixth centuries, or the cult of the Earth Mother, which flourished among the Celtic peoples of the early Middle Ages). These pre-Christian priestesses usually prayed, made sacrifices, or participated in magical tradition that often included conjurations.[5]

Toward the end of the Middle Ages, specifically the thirteenth century with the rise of Scholasticism à la Thomas Aquinas, the devil's powers became less ambiguous as it started to be identified with entire groups of people. During the Middle Ages, women, specifically the traditional village wise woman, were considered the vessel of ancient knowledge, as manifested in herbal and nature-based healings. In many cases, she can be understood as the town healer or midwife. But if she could use magic to do good, could she not also use magic to do evil? Regardless, to engage in certain forms of magic, whether to do harm or good, was characterized as witchcraft. Ironically, there was a much older tradition known as "white magic" or Christian magical theology (*theologia magica Christiana*) that was reserved for male practitioners who generally were not condemned for their dangerous alchemical games and experiments. Thomas Aquinas and his teacher Albertus Magnus were among the renowned Scholastic theologians whose names were often associated with this type of beneficent or alchemical magic aimed at understanding the natural world and amplifying Christian knowledge. All other magical practices not approved of by the church were deemed as malevolent or "black magic" and regarded as under the auspices of Satan, the conjuring of demons as part of the so-called "Devil's pact."

It was during the late Middle Ages that thinkers and theologians began to ask through what power witches performed their magic. To answer this concern, a demonology was attached to witchcraft, a move that created a simple dichotomy: those who used magical power (for example, witches) did so through the power of Satan; furthermore, anyone who was not a Christian was a follower of Satan. Not to follow Christ according to the dictates of the church was to be in league with the devil. This of course was not a new position, since the Church Fathers had developed similar discourse centuries earlier to discredit rival religions and philosophical schools in the ancient world. The persecution and punishment of witches became the established European Christian church's attempt of eliminating these practitioners of ancient traditions, who usually were women, of suppressing any competing spirituality or cultural tradition. It was to female practitioners of magic, to witches, that the various misfortunes that befell an individual, a community, a ruler, or a state were attributed.

The witch became the accomplice, lover, and covert human presence of Satan. She ceased using magic to achieve some desire or mere personal goal; rather she was now used by Satan to achieve his goals on a grand scale. Because Satan lacks generosity, medieval scholars concluded that a reciprocal relationship had to exist. Acquiring magical powers implied that a pact with the Devil had to have been made, with the witch's soul being traded for supernatural knowledge. For the audacity of interpreting reality or healing the sick through folk-medicine and natural magic apart from the church, the penalty was severe, even though many of those who perished during the witch hunts were innocent victims that probably were not engaged in any specific indigenous non-Christian European religious or magical tradition. Still, in the zeal to strengthen the official church hold on the political and religious milieu, those seen as opponents were sacrificed on the altar of Christ in conformance with the biblical mandate: "You shall not allow a witch to live" (Ex. 22:18).

As the threat of witches to Christian society spread, specifically in parts of Northern Germany, Pope Innocent VIII released the bull exhorting magistrates to hunt down these witches. He decreed that "all heretical depravity should be driven far from the frontiers and bournes of the Faithful."[6] In response to the Pope's wishes, two Dominicans, Heinrich Kramer (Henricus Institoris) and Jakob Sprenger produced the *Malleus Maleficarum* (Hammer of She-witches) around the year 1486, the first major treatise providing guidance on how to hunt down witches. In the age of the printing press, their manuscript was widely circulated, quickly becoming the normative understanding of witches and their unholy alliance with the Devil. These witch hunts led to tens of thousands, mostly women, being executed, usually by being burned at the stake. The number of those persecuted is difficult to determine. Estimates range from the thousands to the millions. From the start of the sixteenth to the late seventeenth century it is estimated that one hundred thousand women perished, half of these in Germany. Records have been lost, and the numbers have been inflated by officials wishing to show their fidelity in eliminating demonic influences from their jurisdictions and by more recent scholars in order to magnify the gravity of the persecution.[7]

According to an earlier anonymous treatise (*Errores Gazariorum*) from 1430, the Devil would usually appear to these witches in the form of a cat while they met in synagogues. During these Sabbaths, the witches would invert the moral and religious norms by doing homage to Satan. Although not much is written in the *Malleus Maleficarum* as to what occurred during these secret nocturnal Sabbaths, popular rumors at the time included orgies, naked dancing to atonal music, aerial transportation by riding tridents or pitchforks (a symbol associated with the Devil) as well as brooms, kissing a cat's anus, ritual intercourse with Satan, engaging in a parody of the Catholic Mass where the Nicene

Creed is recited backward, and eating the corpse of exhumed deceased children. Also contributing to the understanding of the demonic were the moralistic paintings of the period, for example, the works of the Early Netherlandish painter Hieronymus Bosch (1450–1516). The medieval surrealistic Hell panels of the triptychs he produced, among his most famous being *The Garden of Earthly Delights*, created a reality based on nightmares where the moral symbols employed elicited fear, a fear that focused on the Devil and on the nature of woman as temptress. Bosch's painting illustrates a disturbing perception of Hell where those who succumbed in life to the devil's temptation find themselves reaping the rotted fruits of eternal damnation—a damnation defined by cruel and brutal scenes of torture and torment.

It is interesting to note that during the late Middle Ages evil most commonly took the *female* human form—a phenomenon that should not be surprising when we consider the prevailing assumption that women were the temptress of holy men. Women, according to the *Malleus Maleficarum*, "know no moderation in goodness or vice...When they are governed by a good spirit, they are most excellent in virtue; but when they are governed by an evil spirit, they indulge the worst possible vices."[8] Women were believed to be more superstitious than men and more carnal than men; they were perceived as intellectually childlike.[9] Hence, they are quicker than men to waver in their faith, making them more susceptible to the influences of the Evil One. Or as Tertullian, the third-century apologist succinctly stated: "You [woman] are the one who opens the door to the devil...you are the one who persuaded [Adam] whom the devil was not strong enough to attack. All too easily you destroyed the image of God, man. Because of your desert, that is, death, even the Son of God had to die."[10] A simple dichotomy is created due to women's weaker nature. They are either virtuous—the Madonna—or wicked—the whore, quick to engage in orgies attended by Satan.

One wonders if the constant portrayal of witches as sexual deviants constantly copulating in all sorts of orgies, coupled with how they were normatively interrogated,[11] encompasses the attempt of those judges to exorcise their own suppressed sexual desires now projected upon female bodies. If so, this might explain the cruel torture the female bodies endured—an offering lifted up by which the male bodies of judges found salvation from their own sexual sins. A simplistic binary relationship is created where the male bodies of holy men are defined through the negation of the demonic bodies of women who are witches. They—witches—are controlled by their flesh; we—holy men—are controlled by the Holy Spirit. They are evil; we are righteous. They belong to Satan; we belong to God. Once the Other is defined in these terms, whether they be women accused as witches or colonized people accused as heathens and pagans, it becomes easy to include one more pair of binary oppositions. They are nonhuman; we are human. Their nonhuman construct allows those who self-define as human to visit all forms of inhumane cruelty upon them in an effort to dehumanize them. Their slaughter becomes justified because we—righteous Christians belonging to God—are acting in God's name against God's enemies.

In the mind of church leaders, these women were evil, if not inhuman, because they were engaged in something more sinister than simply providing the sick some herbal medicine. The power of healing they demonstrated could only be gained by making a pact with the Devil, whose prerequisite was the renouncement of Christ and Christianity. How else could these uneducated women hope to match the erudition and sophistication of male doctors who had studied the healing arts at church-approved universities and colleges? These women dealt in petty potions and petty evils while pretending to heal the sick and counsel the afflicted. Such a pact is important because without the assistance of witches, devils could not "bring about evil...either substantial or accidental, and...they can[not] inflict damage without the assistance of some agent [i.e., witch], but with such an agent diseases, and any other human passions or ailment, can be brought about."[12] In other words, while demons who are permitted by God can visit havoc upon humans, they prefer the assistance of witches.[13] Any misfortune or sickness that befalls an individual, town, or country occurred because some witch channeled the power of devils. Employing herbal medicine was not some quaint innocent practice based on some benign ancient tradition—it was part of a pact that made the witch more malevolent and dangerous than Satan. Her ultimate goal was the same as Satan's, namely, the overthrow of the religious and political structures of the time. Not much has changed when we notice that even to this day; those who challenge or attempt to change the economic and political status quo are also characterized as demonic.

Anyone who renounced the true faith so as to participate in such diabolical practices deserved no mercy. The crimes of witches exceed the sins of all others, even exceeding the sins and fall of the angels who followed Satan in rebelling against God.[14] They have chosen to become enemies of God, and, as such, have no one to blame but themselves for the suffering awaiting them. Likewise, to argue that witches making pacts with the Devil really do not exist only proves that those holding this position "are to be regarded as notorious heretics."[15] For those who administer public justice against witches or prosecute them in any public official capacity (i.e., Inquisitors) cannot be injured, afflicted, or influenced by their witchcraft.[16] And if these administrators and public officials are negligent in their pursuit and persecution of witches, then it is God who is injured by their neglect and thus will permit witches to bring great affliction upon those lacking the zeal to prosecute and persecute these evil doers.[17]

Evil ceased being a sole matter of human nature or an inclination of the human heart. During this the time of the burnings it became more enfleshed, more concrete—even able to produce a child that, while not being of the Devil, is born with a propensity for evil. But how? After all, how can demons—as spirits—impregnate a woman? According to Thomas Aquinas, a demon would shape-shift into a woman (succubus) and either seduce a man, or visit him while he is asleep for the purpose of extracting his semen (hence explaining why men at times have nocturnal emissions, known as "wet dreams"). Then the demon would shape-shift into a man (incubus) and plant the stolen sperm into a woman.[18] This idea that demons can collect male semen and deposit it within women can be further traced back to Augustine.[19] The *Malleus Maleficarum* shows how witches could be found in fields or forests, lying on their back with the bottom half of their bodies exposed. Based on "the agitation of their legs" and the "disposition of their sexual organs" it was seemingly obvious that they were "copulating with incubus demons which are invisible to the onlookers."[20]

Not only can demons take the form of humans to conceive satanic children, but they can take the form of well-known Christians to destroy their reputation. This was the case with archbishop Silvanus of Nazareth. The demon, transformed in the archbishops' likeness, entered the private quarters of a respectful lady and attempted to rape her. Crying out for help, several came to her aid, finding the demon—in the form of the archbishop—hiding under her bed. The innocent archbishop's reputation was thus defamed; only to be restored when the demon in question was forced to confess at St. Jerome's tomb.[21]

Witch hunts were not limited to Roman Catholics. In fact, the high point of the late medieval witch-craze was a phenomenon of the Reformation period. Throughout the sixteenth and seventeenth centuries both Catholic and Protestant officials tried and executed tens of thousands of women on the charge of witchcraft. Leaders of the Protestant Reformation like Martin Luther and John Calvin, may have done much to debunk Catholicism along with its theology and rituals, but their Protestant views of Satan and witches did not deviate much from their medieval Catholic counterparts. Protestants were quick to point out that the papacy was occupied, indeed possessed, by the Anti-Christ, while Catholics concluded that it must have been Satan who inspired the Protestant Reformation. Although Protestants and Catholics each charged the other as being satanic, agreement existed concerning the reality of Satan. Luther, whose own physical seizures were attributed to Satan, concludes during his lectures on Galatians that "it cannot be denied but that the Devil liveth, yea, and reigneth throughout the whole earth." Humans "are all subject to the devil" who is "the prince and god" of this world and responsible for "sorcery and witchcraft."[22] John Calvin would agree. He writes, "For the devil is said to have undisputed possession of this world...In like manner, he is said to blind all who do not believe the Gospel, and to do his own work in the children of disobedience."[23] In short, whatever did not come from God, according to Reformation leaders, was evil. A simple dichotomy was created and maintained. Either you believe in the Protestant interpretation of the Gospel or you are among the "wicked [who] are vessels of wrath."[24] For Martin Luther, Catholics who remained faithful to the church, Jews who refused to recognize the Messiahship of Jesus, peasants who rebelled against aristocratic landholders, and Protestants who were not followers of Luther were dismissed as being "agents of Satan."[25]

Leaders of the Reformation exaggerated Satan's power, making his influence even more pervasive than their fellow Catholics. In so doing, increased the fear of him. Reformation leaders saw their earthly existence as a battle against the Evil One that could be won through the extirpation of witches. Martin Luther calls for the eradication of witches in 1526 when he delivers his *Sermon on Exodus*. "Women are more susceptible to those superstitions of Satan. . . They are commonly called 'wise women'. *Let them be killed.* . . The law that sorceresses should be killed is most just, since they do many cursed things while they remain undiscovered. . . .Therefore, let them be killed."[26] It is important to note that the first century of the Reformation coincides with the most intense period of the witch hunts that began during the 1560s. Ironically, while Protestants and Catholics saw each other as demonically influenced, Protestants still joined their Catholic opponents in ferreting witches and cleansing society of these female induced evils.

Like Martin Luther,[27] John Calvin captured the common theological understanding that Satan could do nothing without the consent of God. "With regard to the strife and war which Satan is said to wage with God, it must be understood with this qualification, that Satan cannot possibly do anything against the will and consent of God."[28] We are left wondering why, if God is so powerful, God allows Satan and his horde of demons such power among humans. It is because God, according to the *Malleus Maleficarum*, is so heavily offended by human sin, that God grants the devil greater power in tormenting humanity.[29] John Calvin would agree.

God thus turning the unclean spirits hither and thither at his pleasure, employs them in exercising believers by warring against them, assailing them with wiles, urging them with solicitations, pressing close upon them, disturbing, alarming, and occasionally wounding, but never conquering or oppressing them; whereas they hold the wicked in thralldom, exercise dominion over their minds and bodies, and employ them as bond-slaves in all kinds of iniquity.[30]

Probably the best-known example of a Protestant-led witch hunt unfolded in colonial Massachusetts from February through May of 1693. Salem Village (later renamed Danvers), where the witch hysteria began, was rife with disputes over grazing rights and property lines. The ministers to the village found themselves thrown into internal disputes over land, with several leaving the parish as a result of the nonpayment of their wages. Eventually, the decision was taken to call Reverend Samuel Parris, though significant levels of division remained within the church given that the vote to send for Parris had only a slim majority in favor. Ironically, the witch hysteria began in the home of Reverend Parris, when his daughter Betty Parris (age nine) and his niece Abigail Williams (age eleven) began to throw uncontrollable fits, barked like dogs, and fell into trances. It was believed that these ailments began with a game these girls played with the household indigenous Caribbean slave, Tituba. Eggs whites were poured into water (creating a type of crystal ball known as the Venus glass) so as to ascertain, based on the shape taken, the occupation of future husbands.

Soon these two girls were joined by others in bizarre fits. When examined by the village doctor, William Griggs, he concluded that there was no physical ailment responsible for their condition; thus, they must be bewitched. The question then became: By whom? The girls subsequently began to accuse neighbors of being witches, responsible for causing their afflictions. They began by first accusing outsiders: Sarah Good, a homeless beggar; Sarah Osborne, who didn't attend church; and the ethnic other, Tituba the slave. Over the course of the hysteria, more than 150 individuals were imprisoned for being witches and consorting with the Devil. Of those accused, fourteen women and five men were executed on the capital felony of witchcraft. The "spectral evidence" that was admitted in the rituals at Salem consisted of the testimonies of the "victims," who stated that they were attacked by phantoms having the form of the various accused. Though these phantoms were invisible to others, such evidence was considered acceptable in the court of law run by chief justice William Stoughton. One man, Giles Corey, was crushed to death under heavy stones (*peine forte et dure*) for refusing to enter a plea on the accusation of being a witch. About five other individuals died while incarcerated. The hysteria comes to an end when Royal Governor William Phips dissolved the court conducting the investigations because accusations were starting to be leveled against the colonial elite.

Although it is difficult to understand such hysteria and outburst as what occurred in Salem, such events did serve a purpose for the villagers. A powerful Satan helps answer the theodicy question. In an era pregnant with war and pestilence, an era of short and brutal life spans, an era of illiteracy and ignorance, having a Satan responsible for human suffering with God's blessings because of human disobedience to God's representative on earth, the church, starts to make solid theological sense. In a perverted form of logic, humans deserve demonic torment and the church-inflicted torture. Whenever misfortune befell good townsfolk, relief from the anxiety of the times could be had by denouncing the witch and projecting upon her all of the guilt and insecurity felt. In a sense, the witch played an important role as scapegoat, carrying upon herself all the sins of society. Through her stripes her neighbors were healed.

According to the influential French philosopher René Girard, scapegoating serves an important task during times of crises, especially crises that remind humans of their mortality, such as political disturbances, famines, or plagues common during the late Middle Ages. Such monumental upheavals like the Black Death of the fourteenth century or the religious wars of the sixteenth century caused the collapse of the "social order evidenced by the disappearance of rules and 'differences' that define cultural divisions."[31] During times of crises, Girard argues, human society unites through what he terms a "victimage mechanism."[32] Those suffering the misfortunes of the time "convince themselves that a small number of people, or even a single individual, despite relative weakness, is extremely harmful to the whole of society."[33] The shedding of blood is required to cover the sins of the many, bringing unity and reconciliation among the perpetrators of violence. Ignorant of the true causes of the crises, those calling for a witch hunt find strength and reassurance in the collective persecution of victims in order to eliminate the perceived cause of the crises.[34] By offering up scapegoats, those in power, namely the church, eliminate potential "troublemakers" and "rebels." Those labeled "witches," who are perceived as openly and aggressively challenging the social and political supremacy of Christianity, quickly find themselves in precarious situations. Normalizing witch hunts becomes a powerful instrument in maintaining the status quo, effectively silencing potential opponents.[35]

Natural cataclysms, wars, and epidemics may have led to the sacrifice of scapegoats accused of bringing about disaster; but there was no need to wait until these calamities occurred. It became profitable for individuals to testify that their political enemies were in league with the Devil in order to remove those who would oppose the accuser's drive for power and/or privilege. In some cases, an accusation would lead to the accuser obtaining the land and possessions of the accused. In other words, there existed profitable incentives to "out" those who were in cahoots with Satan or who practiced black magic and sorcery. This form of scapegoating for profit began in the early fourteenth century, when the king of France, hoping to overturn the papal decisions of the deceased Pope Boniface VII (whom ironically Dante placed in the inner circle of Hell where simony is punished), posthumously accused him of obtaining his position as Pope with the help of demons.[36] As recently as 2006, Governor Timothy M. Kaine officially pardoned Grace Sherwood of Pungo, Virginia who was accused of witchcraft on July 10, 1710, and served seven years in prison after being dunked in the Lynnhaven River. The fact that she had floated back up to the surface of the water was taken as proof of her diabolical identity as a witch. Notably, Pungo is located in the central part of Virginia near Norfolk and Virginia Beach, and Grace Sherwood was a widow with good grazing lands and desirable property that local rivals hoped to confiscate following her trial and conviction. After she was released from prison, she lived to be about eighty years old. The case of Grace Sherwood passed into the lore and legends of colonial America as the infamous "Witch of Pungo," a homegrown historical incident that reminds us of how very recent and factual the witch-craze nightmare really was....

PART SIX

———

Confronting Sexism

16

Beyond Machismo:
A Cuban Case Study[1]

Abstract

This article explores the multidimensional aspects of intra-Hispanic oppression by unmasking the socio-historical construction of machismo. Usually, traditionally disenfranchised groups construct well-defined categories as to who are the perpetrators and who are the victims of injustices. All too often, Hispanic ethicists tend to identify oppressive structures of the dominant Eurocentric culture while overlooking repression conducted within the Hispanic community. The author suggests that, within the marginalized space of the Latino/a community, there exist intra-structures of oppression along gender, race, and class lines, and that these require a type of analysis that moves beyond (what Edward Said terms) "the rhetoric of blame." One form of such analysis is developed here, as the author examines intra-Cuban sexism, racism, and classism.

I am a recovering *macho*, a product of an oppressive society, a society where gender, race and class domination do not exist in isolated compartments, nor are they neatly relegated to uniform categories of repression. They are created in the space where they interact and conflict with each other, a space I will call *machismo*. The understanding of *machismo* requires a full consideration of sexism, heterosexism, racism, ethnocentrism and classism. All forms of oppression are identical in their attempt to domesticate the Other. The sexist, who sees women playing a lesser productive role than men, transfers to the non-elite male Other effeminate characteristics, placing him in a feminine space for "easy mounting."

This article explores the multidimensional aspects of intra-Hispanic oppression by unmasking the socio-historical construction of *machismo*. Usually disenfranchised groups construct well-defined categories as to who are the perpetrators and the victims of injustices. All too often, we who are Hispanic ethicists tend to identify the oppressive structures of the dominant Eurocentric culture while overlooking repression conducted within our own community. I suggest that within the marginalized space of the Latino/a community there exists intra-structures of oppression along gender, race and class lines, creating the need for an ethical initiative to move beyond what Edward Said terms, "the rhetoric of blame."[2] Specifically, this article will present a paradigm called *machismo*, which explicates intra-Hispanic oppression. The article then employs this paradigm to the Cuban experience by examining intra-Cuban sexism, racism and classism.

The Machismo Paradigm

To be a man, a *macho*, implies both domination and protection of those under you, specifically women. It becomes the *macho*'s responsibility, his burden, to educate those below his superior standards. Because of my gender, I confess my complicity with sexist social structures, complicity motivated by personal advantage.[3] All things being equal, I prevail over women in the marketplace, in the church community and within our Hispanic community because I am male. It is not my intention to speak for women about their oppression, or to provide them with the necessary pedagogy to achieve liberation. Several, although unfortunately not enough *mujerista* theologians are presenting this voice.[4] My contribution to the discourse must be limited to how I, as a male, as a *macho,* facilitate the oppression of my gender Other.

Because sexism reflects only one aspect of *machismo*, it is appropriate to expand the meaning of this term to include all forms of oppression imposed on those who fail to live up to the manly standards of being a white, elite, Cuban male.[5] *Machismo* is as much about race and class as it is about gender. For Cubans, seriously dealing with our patriarchal structures must be the first stage in the process of dismantling all forms of oppression, providing for the liberation and possible reconciliation of all, including women.

History is forged through one's *cojones* (balls). Women, nonwhites and the poor fail to influence history because they lack *cojones*, a gift given to *machos* by the ultimate *Macho*, God. To call a man *lavándole los blumes de la mujer* (one who washes his wife's bloomers) is to question his *machismo*. "*El colmo*" (the ultimate sin) is to be called a "*maricón*" (a derogatory term meaning queer or fag), the antithesis of *machismo*. We, white Cuban elite males, look into Lacan's mirror and recognize ourselves as *machos* through the distancing process of negative self-definition: "I am what I am not." The formation of the subject's ego constructs an illusory self-representation through the negation of *cojones*, now projected upon Others, identified as non-*machos*. Ascribing femininity to the Other forces the construction of female identity to originate with the *macho*. In fact, the feminine Object, in and of itself, is seen as nothing apart from a masculine Subject that provides unifying purpose.

The resulting gaze of the white Cuban elite male inscribes effeminacy upon Others who are not *macho* enough to "make" history, or "provide" for their family, or "resist" their subjugation to the dominant *macho*. Unlike in the United States, sexual identity for Cubans is defined in terms of masculinity not in terms of gender. Women are "the not male." When the gendered Other demonstrates hyper-*macho* qualities, she can be praised for being *macho*. This was the case with both General Maceo, who was black, and his mother,[6] thus both were described as *macho*.

The phallic signifier of *machismo* is located in the *cojones*. For Cubans, *cojones*, not the penis, become our cultural "signifier of signifiers." The Other, if male, may have a penis, but lacks the *cojones* to use it. I conquer, I subdue, I domesticate *por mis cojones* (by my balls). A distinction is made between *cojones*, the male testicles, and *cojones*, the metaphoric signifier. Power and authority exhibit *cojones*, which are in fact derived from social structures, traditions, norms, laws, and customs created by *machos*, who usually are white and rich.

From one perspective, no one has *cojones*. The *macho* lives, always threatened by the possible loss of his *cojones*, while the non-*macho* is forcefully deprived. The potent symbolic power invested in the *cojones* both signals and veils white elite Cuban male socioeconomic power. Constructing those oppressed as feminine allows white Cuban men with *cojones* to assert their privilege by constructing oppressed Others as inhabitants of the castrated realm of the exotic and primitive.[7] Lacking *cojones*, the Other does not exist, except as designated by the desire of the one with *cojones*. Like a benevolent father (*el patrón*), it becomes the duty and responsibility of those with *cojones* to care for, provide for and protect those below. The castrated male (read: race and class Other) occupies a feminine space where his body is symbolically sodomized as prelude to the sodomizing of his mind.

The non-*macho* becomes enslaved by the inferiority engraved upon their flesh by the Cuban ethos. Likewise, the *macho* is also enslaved to his own so-called superiority that flows from his *cojones*. While non-*machos* are forced to flee from their individuality, the *macho* must constantly attempt to live up to a false construction. Both are alienated, both suffer from an obsessive neurotic orientation, and both require liberation from their condition. For Cubans, Gutiérrez' "preferential option for the poor" must be expanded to include a preferential option for those castrated by the *macho*, be they women, homosexuals, Taínos, Africans, Chinese, or the poor.

How did our neurotic state develop? Cuba, unlike other Latin American nations that enslaved the indigenous people, reduced the Taínos to near extinction. To replace this vanishing population, Mayans and Africans were imported as slaves. Later, the Chinese began to take their place. The Cuban concern was the acquisition of cheap labor. Hence, slave merchants did not bother bringing women, contributing to a predominant male society. By the same token, the white overlords were also mostly men, searching for gold and glory. Cuba was a stopping off point to somewhere else. Those passing through were on their way to discover riches on the mainland. Few women accompanied these *conquistadores*. Since the beginning of Cuban European history, its population lacked sufficient number of women of any color. This absence of women contributed to the creation of an excessively male-oriented society, where weaker males (non-*machos*) occupied "female" spaces. They washed; they cooked; they "entertained."

Cuba was the last Latin American nation to gain its independence from Spain. Rather than having a century of nation building, Cuba spent the nineteenth century preoccupied with military struggles, contributing to a hyper-*macho* outlook. The physical bravado characterizing a century of bloody struggle for independence fused manhood with nationhood. *Machismo* became ingrained in the fabric of Cuban culture. Both sides of the Florida Straits proclaim the same message: *patria* is real man's work.[8] Women, gays and blacks are not *macho* enough to construct *patria*.[9] Hence Cuba, a predominantly black nation, is ruled by a predominantly white hierarchy, while in Miami, the Cuban American National Foundation (CANF) was established by fifty white business*men* organizing to create a post-Castro Cuba. Exilic Cuban anthropologist Behar describes the amalgamation of *machismo* with nationhood when she writes:

> In seeking to free Cuba from its position as a colony of the United States, the Cuban Revolution hoped to redeem an emasculated nation. Manhood and nationhood, in the figure of the Cuban revolutionary hero, were fused and confused...Manhood is an integral part of the counterrevolution too. As Flavio Risech points out, "neither *revolucionario* nor anticommunist *gusano* can be a *maricón*"...If national identity is primarily a problem of *male* identity, how are Cuban women on both sides to write themselves into Cuban history?[10]

With colonization by the United States immediately following "independence" from Spain, Cuba continued in its emasculated status. The long United States' military occupation, the Platt Amendment, and the transformation of La Habana into a Western Hemisphere whorehouse for Anglo consumption meant Cubans lost their manhood, their *machismo*. To regain their *machismo*, Cubans learned how to imitate their oppressor by enhancing forms of domination over non-*machos*, specifically women. We, who came to this country as infants or small boys seek now to reinstate our *machismo*. The first generation of the Exilic-Cuban adolescent boys experienced both peer and parental pressure to "prove their manhood." *Machismo* means to be sexually ready for anybody, anywhere, anytime.[11] Conquering *la americanita* (the North American girl) became an adolescent ritual of *machismo*. Exilic Cuban boys were encouraged to date the *americanita* in order to prove their manhood, as long as they remembered to marry *la cubanita* (Cuban girl).

This generations of Exilic Cubans who arrived in this country as children were forced to navigate simultaneously both sexual maturation and cultural adaptation. Both these processes, as Gustavo Pérez Firmat points out, became interwoven so that gender and cultural identity became integrated. Thus, cultural preference merged with sexual preference. In trying to become a mature man in exile, both regression and assimilation remain constant temptations as I attempt to construct my identity on the hyphen in Cuban-American.[12] To Firmat's description of the attempt to live on the hyphen, I would add the sexual conquest of the *americanita*. For as Fanon points out, "When my restless hands caress those white breasts, they grasp white civilization and dignity and make them mine."[13] Conquering the *americanita* provided an opportunity for the Exilic *macho* to converse with the dominant culture from the position of being on top (pun intended).[14]

To tell a man not to be a *maricón* also means "don't be a coward." Cuban homophobia differs from homophobia in the United States. We do not fear the homosexual; rather we hold him in contempt for being a man who chooses not to prove his manhood. Unlike North Americans, where two men engaged in a sexual act are both called homosexuals, for Cubans only the one that places himself in the "position" of a woman is the *maricón*.[15] Only the one penetrated is labeled *loca* (crazy woman, a term for *maricones*).[16] In fact, the man who is in the dominant position during the sex act, known as *bugarrón*, is able to retain, if not increase, his *machismo*.

While visiting the home of an Exilic Cuban radio commentator (who contributes to the anti-Castro rhetoric common on Miami's airwaves), I noticed a statue proudly displayed on his desk. The statue was of a cigar smoking Fidel Castro on all fours with his pants wrapped around his ankles while a standing Ronald Reagan sodomized him. In the mind of the sculptor and the Cuban men who see the statue, Ronald Reagan is not in any way a homosexual. Quite the contrary, the statue celebrates the *machismo* of Reagan who forces Castro into a non-*macho* position.

Carlos Franqui, director of *Radio Rebelde* and one of Castro's twelve disciples who came down from the mountain in 1959 to serve as editor of the newspaper *Revolución*, describes how *machismo* affects politics. He wrote:

> The politics of gang warfare in the mid-1940's is disguised as revolutionary politics. Actually, it was a collective exercise in *machismo*, which is its own ideology. *Machismo* creates its own way of life, one in which everything negative is feminine. As our Mexican friends Octavio Paz and Carlos Fuentes point out, the feminine is screwed beforehand…[*Machismo's*] negative hero is the dictator (one of Batista's motto was "Batista is the Man"), and its positive hero is the rebel. They are at odds in politics, but they both love power. And both despise homosexuality, as if every *macho* had his hidden gay side…The two brands of *machismo*, conservative and rebel, are quite different. The conservatives (generals, soldiers, police) always defend the establishment, while the rebels attack it. Nevertheless, both groups share the same views about morality and culture. They hate popular culture, and all the Indian and black elements in it. Anything that isn't white is no good.[17]

Sexism

Machismo moves beyond the oppression of women. Although a detailed review of the Cuban patriarchal system would reveal a multitude of examples showing how sexism maintains women's repression, this article will instead examine how the overall conquest of "virgin land" was made possible by the initial conquest of female bodies. Cuban *machismo* and the establishment of *patria* (Motherland) occurred within the zones of imperial and anti-imperial power. Here, land and nationalism are gendered. The land requiring subjection is assigned a female body. Several postcolonial scholars perceive nationhood as resting on this male projection of identity.[18] The construction of *patria, la Cuba de ayer* or *Cuba Libre,* along patriarchal lines, can be understood as a gender discourse. For Resident Cubans, Fidel Castro serves as the father figure, *el señor*. For Exilic Cubans, the late Mas Canosa was the head of the household, *el patrón*. Below both exists feminine land, needing the masculinity of those who will construct *patria* upon her.

Earlier, the first creation of Cuba required the reduction of women to the status of representational objects.[19] As Mörner suggests, the European conquest of the so-called "New World" began with the literal sexual conquest of the native American woman.[20] Todorov recounts an incident involving Miguel de Cuneo who participated in Columbus's second journey. Cuneo attempted to seduce an indigenous woman given to him by Columbus. When she resisted, he whipped her and proceeded to rape her.[21] The image of land and woman merge. Another example illustrates how Columbus saw the world. To him, "[The world] is like a very round ball, and on one part of it is placed something like a woman's nipple."[22] The concept of "virgin land" represents the myth of empty land. If land is indeed virgin, then, according to McClintock, the indigenous population has no aboriginal territorial claim, allowing for the colonizer "the sexual and military insemination of an interior void."[23]

The first European to gaze upon the naked female body of the indigenous people and the virgin land under their feet was Christopher Columbus.[24] Mason shows Columbus's first reaction was not to the lack of political organization of the island's inhabitants nor to the geographical placement of these islands within the world scheme. Rather, by eroticizing the naked bodies of these inhabitants, visions of Paradise were conjured up, with Columbus receiving the Amerindians' awe and love. Columbus and his men are invited to penetrate this new erotic continent, which offered herself without resistance.[25] These naked bodies and "empty" land merge the sexual and the economic preoccupations of the would-be colonizers.[26] Virgin land awaits to be inseminated with man's seed of civilization. A reconstruction and reversal exposing the hidden transcripts of oppression through *machismo*, provide a fundamental step toward dismantling Cuban oppression as manifested on both sides of the Florida Straits. On our way to that task, we must address next the issue of racism.

Racism

Race is not a biological factor differentiating humans, rather, it is a social construction whose function is the oppression of the Object-Other for the benefit of the Subject. Racism toward the Cuban's Others (Amerindians, Africans, Chinese and any combination thereof) is normalized by the social structures of both Resident and Exilic Cubans. Because domination of a group of people by another is usually conducted by the males of the dominant culture, it becomes crucial to understand the construction of this domination as seen through the eyes of the oppressor. Our patriarchal structure projects unto my "darker" Other the position occupied by women regardless of the Other's gender. For this reason, it is valid to explore Cuban racism as a form of *machismo*.

By examining the Spaniard's domestication of the Taínos (of the Arawakan nation), I will expose the original typology of intra-Cuban oppression. As previously mentioned, the *macho* subdues virgin land, relegating her inhabitants to landlessness. According to Kant, "When America was discovered...it was considered to be without owners since its inhabitants were considered as nothing."[27] The gendering of Taíno men as non-*machos* occurred early in the conquest, and provides a prototype for all subsequent forms of Cuban oppression.

By 1535 Gonzalo Fernández de Oviedo, chronicler of the colonization venture referred to the Amerindians as sodomites in the Fifth Book of his *Historia General y Natural de las Indias* (General and Natural History of the Indies). There exists no hard evidence about attitudes toward homosexuality among the aborigines, but de Oviedo claims that anal intercourse by men with members of both sexes was considered normal.[28] In a report given to the Council of the Indies by the first bishop of Santa Marta, Dominican friar Tomás Ortiz wrote, "The men from the mainland in the Indies eat human flesh and are more given to sodomy than all generations ever."[29] Juan Suárez de Peralta, a resident of Mexico in the late sixteenth century, describes with obvious distaste, the inverted patriarchal of Amerindian society when he writes:

> The custom [of the Amerindians is] that the women do business and deal with trade and other public offices while the men remain at home and weave and embroider. They [the women] urinate standing while the men do so seated; and they have no reluctance to perform their natural deeds in public.[30]

By the eighteenth century, the supposed prevalence of homosexuality among the Amerindians was assumed. Like other "primitives" of the world, the typical Amerindian was regarded as a homosexual and an onanist, who also practiced cannibalism and bestiality. These sins against nature threatened the institution of the patriarchal family and by extension, the very fabric of civilized society. The supposed effeminacy of the Amerindians was further demonstrated by emphasizing their lack of body hair and pictorially displaying their supposedly small genitals. Simultaneously, the Amerindian woman was portrayed with excessively masculine features and exaggerated sexual traits, justifying the need for *macho* Spaniards to enter the land and restore a proper, phallocentric social order.[31]

By constructing people of the periphery as non-*machos*, one assigns them a function in life: service to the Spaniard *machos*. Colonization becomes a form of sexism, the domestication of the indigenous male Other as woman. Thus, Sepúlveda illustrates the masculine superiority of Spaniards to Amerindians by saying that they relate "as women to men."[32] This feminine space constructed for Amerindians was established through brutality. By linking sodomy to cannibalism and bestiality, the Spaniards justified the treatment of Amerindians, the latter were seen as violators of both divine rule and the natural order of both men and animals. The enslavement of the Amerindian was God's punishment for sins and crimes committed against nature.

Spaniards seeing Taínos in the position of women, waged a ruthless war against *el vicio nefando* (the nefarious sin—a euphemism for sodomy).[33] This crusade was waged with righteous indignation on the part of the colonizers, who had the Amerindians castrated and forced them to eat their own dirt-encrusted *cojones*.[34] So also, conquistador Vasco Núñez de Valboa had forty Amerindians thrown to the dogs on charges of sodomy.[35] Spanish *machismo* entailed contempt and rage toward the non-*macho*, which displayed itself in barbarous acts. Las Casas writes, "[The Spanish soldiers] would test their swords and their *macho* strength on captured Indians and place bets on slicing off heads or cutting of bodies in half with one blow."[36] According to the *licenciado* Gil Gregorio, the only hope for the Amerindian was acquiring civilization by working for the Spaniards so that they could learn how to live "like men."[37] Meanwhile, their not being *machos* allowed the Spaniards to take Amerindian women and daughters by force without respect or consideration for their honor or matrimonial ties.[38]

Cuba's African population also was categorized as feminine. Undergirding the construction of race is the perception that blacks are non-*machos*.[39] Quoting various anthropologists of his time (i.e., Klemm), Fernando Ortiz, the Cuban sociologist, classified humans into two groups: active or masculine, and passive or feminine. Using morphology, he decided that African skulls reveal feminine characteristics.[40] *Machismo* manifested as racism can be observed in the comments of the nineteenth century Cuban theologian José Augustín Caballero, who wrote, "In the absence of black females with whom to marry, *all* blacks [become] masturbators, sinners and sodomites."[41] Until emancipation, the plantation ratio of males to females was 2:1, with some plantations imbalances reaching 4:1.[42] Usually, black women lived in the cities and towns. Hence, slave quarters, known as *barracónes*, consisted solely of men, creating the reputation of their non-*macho* roles as voiced by Caballero. Skewed sex ratios made black males the targets of the white master who as *bugarrónes* could rape them. The wives and children of the male slave were also understood to be the master's playthings.[43]

Paradoxically, while the African man was constructed as a non-*macho*, he was feared for potentially asserting his *machismo*, particularly with white Cuban women. White women who succumbed to the black man, it was thought, were not responsible for their actions because they were bewitched through African black magic.[44] Thus, attraction becomes witchcraft and rape. Likewise, the seductive *negra* (Negress) was held responsible for compromising the virtues of the white men.[45] A popular Cuban saying was "there is no sweet tamarind fruit, nor a virgin mulatto girl." Fanon captured the white Caribbean's sentiments when he wrote:

As for the Negroes, they have tremendous sexual powers. What do you expect, with all the freedom they have in their jungles! They copulate at all times and in all places. They are really genital. They have so many children that they cannot even count them. *Be careful, or they will flood us with little mulattoes...*One is no longer aware of the Negro but only of a penis; the Negro is eclipsed. He is turned into a penis. *He is a penis* (Fanon: 57–59, 170). (italics mine).[46]

The African-Cuban may be a walking penis, but a penis that lacks *cojones*. White Cubans projected their own fears and forbidden desires upon the African-Cuban through a fixation with the black penis that threatened white civilization. The black penis is kept separate from power and privilege that come only through one's *cojones*. Casal documents this white Cuban fixation with the black penis in recounting an oral history of blacks being hung on lampposts by their genitals in the central plazas throughout Cuba during the 1912 massacre of blacks.[47] The massacre was fueled by news reports of so-called black revolt leading to the rape of white women. This peculiar way of "decorating" the lampposts perfectly expressed the sexual mythology created by Cuban white racism.

In this analysis we must also include Asians. Asian laborers were brought to Cuba as "indentured" servants, an alternative to African slavery. Landowners were not necessarily interested in obtaining new slaves. Their concern was to procure domestic workers. Although Coolies were technically "free," their conditions were as horrific, if not worse than slavery.[48] Many died during their long voyage to Cuba, ironically, on the same ships previously used to transport Africans. As in slave ships, an iron grating kept Coolies separated from the quarterdeck. Cannons were positioned to dominate the decks in the event of a rebellion. A Pacific version of the Middle Passage, was thus created. In some instances, almost half the Coolie "cargo" perished in transport.[49]

Cuban structures of white supremacy constructed the Coolie laborer similarly to African slaves. Like Africans, few Chinese women were transported to Cuba. Market demand dictated the need for young men, not women, to work the sugar fields. According to an 1861 Cuban census, there were 34,834 Chinese in Cuba; of these, 57 were women. By 1871, out of 40,261 Chinese in Cuba, only 66 were women.[50] As with Africans, the lack of women fostered the construction of the Chinese sexual identity as homosexual.[51] Cuban ethnologist Ortiz credits the Chinese for introducing homosexuality (as well as opium) in Cuba.[52] For Martinez-Alier, the consequence of Chinese rejection by the white and black woman led society to conclude that the Chinese succumbed to "unspeakable vices," a euphemism for sodomy.[53]

The Cuban Asian, African, and Amerindian share a sacred bond. These three represent God's "crucified people," victims in the expansion and development of capitalism, who literally bear the sins of the modern world. As a crucified people, seen as the feminine Other by *machos*, they provide an essential soteriological perspective on Cuban history.[54] Sobrino, developing the concept of a crucified people, maintains that God chose those oppressed in history and made them the principal means of salvation, just as God chose the "suffering servant," the crucified Christ, to bring salvation to the world.[55] This theme of solidarity between the crucified God and the suffering of the non-*machos* (Amerindians, Africans, and Asians) leads to atonement for the *macho* perpetrators (the Europeans: Spain and the United States). Through the emancipation of the non-*macho*, crucified people liberate the rest of society.

Classism

The Amerindian, African, and Asian were constructed as feminine for the benefit of the *machos*. Similarly, those who were poor, regardless of their whiteness, were also seen as being emasculated. Whatever wealth Cuba produced was accomplished by the sweat, blood and corpses of God's crucified people. If Amerindians, African, and Asians represent the oppressed elements of our culture, then our Spanish and Anglo roots represent the oppressive elements. Classism among Cubans can be understood as a manifestation of *machismo* whereby a dialectic is created between the subject (Spaniard and Anglo men) and the object (Amerindian, African, and Asian), consisting of the continuous progressive subordination of the object for the purposes of the subject. Writing of the narrative process by those with *cojones* constructs non-Europeans as a secondary race that needs civilization to be mediated through the paternal white hands of the *macho*.

The *macho* subject sees himself in the mirror of commodity purchasing as one able to provide for family, thus strengthening the patriarchal system. For Exilic Cubans, Cuba's economic difficulties proved Castro's inability to provide. Castro thus forfeits his role as *patrón*, as the head of family. Remembering *la Cuba de ayer* as economically advanced, like the United States, justifies the need to reeducate Resident Cubans in a post-Castro Cuba so as to return to her former glory. Their inability to provide demonstrates the Resident Cubans' lack of manhood. Like children, they require instruction in the ways of freedom and capitalism. The relationship Exilic Cubans hope to reestablish is one where Miami positions itself "on top of" La Habana.

Historically, the highest rung of Cuba's social hierarchy was occupied by whites, divided into a variety of stratified economic classes. Regardless of the degree of whiteness, all enjoyed equal political privileges: namely, the right to own as many slaves as desired, and the right to acquire wealth in any manner whatsoever. The apex consisted of whites born in Spain called *peninsulares*, who dominated the property market. They also dominated the commercial sector and held the majority of colonial, provincial, and municipal posts. They were preponderant in the Cuban delegation to the Spanish parliament, and in the military and the clergy. They represented the majority of high court presidents, judges, magistrates, prosecutors, solicitors, clerks, and scribes. More than 80 percent of the *peninsular* population was qualified to vote, compared to 24 percent of the entire Cuban population.[56] The *peninsulares* saw themselves in Lacan's mirror as *machos*, while viewing the white *criollos* (those born on the Island) as effeminate and culturally backward. A frequent *peninsular* charge against the *criollos* was their effeminacy, their non-*macho* position.[57]

Below the *peninsulares* in the social hierarchy were these same white *criollos*. Antagonism between them and the *peninsulares* was checked by a shared racial fear. At the bottom of the white stratum were the *monteros* or *guajiros* who lived in the shadows of the white elite. While their lifestyle economically differed little from the slaves, *peninsulares* and white *criollos* conferred upon them the distinction of being superior to all the nonwhites.[58] Valuing their elevation above blacks, they served as vigilantes during "slave revolts," showing intense viciousness in their suppression of blacks.

After the Spanish-American War, a dependency relationship with the United States developed. It was, then, on the safe domain of Cuban land where the United States first launched its venture into world imperialism. Maturing as an empire, the United States was less interested in acquiring territory than in controlling peripheral economies to obtain financial benefits for the center. A dependency relationship with Cuba, masked by the guise of New World independence, was preferable to incorporating an "effeminate" people into the Union. Theodore Roosevelt and his virile "rough riders" established the myth of United States' masculinity later incarnated in John Wayne and the Marlboro man. Attributing effeminacy to the Cubans justified the economic control of the Cuban periphery. Secretary of War Elihu Root, referring to Cuba, said it best: "It is better to have the favors of a lady with her consent, after judicious courtship, than to ravish her."[59]

On March 16, 1889, an article published in the *Manufacturer* questioned whether the United States should annex Cuba. Developing a case against it, the author writes:

> The Cubans are not...desirable. Added to the defects of the *paternal* race are *effeminacy* and an aversion to all effort, truly to the extent of illness. They are helpless, lazy, *deficient in morals*,

and *incapable by nature* and experience of fulfilling the obligations of citizenship in a great and free republic. Their lack of *virile strength* and self-respect is shown by the apathy with which they have *submitted* to Spanish oppression for so long (italics mine).[60]

According to the *Manufacturer*, Cuban submission to Spain identified the Cubans as an emasculated people, unworthy of being accepted into the *macho* Union.[61]

The economic result of colonialism was the reduction of *machos* to effeminate positions. The 1959 revolution was an attempt to reclaim our masculinity. Likewise, the exilic experience for those of us who came to the United States was in part the establishment of our *machismo* in terms of North American paradigms, accomplished through the capture of Dade County's political, social, economic, and cultural power structures. To my mind, white Cuban men with power and privilege in both resident and exilic communities continue to benefit from repressive social structures built around the concept of *machismo*.

Conclusion

When *machos* gaze upon the Other, what do they see? How we "see" them, defines our existential selves as *machos*. To "see" implies a position of authority, a privileged point of view. "Seeing" is not an innocent metaphysical phenomenon concerning the transmittal of light waves. It encompasses a mode of thought that radically transforms the object being seen into an object for possession. The white Latino elite *macho* understands who he is when he tells himself who he is not. *Machos* as subject are defined by contrasting themselves with the seen objects: Amerindians, Africans, Asians, women, and the poor. In defining what it means to be a *macho* by emphasizing the differences with our Others, one reflects established power relations exist that give meaning to those differences.

Specifically, when a *macho* gazes upon one of God's crucified peoples, he perceives a group that is effeminate. When the *macho* looks at himself in Lacan's mirror, he does not see a *maricón*; hence he projects what he is not into his Other, defining himself as a white, civilized *macho*. The power of seeing becomes internalized, naturalized, and legitimized in order to rationalize the dominant culture's position of power. Our task as Hispanic ethicists is to move toward dismantling *machismo*, to go beyond *machismo*, by shattering the illusions created in our hall of mirrors.

17

Testimony of Rebekah[1]
Genesis 24:1–67:

In modern terms, Rebekah and Isaac's family puts the "funk" in dysfunctional! ...We know that Isaac is a mama's boy...He watched his father expel his older brother and stepmother into the wilderness. He witnessed his mother's anger, jealousy, and resentment toward Hagar and Ishmael. He had heard the story of how his father almost forced his mother into adultery because he was afraid to be honest about being her husband. Isaac grew up in a dysfunctional family filled with tension, deception, and violence. . . His hopes for a happy and healthy family are doomed from the start.

—BARBARA J. ESSEX[2]

The chapter opens with the elderly Abraham entrusting his faithful servant with the task of finding Isaac a suitable wife....The faithful servant is instructed to return to Abraham's kinfolk, and from among them find a wife for his son. Isaac is not permitted to find for himself a wife from the daughters of the Canaanites among whom they live. Not to marry a Canaanite woman could be based on the fear of diluting the purity of Abraham's stock or the purity of his religious practices. With these instructions, Abraham sets in motion the norm of endogamous marriages, that is, marriages that occur within the same extended family or clan. Abraham's instruction concerning marriage eventually takes form as law. According to Exodus 34:14–16, Jewish men are not to marry foreign women because "their daughters who prostitute themselves to their gods will make [Israel's] sons also prostitute themselves to their gods." . . .

With the faithful servant's hand on Abraham's genitals, an oath is sworn to bring back a wife for Isaac from his own people and not take him to his kinfolk's home lest he does not return and thus forfeits the promise made by God to Abraham. . . .Trusting that God will send an angel or messenger before him to prepare the way in faith, the servant goes about his task of fulfilling his oath, confident God will bless his venture. When the servant reaches Nahor he "puts out a fleece" that allows God to act (cf. Judg. 6:37–40). He would stand by the spring outside of the town where the young women come to draw water. Springs, along with wells, are locations where the possibility for marriage usually begins (Gen. 16:7–14, 21: 8–21, 29: 1–12; Ex. 2; Jn. 4). No doubt the earth's water is associated with the possibility of fertility. While standing by the spring, the servant decides to ask one of the girls to tilt her pitcher so that he can drink. If she does so, and offers to also water his camels, then she would be the one God has chosen for Isaac.

He has not finished setting the parameters for the test when Rebekah comes out of the town to draw water. Verse 16 tells us that she is beautiful and a virgin untouched by any man. It is interesting to note that the text tells us nothing about Isaac's virginity, or lack thereof. When the servant asks her for some water, she replies by calling him "my lord" and offers to also water his camels, a laborious task; to provide drink for ten thirsty camels that just crossed a desert is an arduous undertaking, requiring multiple trips to the spring to obtain sufficient water for them to drink. Camels can drink from twenty to thirty gallons of water in ten minutes. That comes to two to three hundred gallons of water she is offering to fetch!

After Rebekah passes the servant's test, he places a gold ring weighing a shekel through her nostrils, and on her arm places two bracelets weighing ten gold shekels. When he asks her who she is, Rebekah responds by stating that she is the daughter of Bethuel, son of Milcah, wife of Abraham's brother Nabor. In most biblical genealogies, only men beget other males. The names of women are mostly absent. Yet here, when it comes to Rebekah's genealogy, her grandmother Milcah, not her grandfather Nabor for whom the town is named, is highlighted. Milcah (Hebrew for "queen") is the family matriarch, who along with Nabor's concubine Reumah (22:20–24) give birth to the original twelve tribes that become part of the Aramaean people. Rebekah's origins are matriarchal, countering the prevalent Abrahamic patriarchy. This self-understanding affects her child rearing, as we shall later note, culminating with her son Jacob identifying himself as the son of his mother rather than his father, Isaac (29:12).

The tension between patriarchy and matriarchy is evident in Rebekah's testimony. She strongly identifies herself through her grandmother and brings the stranger to her mother's, not her father's, house. She does not wait for her father or brother to extend hospitality to the stranger, customarily the responsibility for men to offer, but invites the stranger to stay at her house. It is interesting to note that father, Bethuel, is mainly invisible throughout the narrative. She is portrayed as an independent woman, speaking to male strangers, an act prohibited in patriarchal social order. Yet while we celebrate her independence, her marriage is still arranged for her.

When Rebekah runs home to recount what had happened to her, her brother Laban runs out to meet the man at the spring, probably motivated by the extravagant gold pieces lavished on his sister.... Although Rebekah is portrayed as an independent woman, she is not so liberated as to determine who she would marry. The servant arranges her marriage with her father and brother without her consent. Even when she agrees to leave with the servant, she is not providing consent to the marriage; she is just agreeing to leave quickly rather than wait ten days. We are left wondering if her rush to depart is based on wanting to leave the family that "sold" her for the lavish gifts bestowed upon them, or her eagerness to meet her unknown new husband.

The servant declines staying ten addition days when asked to do so, no doubt wishing to return quickly due to Abraham's imminent death. Rebekah leaves with her nurse, who we later discover is named Deborah. In a way, her journey to Canaan parallels that of Abraham (12:1) who also voyaged to a foreign land leaving behind kinfolk, home, and the familiar. It is Rebekah, not her intended husband Isaac, who truly walks in Abraham's steps—following in his life experience of alienation.

After a long journey back to Canaan, Isaac finally sees his "mail-order" bride. We are told by the text that Isaac immediately fell in love with Rebekah. Not surprisingly, Rebekah's feelings toward Isaac are unknown, and remain unknown throughout the rest of the book of Genesis. We are not told if she is happy with her new husband, or if she is homesick for what was left behind. All we know is that she comforts her new husband, who was distressed over his mother's death.

The chapter ends with Isaac bringing Rebekah into his mother's tent to consummate the marriage. Once consummated, Isaac is finally consoled over the loss of his mother. An ambiguous space is created in this tent where one woman (mother) is replaced by another (wife) through sexual union. It may be true, as we shall soon discover, that Rebekah will remain barren for the next two decades, but that does not stop her from having to take up the task of mothering—physically taking Sarah's place in her tent as Isaac's mommy. The reader is left wondering if Isaac obtained a wife or a replacement (with benefits) for his mother. Rebekah becomes the wife-mother expected to continue doting and spoiling what appears to be the man-child.

18

Testimony of Tamar[1]
Genesis 38:1–30:

Rid society of prostitutes and licentiousness will run riot throughout. Prostitutes in a city are like a sewer in a palace. If you get rid of the sewer, the whole place becomes filthy and foul.

—St. Thomas Aquinas[2]

The Joseph novella is briefly interrupted with an interpolated story concerning Tamar (whose name means "palm tree") and her father-in-law, Judah, one of Joseph's brothers. Judah, the fourth son of Jacob and Leah, leaves his family to stay with Hirah, of whom we know nothing, in a small town called Adullam, located some twelve miles southwest of Bethlehem. While there, he marries an unnamed Canaanite. That he is not condemned for marrying a "foreign" woman (even though it is Judah who is the foreigner) indicates that this text must be a very old story. Judah's unnamed wife bears him three sons: Er, Onan, and Shelah. After some time, Judah chooses a wife from the local people for his eldest son. Her name is Tamar.

The purpose of this story is to ensure the establishment of Judah's male line, told from and for the male's point of view, and connect this bloodline with the land of southern Canaan. Tamar, the foreign woman in the story, even though she is on her own land, becomes the object by which the subject's goal of producing an heir is accomplished. In patriarchy one must dominate (usually the male), while another must submit (usually women, children, and men conquered through war). A careful reading of the Hebrew text reveals few exceptions. For example, Deborah the judge (Judg. 4) and Queen Esther (in the book of Esther) are able to maneuver within the patriarchal structures and carve out a space for themselves from which to exercise leadership. The identities of women are reduced in the biblical text to an extension of their male

134

counterparts, who are presented as the possessors of their female bodies. Tamar is no exception.

A woman's main purpose within the book of Genesis is to produce heirs, specifically male heirs—a theme often repeated throughout the rest of the biblical text. The barren matriarch Sarai offers her slave girl Hagar to Abram for rape so that he can have an heir (16:2). Rachel, Jacob's wife, demands of her husband, "Give me children, or I shall die!" (30:1), as she competes with her sister Leah, also Jacob's wife, for his attention—an attention obtained through the birthing of men. In the minds of these women, barrenness was a humiliation. And yet, Johanna W.H. Bos reminds us:

> The story of Tamar points in the direction of a gynocentric bias. The men in the story are wrongheaded irresponsible bunglers, who don't see straight. They are shown up as such by Tamar, who notices correctly and who causes Judah such an "eye-opener" that his view of reality is restored. The tone in which the men are discussed, summarily dispatched by God, or acting as if they were in charge and all the while making fools of themselves, points to a gynocentric bias as well.[3]

According to the story, Tamar married Judah's oldest son, Er; however, Er offended God (we do not know how) and as a result died....Unfortunately, Er died childless. Following ancient tradition, Onan, Er's brother, took Tamar as his wife to perform his duty of impregnating her so that a child could be born in his brother's name. It was considered disastrous for a man to die without an heir to perpetuate his name, hence the development of the custom of levirate marriage—a custom that eventually was canonized in Deuteronomy 25:5–10. Besides ensuring the deceased man had an heir, the act of marrying one's dead brother's widow kept property within the deceased husband's family, preventing it from going to the household of another man whom the widow might marry.

Onan, for reasons we do not know, refused to impregnate Tamar. Whenever he copulated with Tamar he would pull out before climaxing and spill his seed on the ground. God found this offensive and "put him to death." Christian commentators have historically understood Onan's sin to be masturbation because he "spilled his semen on the ground." Hence a synonym for masturbation is onanism, an eighteenth-century term derived from his name. But the sin of Onan was not masturbation. According to the text, he spilled his seed on the ground because he deliberately abdicated his duty of ensuring that his brother's name would continue. To be specific, his sin was avoiding his levirate obligation to his dead brother by performing coitus interruptus. Maybe he selfishly hoped to split his father's inheritance with his younger surviving brother, leaving out any possible descendants of Tamar. . .

Tamar, twice widowed, found herself with no husband or children, a precarious situation for any woman living within a patriarchal society. Her only hope in maintaining a "good" name for herself and obtaining financial security is to be married to the next brother. But Judah, fearful that his youngest might meet the same fate as his older brothers, tells Tamar to return to her father until Shelah comes of age. Prohibited from marrying any other man but her dead husband's brother, she becomes marginalized, with no way of securing a future. Judah must have thought that there had to be something wrong with Tamar, who, like the black widow spider, seemed to lose her husbands to death. It never occurred to him that his sons may have been responsible for their own demise. With the passage of time, Tamar realized her father-in-law was not going to honor the tradition that would have required Shelah marrying her. Even though she had custom and the law on her side, she, as a woman, was powerless, relegated to the margins. She lacked the means of holding those with power over her accountable.

When she hears that her father-in-law will be visiting her town on business (it was the season of sheep shearing), she starts pondering how to force his hand so that he meets his obligations. Unable to confront Judah directly, Tamar devises a plan, using the power of her sexuality, to force Judah to act "justly" according to tradition. Like so many women throughout history, she uses her body in order to survive in a patriarchal society. She plays the prostitute and tricks the recent widower Judah to lie with her. Although Tamar engages in a bold and risky act—risky because she could be killed for becoming pregnant while not being married—she overshadows Judah for a brief moment in time, only to rapidly disappear from the narrative as soon as she accomplishes her assigned task and produces an heir.

The initiative Tamar shows makes her an archetype for all who are marginalized, not just women. Tamar shows how playing the role of the trickster to subvert prevailing oppressive structures is necessary to force those oblivious of their power and privilege to do justice. Tamar removes her widow's garbs and puts on a veil commonly used by prostitutes, for a harlot, according to the book of Proverbs, is known by her attire (Prov. 7:10). She sits by the side of the road where she expects Judah will be traversing. Noticing her, Judah is enticed to employ her services. Strange that he does not recognize his daughter-in-law, the wife of his two deceased sons. Surely Judah suffers from a lack of vision.

Tamar plays the prostitute, participating in what has come to be known as the oldest profession. For many, prostitution is immoral, and they are right, but not because it involves sex. Prostitution is immoral because it relies on exploiting the vulnerability of women or men (mostly women) by exchanging their worth and dignity for a few dollars. Regardless that some have attempted to portray prostitutes as fully liberated women in control of their sexuality, the truth remains that it is a system predominantly run by men, at the service of men, for the profit of men. Prostitutes are objects created and condemned by the same male-centered society that benefits from their existence, making prostitution one of the oldest male-dominated and sexually abusive social structures.

Yet the women like Tamar, who are forced into prostitution for economic reasons, are defined and scorned because of their sexual activities. They become "whores," yet when a Solomon takes seven hundred wives of royal birth and three hundred mistresses (concubines), we fail to apply the same terms to him. Men are seldom negatively defined by their sexual activities, nor are they held liable for procuring the sexual services of women. Regardless of society's bias toward prostitutes, for Jesus they were the ones entering heaven before the religious leaders of his day who observed God's commands and dictates (Mt. 21:31), perhaps because Jesus understood that these women were the oppressed victims of a so-called victimless crime where intercourse is reduced to a commercial transaction.

The Bible distinguishes between secular prostitution and prostitution connected with a religious cult. The biblical text appears to treat secular prostitution as natural and necessary. Among the sexual laws appearing in the Hebrew Bible, none forbids a man from visiting a secular prostitute, as illustrated by the Hebrew spies visiting Rehab's brothel in Jericho (Josh. 2:1), or Samson spending the night with a prostitute (Judg. 16:1–3). In these stories the women are not stigmatized. None of these secular prostitutes who serviced these holy men of God are condemned; rather, most of them are portrayed as heroines, with Rehab finding a favorable spot in Jesus' genealogy (Mt. 1:5). Yet if a man was to marry, and discover on his wedding night that his bride was not a virgin, then he had every right to have her stoned for "prostituting herself in her father's house" (Deut. 22:21). What made prostitution wrong in the Hebrew Bible was not the exchange of currency for the chance to copulate, but rather the removal of intercourse from the social system that reduced women to property within a hierarchical male-centered power structure.[4]

The only time the biblical text condemns prostitution is when such action is linked to temple worship. It is important to remember that Yahweh's principal nemeses were the fertility god Baal and the female goddess Asherah. Priests of these fertility gods practiced what is called an imitative or homeopathic magic.[5] The rituals practiced by these priests consecrated to fertility gods were based on the law of similarity, which maintained that like produces like. Because they thought that an effect resembled its cause, these priests believed that they could produce any desired effect merely by imitating it. The ritual, hoping to create fecundity for crops and livestock, consisted of sexual acts by and with temple prostitutes in the sanctuary to imitate what they hoped to accomplish in the fields. Those who served as temple prostitutes were male and female. For these cultic reasons, these temple prostitutes are banned from God's people as a "abhorrent" or "detestable thing," occupying the lowest levels of social status (Deut. 23:19).

None of Yahweh's priests could marry a prostitute (Lev. 21:7), and if one of the priest's daughters was to become a prostitute, her father was obligated to burn her alive (Lev. 21:9). Yet Jesus' dealings with prostitutes seem to have been influenced by the book of Proverbs. Although the speaker in Proverbs looks down on the prostitutes as the antithesis of wisdom (Prov. 7), condemnation is mainly reserved for the man who hires her services. It is he who is the fool, frittering away his wealth (Prov. 29:3).

Consequently, Jesus was not afraid to associate with women with so-called bad reputations (Lk. 7:36–50), using prostitutes as positive examples for religious leaders to emulate (Mt. 21:31). Why not condemn the prostitute? Because in a patriarchal social order where a woman's primary means of survival is to be under the authority of a father, husband, or son, she who is without a man has little choice for survival other than to earn her meals by selling her body. It is not the woman who is to be blamed, but the men who designed the social structures that prevent her from surviving apart from a man. The man is the one who creates the circumstances for a woman to turn to prostitution, and then takes advantage of her situation by paying her.

Prostitution, as a lawful immorality, was tolerated throughout most of Christian history because it protected virtuous Christian wives from the lustful demands of their husbands and maintained harmony within the political sphere. Its absence, it was believed, would disrupt society, casting it into a debauched chaos. Early Roman moralists, like Cato the Censor, Cicero, and Seneca, regarded prostitution as necessary because it prevented men from breaking up the marriages of others. During the Crusades, prostitution increased. Pious warriors for the Lord were not expected to abstain from intercourse just because they were away from their wives. According to calculations kept by the Templars (the order responsible for keeping records of the Crusades), thirteen thousand prostitutes were required in one year alone just to satisfy the desires of these saintly warriors.[6] St. Thomas Aquinas, relying on the writings of Augustine, who urged husbands to go to prostitutes rather than commit adultery (with another man's woman),[7] believed that prostitution served a crucial and necessary social function. Besides relieving the wife from her husband's sexual advances, prostitution was believed to be a safety valve geared to reduce sodomy, adultery, rape, incest, and domestic violence.[8] In Aquinas's mind it appeared better to exchange money for sex than to relieve sexual "lust" within a marriage.

The Curia, the ensemble of ministries responsible for assisting the pope to govern the Catholic Church, partially financed the building of St. Peter's Cathedral in the Vatican through a tax on prostitution. The sum collected was four times more than what Pope Leo X expected to collect from the sales of indulgences in Germany. Yet it is the sale of indulgences that is most remembered as the main means for the construction of St. Peter's,[9] while most ignore that the cathedral was partially built on the backs of women (or more accurately stated, women on their backs). With the coming of the Protestant Reformation, a focus on adultery, which included prostitution, was rethought by men. Martin Luther used harsh comments when referring to both adulterers and prostitutes. He attempted to eradicate prostitution, but eventually left the brothels alone, concerned that their closure might create social unrest.

Judah, like so many great religious leaders after him, secures the services of the supposed prostitute, but first he negotiates a price in the form of a goat. To secure that payment was to be made at the conclusion of the interaction, he leaves behind some collateral: the insignia that signifies his rank and status, in the form of his signet (the official means of identification), cord (which holds his signet around his neck), and staff (used to control is flock, symbolizing his authority). After meeting his needs and returning to camp, he sends his friend Hirah the Adullamite to deliver payment, but the "temple prostitute," according to the text, disappeared; and to make matters worse, no one in the village has ever heard of or seen her. That none of the townsmen even thought of Tamar serves as a testimony to her virtue, for none considered her to be promiscuous even while waiting for Judah to act justly. What is damning for Judah is that Hirah is looking for the temple prostitute, not a secular prostitute, thus indicating that Judah's sin may have been religious unfaithfulness to God. Maybe in Judah's mind sexual intercourse with sacred prostitutes would ensure fecundity among his flock through a sympathetic magic that reproduces the act of fertility. Judah, fearful he would become a laughingstock, quickly dismisses the matter.

Three months pass, and Tamar is discovered to be with child. Judah is publically shamed by a woman under his authority who became pregnant; patriarchy conferred on him the right to restore his honor by finding the man who trespassed on his "property" and have them both stoned. But Judah is impetuous, calling for her and her unborn child to be burned at the stake in accordance with the eventual biblical law concerning daughters of priests who played the harlot (Lev. 21:9). Maybe he is seeking revenge for what he has always believed was the cause of death of his two eldest sons? At the moment of crises, Tamar acts, producing the symbols identifying the man responsible for her pregnancy so that she, along with the father of her unborn child, could be sentenced to death. Of course, the symbols belong to Judah. To condemn her is to condemn himself. Less an act of magnanimous rectitude and more an attempt of self-preservation, Judah, with his back against the wall, is forced to publically acknowledge her righteousness, a righteousness that surpasses his own. The subversive act of Tamar as trickster forces Judah to live up to the justice that was always due her.

The story ends with Tamar giving birth to two children, twins by the names Perez and Zerah, echoing the similar birth narrative of Esau and Jacob by Rebekah. And while Tamar disappears from the narrative, accomplishing her assigned task of producing male heirs, we are left questioning if these children are the result of incest. The book of Leviticus prohibits a man from engaging in sex with his daughter-in-law, punishable with both being put to death (Lev. 18:15, 20:12). Nevertheless, Tamar does make one more brief appearance in the biblical text—in Jesus' genealogy (Mt. 1:3).

PART SEVEN

Confronting Heterosexism

19

When the Bible Is Used for Hate[1]

Are you ready kids? Whoooo lives in a pineapple under the sea? SpongeBob SquarePants! Absorbent and yellow and porous is he. SpongeBob SquarePants! But wait, this silly frolicking sponge is really a sexual pervert teaching our innocent children to be pro-homosexual—at least according to Dr. James Dobson of Focus on the Family. I always knew there was something fishy about a sponge who openly held hands with a pink starfish. God only knows what illicit acts are taking place at SpongeBob's neighborhood appropriately named Bikini BOTTOM.

Thanks to the vigilant eyes of James Dobson, who credits himself for bringing about [the George W. Bush] reelection, we can now shield our children from SpongeBob the sex fiend. Yes folks, Dr. Dobson outed SpongeBob during an inaugural feast held for members of Congress. It appears that SpongeBob joined other so-called "gay lovers" like Winnie the Pooh, Kermit the Frog, and Barney the Dinosaur on a new video asking children to take a "tolerance pledge"—a pledge to show dignity and respect for those who are different, whether it be different gender, race, ethnicity, faith, and yes, orientation.

Heaven forbid we teach our children to demonstrate agape (unconditional) love toward those who are different, when fear and ignorance are more useful tools for winning elections. Furthermore, our fear of gays requires we smoke them out and persecute them, even if it endangers the security of our nation. After the first terrorist attack on the World Trade Center in 1993, our intelligence agency revealed an alarming shortage of Arabic-speaking translators. The mountains of data collected concerning possible terrorist attacks remains practically useless because of the backlog of vital information that remains untranslated. Last year's backlog alone encompasses 120,000 hours of potentially vital information concerning possible threats to our security. Of the 279 Arabic translators at the State Department, only five are fluent enough to handle the regional dialects and language subtleties. Yet, since 1998, twenty Arabic-speaking government translators were discharged from the military for being gay. We had trained and skilled people who could do their job well and help save American lives, but because they are gay we would rather not take advantage of their skills and instead choose to endanger lives? Does sexual orientation really affects someone's ability to do their job well?

But why should we be surprised. Those today who use the Bible to advocate hate, disgust, and fear toward homosexuals are the spiritual descendants of those in this nation who have used the Bible to persecute those who are different and have refused to conform to powers and principalities of the privileged social order. Following God's biblical call to missionize the heathens and fulfill our Manifest Destiny, we committed genocide upon the indigenous nations of this land. Based of the Word of God, we [hung] independent-thinking women…in Salem on the charges of being witches. Following God's ordained order for the universe as laid out in the Bible we kidnapped, raped, enslaved, and murdered Africans. Maintaining God's scriptural command that men are to rule over women, we denied them the right to vote, and even today, pay them 75 cents on the dollar for the same work they do as men. And when the Reverend King voiced the call for freedom and liberation to flow like living water, most of our white churches stood against what was seen at the time as a communist wolf in sheep's clothing, because the desegregation he advocated contradicted how we've been taught to read the Bible. Sadly today the Bible is being used to oppress, dishonor, and persecute our queer brothers and sisters, who like the rest of us, are also created in the image of God. I am repulsed by politicians who have fanned the flames of hatred and fear toward gays in order to score votes with evangelical Christians. I am dismayed that the universal church of Jesus Christ has changed the message of salvation as an act of unconditional love to one where gays cannot be included among the saved. But does not Christ call us to love our (white, black, Latino/a, Native American, and yes gay) neighbor as ourselves?

Now, if you excuse me, my favorite TV show comes on in ten minutes—*SpongeBob SquarePants*.

An Apology to Homosexuals

(follow-up to article above)

To my gay bothers and sisters. May the grace of our Lord Jesus be with you. I've received numerous communiques demanding an apology for a previous column I penned. And I agree. But if any apology is due, it is one that should be made to the gay community. I am sorry if I inadvertently made you the Object of my discourse rather than the subject. I never intended to speak for you or about you, but rather to highlight what I continue to see as a moral travesty—the use of sacred text to justify cultural bigotry.

The purpose of said article was that gays and lesbians are fired because of their sexual orientation, and specifically how the firing of trained Arab translators places this nation's security at risk. This injustice is undergirded in the name of God, as have past oppressions. Use of the Bible to justify crusades, genocide, slavery, and sexism is historical fact. My fear is that we are repeating history.

Hurt feelings of public religious political figures, myself included, are not the issue. What is important, my gay bothers and sisters, is that God loves you, God cherishes you and God suffers in your sufferings. You should know that Christ dwells in you, and you should not reject the good news of the salvation and liberation because of how those claiming to be Christ's disciples interpret his words. You should know that you are created in the image of God, created for dignity because you have worth. And because all that God creates is good, you should never settle for being "tolerated." Like all humans, you should be accepted into the fabric of society.

It is one thing for some to disagree with your lifestyle; it is another for them to use their power and prestige to impose their views, and in doing so, deny you humanness. And we who are heterosexuals should know that your orientation, like ours, is but a part of who you are, not the total means of defining your identity. You are more than gay. You are parents, siblings, children, teachers, scientists, ministers, politicians, military personal protecting our freedoms, and world leaders.

At first glance it appears that Jesus makes no reference to homosexuality. But several of my gay brothers and sisters point to Matthew 19:12: "There are eunuchs who are born thus from their mother's womb, and there are eunuchs who are made eunuchs by men, and there are eunuchs who make themselves eunuchs for the sake of the reign of Heaven." Those who are made eunuchs, like Nehemiah the cupbearer, refer to those who were castrated in order to be the king's servant. This insured their ability to serve the monarch without dishonoring the king's possessions, specifically his queen or harem. Eunuchs for the sake of God's reign, are those who chose celibacy as a religious calling.

But how do we interpret eunuch from birth? Some gay scholars believe that this verse refers to them as modern-day sexual outcasts or transgendered persons. The eunuchs from birth represent men who have not been with women because of their orientation from birth. Eunuchs were considered spiritual outcasts, unable to participate in the cultic practices of the faith community: "He shall not enter the assembly of Yahweh if his male member is wounded, crushed, or cut (Deut. 23:1)." By referring to himself as a eunuch, Jesus seeks solidarity with the sexually oppressed of his times, while fulfilling the promise stated in Isaiah 56:3–5: "Do not let the eunuch say, 'Behold, I am a dried up tree,' for thus says Yahweh to the eunuchs who keep my Sabbaths, and chooses things with which I am pleased, and take hold of my covenant. I will even give them in my house and in my walls a name better than sons and daughters, I will give them an everlasting name which shall not be cut off."

Jesus' inclusion of the sexual outcast served as a model of welcoming and affirming everyone into the early Christian church. Love for all people, including the outcasts, becomes the acceptable norm established by Jesus. Love is an action word, not an abstract concept based on unexpressed feelings. The real test of love is that it be unconditional, not for the devious purpose of changing them (which in effect transforms people into objects), but rather love for the sake of the person, as she or he is.

When the disciple Philip (Acts 8:26–40) encounters an Ethiopian eunuch on the road to Gaza, who is reading the prophet Isaiah, Philip is quick to share the affirming message of the gospel and to welcome the sexual outcast into the fellowship of believers. But what if I'm wrong? What if homosexuality is a sin? Then, when I stand before the throne of the Almighty, I can stand with confidence. For I rather have erred on the side of grace and mercy than on the side of judgment and condemnation.

20

Confessions of a Latino Macho: From Gay Basher to Gay Ally[1]

Tommy (not his real name) was a good friend of mine. We met in the 1980s at our local Southern Baptist Church, where I served as a deacon and Sunday school teacher. At the time we were young, single, "good-looking," and took our faith seriously. We were also "backsliding" Baptists, which meant we enjoyed dancing—and if truth be known, an occasional glass of wine. Every so often we would invite fellow church singles to join us for a night of fellowship, conversation, music, and, of course, dancing. We all became close friends; a family that at times planned vacations together. One night, Tommy stopped by my house for a talk. Considering our youth and availability, it should not be surprising that our conversation eventually led to the topic of sexuality. I shared with him the struggles I was undergoing with my commitment to celibacy. The temptations, I felt, were many. I shared with Tommy about a particular young lady, whom I feared would be a stumbling block, making it difficult to maintain my present sexual abstinence, if I started dating her. At this point Tommy shared that he too struggled with sexual temptation; however, for him, the temptation was for other males.

Tommy, to my shock, and yes, *horror*, was gay. How can a good committed Christian, let alone a Southern Baptist, be a homosexual? There was a long silence. Tommy wondered if his confession would bring about the end of our friendship. I feared that he might make a pass at me. I finally broke the silence by reminding him that homosexuality was a sin, an abomination before God, and a free choice he was making that was morally indefensible. How did I know this? Because my church told me.

I converted to Christianity in my early twenties when I walked down the aisle and made a public confession of giving my heart to Jesus. The church I joined was a large, loving congregation. For the first time in my life, I felt as if I belonged. People embraced me as if I was family. These loving, gentle people began to teach me about God, the Bible, and what it meant to be a Christian. Among the many lessons taught to me, one was that homosexuality was a sin. Why would I have doubted people I admired and wanted to emulate? These were sincere, faithful Christians. Why would they purposely lead me astray? They pointed to the chapters and verses in the Bible that showed God's anger towards gays.

Keep in mind that prior to my conversion, I was a gay-basher, participating in contributing to their public humiliation. Living in Miami during the late 1970s, I found myself participating in Anita Bryant's very public campaign against gays. Converting to Christianity some years later found me in a church that taught the proper Christian response was to hate homosexuality while still loving the sinner. If I wanted to belong to this group of Christians and make this church my home, I had to make sure that my actions toward gays were consistent with what my church said God's view was toward homosexuals—a type of kinder, gentler form of gay-bashing.

So here I was with my dear friend Tommy. We had become close friends, so shunning him was no longer an option. How could I hate the sin while loving the sinner? I asked Tommy if he wanted to break free from the bondage of sin. He said yes. I asked him if he wanted to be a heterosexual. "Dear God Almighty, yes," he burst out before emotionally breaking down. Tommy, I felt, was well on the road to healing and salvation.

I agreed to be his spiritual partner in the struggle against the evils of homosexuality. We covenanted to pray together. We fasted. We cast out the demon of homosexuality. If anyone ever truly wanted to be a heterosexual, if anyone ever truly wanted to stop finding men attractive, if anyone ever truly humbled himself before God to faithfully live a Christian life, it was Tommy. Years went by, and—you know what?—Tommy was still gay. Tommy did not change, but I did. In a very real sense, Tommy taught me something important about God. For you see, either God is impotent in saving a willing believer from her or his sins, or maybe, just maybe, I have been taught to read the Bible through the eyes of oppressors, regardless as to how loving and sincere these oppressors appeared.

Irrespective of how earnest and caring Christians may actually be, their use of the Bible to advocate hate, disgust, and fear toward homosexuals makes them the heirs of those who previously used the Bible to persecute women and marginalized racial and ethnic groups. Like their spiritual ancestors who perpetrated genocide upon indigenous nations in obedience to God's call to evangelize the heathens and fulfill their Manifest Destiny, they commit atrocities even though they are sincere about their faith. It matters not that they spend hours on their knees seeking God's guidance, they fall into the same mortal sin that their spiritual ancestors of Salem, who executed independent-thinking women on the charge of witchcraft. Like those other Christians who came before that used God's Word as a light unto their feet and a lamp unto their path, they boldly marched forward to enslave Africans, steal the land of Mexicans in the Southwest, and deny women basic voting rights. The folks at my church were really nice people, God-fearing, and decent; nevertheless, the way they understood their faith oppressed and dishonored our queer brothers and sisters, who like the rest of us, are also created in the very image of God.

The sin that I had to wrestle with was not Tommy's homosexuality, but my heterosexuality. It is not homosexuality that displeases God, but as Marvin Ellison [has] argue[d]...it is my sin of heterosexuality—that is, making my sexual experience compulsory on everyone else.[2] That is the true abomination. The Christian church has, for nearly two thousand years, affirmed my heterosexual experience, making it the normative behavior for all of humanity. This patriarchal understanding of sexuality has been justified and legitimized by my Christian faith, creating multiple oppressive structures to be imposed, not just on the LGBT community, but also on women, children, and people of color. If I wanted to move beyond such oppressive structures, which included manifestations of gay bashing, I would need to move away from conservative *and* liberal interpretations of scripture. I would need to adopt a liberationist reading of Scripture and a liberationist approach to theology—that is, an approach that seeks to understand sexuality from the perspective of those who have been oppressed by how sexuality has historically been defined by Christianity.

I had to begin to understand that the binary roles of men and women, specifically in my Hispanic context of macho men and passive women in the vein of *la Virgin de Guadalupe*, existed and flourished within a set of normative rules, traditions, and customs. Enforcing these gender roles, either through personal behavior or societal structures, legitimized whatever abuses I visited upon the queer community as morally justified. Their refusal to adopt my heterosexuality became an outward expression of their rejection of God, thus justifying my "righteous indignation." Their rejection of Jesus, and his suffering atonement on the cross for their "sins," meant that they chose to be responsible in paying for "the wages of sin." Rather than simply continuing the "bashing gay lifestyle" lived prior to my conversion to Christianity, I now had a prophetic mandate to lead them to salvation through their adoption of my sexual orientation. For some, because such a mandate comes from reading the Bible through heterosexual eyes, the imposition of heterosexual patriarchal structures must be enforced by whatever means necessary. If we remember that the greatest evils against humanity occur when good religious folk safeguard against the evils of others, then it should not be surprising that by defending "traditional" marriages from the "abomination of the gay lifestyle," abominable acts, in the name of the Lord, become legitimized.

Fortunately for me, my failure to convert Tommy to heterosexuality led me to some disturbing questions. Could it be that homosexuality was not a sin? Could it be that God loves and accepts Tommy just as he is? And, finally, could it be that it was *I* who needed to repent of my sin, and not Tommy? Repent from the abomination of a heterosexual lifestyle that uses all the religious and cultural structures of society to rob Tommy of his dignity of being the beloved of God, created in the very image of the Rock of my salvation? In this chapter, I hope to explore my complicity with heterosexism. Because of my orientation, I can never speak for the queer community, nor provide them with the necessary pedagogy to achieve liberation. To do so would be paternalistic. Yet, to remain silent in the face of oppressive structures because "homosexuality" is not my issue makes me complicit with social structures designed to protect and advance my heterosexual privilege within society, similar to the way white privilege benefits Euro Americans regardless of their beliefs in or rejection of white supremacy. We who are not gay but participate in the struggle for liberation must guard from inadvertently making the queer community the *object* of our discourse, rather than the *subject*. This is usually done when heterosexuals debate if gays have worth or dignity. The only thing that I, as a heterosexual, can say with any integrity concerning LGBT issues is how I benefit and am privileged by my heterosexual orientation.

In the final analysis, those of us who are heterosexuals must become involved in civil rights for homosexuals because this is fundamentally a justice issue. Martin Luther King Jr. probably said it best, "Injustice anywhere is a threat to justice everywhere."[3] I, and I hope my fellow Christian believers, have no choice but to prophecy against injustices—even when the issues do not directly affect us. To be a liberationist means that whenever a group—any group—is oppressed, then one must stand with that group in solidarity. If not, as James reminds us, one's faith, minus works, is useless (Jas. 2:20).

As a Latino, who also knows a thing or two about discrimination, I must be cognizant that at times the oppressed are also oppressors. Within my marginalized Hispanic community, oppressive structures also exist. Edward Said coined the term "rhetoric of blame" to describe the activity of minorities who attack the dominant culture for being white, privileged, and insensitive to the structures of oppression. To solely attack the United States for being complicit is not an alternative to blaming the victim for his or her predicament. Said advocates studying oppression as a "network of interdependent histories."[4] Even though

Hispanics face ethnic discrimination at the hands of the dominant Euro American culture, within our own Latina/o community we uphold our own oppressive structures—structures that are specifically degrading to women and gays. With this in mind, I begin by proclaiming that I am a recovering heterosexist, that is, a recovering *machista*.

On Being a Macho Man

It is important to note, from the outset, that the usage of the terms *macho* or *machismo* occurs because I am specifically writing from my Hispanic social location. Obviously, comparable English terms exists. Nevertheless, I am troubled when Euro Americans insist on using the Hispanic words *macho* or *machismo*, as though to imply that Latino men are somewhat more sexist or heterosexist than their Euro American counterparts, and in the process, absolve Euro American culture of its own oppressive dispositions. Sexism and heterosexism exist in both the Hispanic and Euro American cultures, and while they may be manifested differently, they are equally oppressive to women and homosexuals.

We who are heterosexuals, specifically those of us who are Latino *machos*, inscribe our genealogies upon the cultural consciousness. Our struggles and accomplishments shape what it means to be a man, to be the head of the household, and to subjugate all who are weaker than us—women, children, those with darker skin pigmentation, and effeminate men. Our understanding is rooted in a *macho* identity that is constructed to ensure a *macho* future that protects the power and privilege of men made of steel, not feathers. This constructed understanding of manliness becomes the norm for the rest of society to emulate, mirroring the actions and values caused by those of us who are forward-thrusted *machos*. Yet, the truth of the *macho* subject is not found in the self-construction of identity.

Jacques Lacan, a psychoanalyst, would have us look for truth in the "locus" of the Other,[5] in this case, the locus of homosexuals. Precisely for this reason, dominant *macho* power must constantly obliterate the Other's "locus." It is not enough to simply be content with imposing a compulsory heterosexuality upon present and future homosexuals. The *macho* does not find satisfaction with merely closeting homosexuals or labeling them as *maricones* (the derogative term for "fag") and thus not worthy of being men. But by some perverted interpretation of scripture, the *macho* must supplant the homosexual's identity, by getting homosexuals to see their identity through *macho* eyes. The *macho* is not satisfied until homosexuals sees themselves as abominations, mired in self-loathing, and recognizing their need for salvation that mercifully is brought to them through the hands of the *macho*.

Nevertheless, to seek the voice of those who are written off from the discourse critiques those of us with heterosexist power and privilege to substitute our norm for their reality. Recalling history from the homosexual underside forces the dominant subject *macho* to view the object as, in fact, external rather than simply a Lacanian projection of the ego's subjectivity. On the other hand, to ignore the voices of our queer neighbors justifies yesterday's sexual domination, while it normalizes today's continuation of that oppression, and prevents tomorrow's hope for liberation.

Missing from analysis of the *macho* is the space occupied by lesbians, known by Hispanics as *marimachos* or *tortilleras* (derogatory terms translated as "dyke"). While *maricones* constitute a "scandal" as men forsaking their manhood, *marimachos* are usually ignored due to the overall *machismo* of the society that grounds its sexuality solely on the *macho's* desires, repressing all forms of feminine sexuality. Tolerance of lesbians is partly due to their unimportance to the *macho's* construction of sexuality. They simply have no space in the dominant construction. Female sexuality does not exist apart from the *macho*. The image of the sex-void sacred virgin becomes the paragon for all women (Catholics and Protestants) to emulate. In fact, same-sexual intercourse engaged in by women becomes for the *macho* (as well as for many Euro American males) a desirable activity in which to participate physically or via voyeurism. While much can be written on the negative impact *machismo* has upon all women who are heterosexuals or lesbians, it will remain beyond the scope of this chapter. The concern of the *macho* is not to fulfill female sexuality. The *macho* is concerned with men who fail to live up to the *macho* construction of what it means to be a man.

On Conquering

Machismo implies clear and distinct gender roles. According to Argentine liberation theologian Marcella Althaus-Reid:

> *Machismo* can be defined as the permeating patriarchal ideology which has characterized Latin American history since the *Conquista* in the fifteenth century. It rules and regulates the behaviour of men, from allowing them to touch women in the streets or public transport, to the complex legal system which condemns women to a life of poverty and brutality. But *machismo* could not exist without women playing a specific part in society, and such is the model called *herbrismo*. . . *Herbrismo* defines a Latin American woman's place, which is her home, or the sphere of the private and domestic. . . Outside of these boundaries is the male territory of paid jobs, politics, church, friends and

lovers; *machista* culture does not condemn men's promiscuity but celebrates it.[6]

Machos are conquerors who emphasize actions over words. They are leaders who are dominant and in control both in the boardroom and the bedroom. Their insatiable sexual appetite defines manliness. Only through seducing women can the *macho* prove his virility. In the mind of the *macho*, he must be sexually ready for anybody, anywhere, anytime. Mirta Mulhare de la Torre's (no relation), who has studied Hispanic sexuality, states it best, "The dominant mode of behavior for *el macho*, the male, [was] the sexual imperative...A man's supercharged sexual physiology [placed] him on the brink of sexual desire at all times and at all places."[7]

To be a man, a *macho*, implies more than simply conquest. The *macho* is also charged with protection of those who are subordinate, specifically women. *Machos* are expected to conduct themselves along certain norms legitimated by the Hispanic culture. It becomes the *macho*'s responsibility, his burden, to protect the honor of the family name by defending and protecting the virtues of *his women*, be they wives, mistresses, or daughters. Yet, simultaneously, *machos* are to be conquerors of other men's possessions, their women. The *macho* state of mind can be summed-up in the popular saying: *Yo suelto mi gallo, los demás que recojan sus gallinas* [I let loose my rooster, let the others gather up their hens]."

A Latino is suspected of being homosexual if his behavior fails to demonstrate *macho* qualities. Such qualities include, but are not limited to, an interest in rough games; a muscular physique; an absence of gentle, quiet, or nurturing sensibilities toward others; a desire to control others; and a drive to posture and aggressively compete with others. To appear strong, virile, and aggressive becomes the essence of *machismo*. Those who fall short of this *macho* paragon are seen as unfit for leadership positions.[8] Thus the term *mariposa* (butterfly, a euphemism for homosexual men) is used to attack one's political enemies.

Women, on the other hand, are expected to be dependent, weak, self-sacrificing and chaste. Thus, by definition, they cannot hold any leadership position within the public sphere. A woman, according to anthropologist Rafael L. Ramírez, "is for pleasure, penetration, *para comérsela* (to be eaten)."[9] To be a non-*macho* accepts a place within society where they are passive, submissive, and accepting of all forms of disrespect and abuse.

All structures (be it the family, the church, or the state) that are patriarchal, hierarchical and non-participative are the outward expressions of the inward sin of heterosexuality. *Machismo* undergirds the violence manifested in domestic spouse abuse, the violence manifested in excluding people from ministering God's Word because of their gender or orientation, and the violence manifested within the political state to maintain the power and privilege of the few. Thus, it can be expected that this understanding of *machismo* will be amplified within the overall sociopolitical culture.

As we can see, we do a disservice to the elucidation of *machismo* by limiting it to just another form of sexism. *Machismo* requires a full consideration of sexism, heterosexism, racism, ethnocentrism, and classism. Manifestations of oppression along gender, racial, class and/or sexual orientation within the Hispanic culture do not exist in isolated compartments, nor are they separate categories of repression. They are created in the space where they interact and conflict with each other, a space we have been calling *machismo*.

In a perverse form of logic, we define this Latino space by gazing back at the overall dominant Euro American culture. We looked toward oppressors to define our standard for manhood. Rather than resist our colonialized status, we adopted and internalized the North American individualistic image and definition of what it means to be manly. The white Euro American heterosexual man became the ideal, incorporated in the consciousness of Hispanic men. The closer a Latino is to this white ideal, the more of a *macho* he is. As Brazilian educator Paulo Freire warned, "*to be* is *to be like*, and *to be like* is *to be like the oppressor*."[10] Colonizing the Hispanic male mind means that we have learned to see ourselves through the eyes of the dominant white Euro American culture. Those closest to this ideal do not wish to dismantle the prevailing oppressive social structures, but to surmount them. Those Hispanic men who are white enough with certain economic privilege desire to become the new oppressors, taking the place in the bedroom of white Euro American males. . . .

On Celebrating Cojones

I will argue that the phallic signifier of *machismo* is located in the *cojones* (balls).... I conquer, I subdue, I domesticate *por mis cojones* (by my balls)....Not only must the *macho* be on "top" when it comes to women, but he must also "top" other men. Why? Because the potent symbolic power invested in the *cojones* both signals and veils the *macho*'s societal and cultural power. The *macho* must prove to other men, and himself, his virility and manliness. Constructing those oppressed as feminine allows *machos* with *cojones* to assert their privilege by constructing oppressed Others as inhabitants of the castrated realm of the exotic and primitive.[11] Lacking *cojones*, the Other does not exist except as designated by the desire of the one with *cojones*. Like a benevolent father, a *patrón*, it becomes the duty and responsibility of those with *cojones* to care for, provide for and protect those below. The castrated male (read: race, class, homosexual Other) occupies a feminine space where his body is symbolically sodomized as prelude to the sodomizing of his mind. The non-*macho* became enslaved by the inferiority engraved upon his flesh through the Hispanic ethos. Likewise, the *macho* is also enslaved to his own so-called superiority, which flows from his *cojones*. While non-*machos* are forced to flee constantly from their individuality, the *macho* must constantly attempt to live up to a false construction of manliness. Both are alienated, both suffer from an obsessive neurotic orientation, and both require liberation from their condition.

It should therefore not be surprising that the construction of homosexuality within the Euro American culture differs from the construct among Hispanics.... Unlike Euro Americans, where two men engaged in a sexual act are both called homosexuals, for Hispanics only the one that places himself in the "position" of a woman is the *maricón*.... In fact, the man who is in the dominant position during the sex act—even with another man—is able to retain, if not increase, his *machismo*. Such a man is called *el bugarrón*.[12]

Reinaldo Arenas, the famed Cuban poet whose homosexuality was persecuted by the Castro government, recounts his experience in obtaining an exit permit to leave the island during the Mariel boatlift of 1980. Because "undesirables" were targeted for expatriation, a large number of homosexuals were able to leave. At the police station he was asked if he was gay. After answering in the affirmative, he was then asked if he was active (*bugarrón*) or passive (*loca*) during sex. He responded passive, to which the lieutenant yelled to another officer, "Send this one directly." Of importance is what occurred to those who confessed in playing the active role during a same-sex act. Arenas claimed that a friend of his who did this was denied permission to leave. For Latinos, those who function as *bugarrón* were not considered to be real homosexuals.[13]

Arenas further insisted that it is not the norm for one homosexual to desire another homosexual. Rather, "she" desires a *macho* who as *bugarrón*, would enjoy the act of possessing as much as the homosexual would enjoy being possessed.[14] For this reason, unlike the United States, violence against gays is not the accepted norm, for *la loca* provides sexual gratification to *el macho* without bringing into question the partner's *machismo*, even though *la loca* is perceived as being a corrupting influence on the *macho*. Although Latino *locas* continue to be held in contempt, they are usually tolerated with humor.[15]

Conclusion

Many years have passed since Tommy and I were buddies. I married and moved away from Miami. Hurricane Andrew hit and I lost touch with almost all of my church friends. Still, I often think of Tommy...I sincerely regret the additional spiritual burdens that I placed upon him due to my biblical ignorance and naiveté. Rather than sharing the good news that God loves him just as God created him, I added to his sense of self-hating. How I wish I had shared that, because he was created in the image of God, he was created for dignity due to his worth; and that, because all that God creates is good, Tommy should never settle for being "tolerated." Like all humans, he should be accepted into the fabric of society. It is one thing for some to disagree with how God created them, it is another for them to use their power within society that is derived from their heterosexuality to impose their views, and, in doing so, deny Tommy's humanness. And we who are heterosexuals should learn that our orientation, like those of gays, is but a part of who we are, not the total means of defining our identity. Those who are homosexuals are more than gay; they are parents, siblings, children, teachers, scientists, ministers, politicians, military personal protecting our freedoms, and world leaders. For not sharing this good news I will remain eternally sorry, while grateful to Tommy for showing me that he no more chose his homosexual orientation than I chose my heterosexual orientation. And, I will always be grateful for the role he unwittingly played in my own conversion from being a gay-bashing *macho* to someone who is now committed to issues of justice for all who are disenfranchised.

21

The Bible: What Our Family Album Has to Say[1]

We take the Bible seriously and see it as offering guide for living in a complex world. Like Jacob, we wrestle with the text in hopes of obtaining the blessing of a clearer understanding. We do not believe, however, that the Bible should be used as a club to beat LGBT Christians into their closets. Who hasn't heard some well-meaning questioner respond to the right for LBGT people to marry or raise children with "But the Bible says . . ."? Because of how these texts have been used, many Christians have remained silent about their orientation or gender identity and many have been forced out of their faith communities or, feeling unwelcomed, have left on their own accord. Family members of LGBT people have also been asked to make a false choice between loving their kin—sons, daughters, brothers, sisters, aunts and uncles, mothers, fathers and so forth—or following the narrow dictates of their church communities. For these reasons, it is therefore imperative that we examine the particular biblical passages that have caused so much heartache and division in our families.

Although we are providing you with an alternative interpretation of select biblical passages than what you may have heard, we do not want to set our interpretation up as a new truth; rather, we ask you to spend time in community wrestling with these texts in an honest, thoughtful, and curious way. We hope these readings will help you to do this and, in the process, see how texts that have been used oppressively can contain the seeds for our liberation.

The Sin of Sodom (Genesis 19:1–29 NIV)

The two angels arrived at Sodom in the evening, and Lot was sitting in the gateway of the city. When he saw them, he got up to meet them and bowed down with his face to the ground. "My lords," he said, "please turn aside to your servant's house.

You can wash your feet and spend the night and then go on your way early in the morning." "No," they answered, "we will spend the night in the square." But he insisted so strongly that they did go with him and entered his house. He prepared a meal for them, baking bread without yeast, and they ate. Before they had gone to bed, all the men from every part of the city of Sodom—both young and old—surrounded the house. They called to Lot, "Where are the men who came to you tonight? Bring them out to us so that we can have sex with them." Lot went outside to meet them and shut the door behind him and said, "No, my friends. Don't do this wicked thing. Look, I have two daughters who have never slept with a man. Let me bring them out to you, and you can do what you like with them. But don't do anything to these men, for they have come under the protection of my roof." "Get out of our way," they replied. "This fellow came here as a foreigner, and now he wants to play the judge! We'll treat you worse than them." They kept bringing pressure on Lot and moved forward to break down the door. But the men inside reached out and pulled Lot back into the house and shut the door. Then they struck the men who were at the door of the house, young and old, with blindness so that they could not find the door. The two men said to Lot, "Do you have anyone else here—sons-in-law, sons or daughters, or anyone else in the city who belongs to you? Get them out of here, because we are going to destroy this place. The outcry to the LORD against its people is so great that he has sent us to destroy it." So Lot went out and spoke to his sons-in-law, who were pledged to marry his daughters. He said, "Hurry and get out of this place, because the LORD is about to destroy the city!" But his sons-in-law thought he was joking. With the coming of dawn, the angels urged Lot, saying, "Hurry! Take your wife and your two daughters who are here, or you will be swept away when the city is punished." When he hesitated, the men grasped his hand and the hands of his wife and of his two daughters and led them safely out of the city, for the LORD was merciful to them. As soon as they had brought them out, one of them said, "Flee for your lives! Don't look back, and don't stop anywhere in the plain! Flee to the mountains or you will be swept away!" But Lot said to them, "No, my lords, please! Your servant has found favor in your eyes, and you have shown great kindness to me in sparing my life. But I can't flee to the mountains; this disaster will overtake me, and I'll die. Look, here is a town near enough to run to, and it is small. Let me flee to it—it is very small, isn't it? Then my life will be spared." He said to him, "Very well, I will grant this request too; I will not overthrow the town you speak of. But flee there quickly, because I cannot do anything until you reach it." (That is why the town was called Zoar.) By the time Lot reached Zoar, the sun had risen over the land. Then the LORD rained down burning sulfur on Sodom and Gomorrah—from the LORD out of the heavens. Thus he overthrew those cities and the entire plain, including all those living in the cities—and also the vegetation in the land. But Lot's wife looked back, and she became a pillar of salt. Early the next morning Abraham got up and returned to the place where he had stood before the LORD. He looked down toward Sodom and Gomorrah, toward all the land of the plain, and he saw dense smoke rising from the land, like smoke from a furnace. So when God destroyed the cities of the plain, he remembered Abraham, and he brought Lot out of the catastrophe that overthrew the cities where Lot had lived.

The Bible tells us that Lot, Abraham's nephew, received unknown visitors. When the men of Sodom heard of Lot's visitors, they surrounded his house, banged on his door, and demanded that the visitors be sent out so that they could be abused and raped. Some preachers and biblical commentators proclaim that the sin of Sodom is homosexuality. But the Bible does not make this case. According to the prophet Ezekiel (16:49 NRSV), Sodom's iniquity was the city's unwillingness, due to their pride and haughtiness, to share their abundance with those who were poor and marginalized. Amos (4:1, 11 NRSV) prophesied the destruction of Israel for following Sodom's example of "oppressing the needy and crushing the poor." Likewise, referring to Israel as Sodom and Gomorrah, the prophet Isaiah urged the Israelites, "Cease doing evil. Learn to do good. Seek justice, reprove the oppressor, be just to the orphan, contend for the widow (1:10–17 author trans.)." Whenever the Bible mentions Sodom, homosexuality is never listed as the cause of destruction. The sin of Sodom and Gomorrah, according to the Word of God, is not providing justice to the "orphans and widows," the biblical euphemism for the disenfranchised. The first to actually say that Sodom's sin was homosexuality was the Jewish philosopher Philo of Alexandria (25 B.C.E.?–50 C.E.?) and Josephus (37 C.E.–100 C.E.?) the historian.

The sin of Sodom, according to the Bible, does not refer to a loving relationship between two consenting adults of the same gender. Instead, it refers to the unwillingness of the people to extend hospitality to the strangers, the aliens in their midst. This could be why Jesus, when giving instructions to his disciples who were about to embark on a missionary journey, states that those cities that refuse them hospitality would face a worse fate than Sodom (Lk. 10:1–12 New Jerusalem Bible). The same xenophobia demonstrated by the Sodomites who sought to physically rape the foreigners among them is with us today in the form of economic rape of those of us who are undocumented. In ancient Sodom, as in the modern United States, the residents in power too often subordinate the stranger, the undocumented worker, and the alien. Rather than using this passage to condemn homosexuality, today's preachers would be more biblically sound if they used Genesis 19 to show how Latina/os are economically treated in this country, which is not so different from what the Sodomites hoped to do with the aliens within their midst.

Even if some want to insist that Sodom's sin was sexual, the only argument they can make is that gang rape perpetrated by heterosexual men is wrong. But even then, we have to remember that rape is not a sexual act. It is an act of domination where pleasure is achieved by subjugating and humiliating the victim. The desire of the men of Sodom to rape the angels was an attempt to subjugate the things of Heaven to the will of humans, an assault on God's authority!

Unfortunately, when we read the story, we ignore the real sexual sin. In Lot's attempt to protect his guests from gang rape, he has no problem in offering up his two virgin daughters instead of his guests. The attempted gang rape of Lot's guests does not suggest a desire for homosexual intimacy but an attempt to demonstrate mastery over the foreigner by sexually subjugating him.

The Sin of Ham (Genesis 9:20–27 NIV)

Noah, a man of the soil, proceeded to plant a vineyard. When he drank some of its wine, he became drunk and lay uncovered inside his tent. Ham, the father of Canaan, saw his father naked and told his two brothers outside. But Shem and Japheth took a garment and laid it across their shoulders; then they walked in backward and covered their father's naked body. Their faces were turned the other way so that they would not see their father naked. When Noah awoke from his wine and found out what his youngest son had done to him, he said, "Cursed be Canaan! The lowest of slaves will he be to his brothers." He also said, "Praise be to the LORD, the God of Shem! May Canaan be the slave of Shem. May God extend Japheth's territory; may Japheth live in the tents of Shem, and may Canaan be the slave of Japheth."

This section of Scripture begins with the sexual union of women with angels (Gen. 6:1–4 NRSV) and ends with the sexual irregularity that takes place between Ham and Noah. According to the story, Noah invents wine, gets drunk, and passes out naked in his tent. His son Ham "gazed" upon his father's nakedness, and for this he and his future children are cursed. In the Bible, "gazing" was a euphemism for desire. In effect, Ham took sexual advantage of his father. Consequently, Noah, upon sobering up, exclaimed in horror for what "Ham has done to him." Like the story of Sodom, this passage has nothing to do with an intimate same-gender loving relationship. It has to do with Ham subjugating and humiliating his father in order to gain control and power over him. Still, if some want to maintain that this is really a reference to a sexual sin, then the sin can only be understood as incestuous rape.

The Law (Leviticus 18:22 and 20:13 NIV)

Do not have sexual relations with a man as one does with a woman; that is detestable. (18:22)

If a man has sexual relations with a man as one does with a woman, both of them have done what is detestable. They are to be put to death; their blood will be on their own heads. (20:13)

There are only two verses in the entire Hebrew Bible that explicitly deal with homosexuality and they are both found in the book of Leviticus in a section known as the Holiness Code (Lev. 17—26). When the Hebrew word "holiness" is used, a better translation would be the word "separate." Thus, "I, Yahweh your God am separate (holy); therefore, you be separate (holy)" (Lev. 19:2 author trans.). The Israelites were called to be separate from the Canaanites who previously occupied the land. This Code concludes, "You shall not do the same deeds as were done in Egypt where you lived, nor must you do the same deeds as are done in Canaan where I am bringing you. You must not walk by their statutes. You must keep my judgments and walk by my statutes" (Lev. 18:3–4 author trans.). In order to survive and maintain their ethnic identity, the Hebrew people taking possession of the land had to make sure they did not adopt the customs of the surrounding people.

Those who violated Leviticus 18:22 and 20:13 (specifically the latter) are to be put to death. If we were to read the Bible literally, should we put all gay men to death? But the injunction does not end with gay men: The Bible calls for the death of those committing adultery (Lev. 20:10), brides who on their wedding night were discovered not to be virgins (Deut. 22:13–21), disrespectful teenagers (Lev. 20:9) and blasphemers (Lev. 24:15).

We usually ignore passages like killing disrespectful teenagers— and we should. But why do we ignore that verse and not the two that mention homosexuality? Putting this question aside, we also need to ask if these two verses are really dealing with homosexuality. Because the word "homosexual" does not exist in the biblical Hebrew language, the direct translation is "not to lie with a man as with a woman." To do so is a detestable act, an abomination. Other abominations include the improper use of incense (Num. 16:39–40); offering a blemished animal as sacrifice (Deut. 17:1); eating unclean animals, such as shellfish (Lev. 11:10), dead carcasses (Lev. 11:11), and the pig, along with other animals with cloven hoofs (Deut. 14:4–8); remarrying a former spouse (Deut. 24:4); or having sex with a woman during her seven day menstruation cycle (Lev. 20:18–24; Ezek. 18:6).

Why is it ritually unclean to "lie with a man like with a woman?" The answer can be found in the prior verse, specifically Leviticus 18:21, which prohibits the offering of children as sacrifices. If we were to link these two verses, a man lying with a man is an abomination because it refers to the "sacred sex" acts that occurred within the religion of the previous inhabitants of the land. Temple prostitution was widely practiced in the ancient world, with a special class of prostitutes serving these needs within many of the religious establishments. Lying with a sacred male prostitute would be considered an abomination because it follows the ritual practices of those from whom the Hebrews tried to separate themselves.

Wearing Women's Garments (Deuteronomy 22:5 NRSV)

A woman shall not wear a man's apparel, nor shall a man put on a woman's garment; for whoever does such things is abhorrent to the LORD your God.

Deuteronomy 22:5 is the one text that speaks to anything approaching condemnation of transgender people. But most biblical scholars say the prohibitions against wearing the garments of the opposite sex are aimed at three other possibilities: keeping women in their place as property, preserving Jewish traditions by prohibiting other worship services where priests donned the garments of female deities, or stopping the mixing of one category with another (it was prohibited, for instance, to wear a garment made from several different fabrics). In all of these cases, the rules were aimed at preserving specific social or religious norms, not at transgender people specifically.

Being True to Our "Nature" (Romans 1:26–27 NIV)

Because of this, God gave them over to shameful lusts. Even their women exchanged natural relations for unnatural ones. In the same way the men also abandoned natural relations with women and were inflamed with lust for one another. Men committed shameful acts with other men, and received in themselves the due penalty for their error.

In this passage, Paul is writing about idolatry, those who exchange "the glory of the immortal God for worthless imitations" (Rom. 1:23 author trans.). He is concerned about those who participate in the unnatural worship of created things found within nature instead of the natural worship of God evident throughout nature. This is not a text about homosexuality but about exchanging what is natural for the unnatural. If this passage is read with a heterosexual bias, it is easy to assume that the term "unnatural" is a reference to homosexuality.

What Paul does mention is that there are heterosexual men who are exchanging "natural intercourse" to be "consumed with passion for each other." In other words, he is condemning men who change their nature. Paul is concerned with heterosexual men exchanging their nature for homosexual practices—a common practice of Paul's time where heterosexual slaves and prostitutes were forced into homosexual activities. Paul is criticizing those who force heterosexuals to engage in same-sex activities against their will. If we wish to apply this teaching today we could say that homosexuals should also not exchange their nature (orientation) for heterosexual practices. This biblical passage also says that women were "turning from natural intercourse to unnatural practices." This is the only place throughout the entire Bible where lesbianism is mentioned. Or is it? Why do we assume that "unnatural practices" here refers to women engaging in same-gender sex? Remaining faithful to Paul's argument against exchanging what is natural for unnatural, could the unnatural practices be a reference to women acting contrary to the patriarchal norms of the time? Could he be discussing women who refuse to be passive in the home?

Exclusion of Sexual Abusers (I Corinthians 6:9 and I Timothy 1:10 NIV)

> Or do you not know that wrongdoers will not inherit the kingdom of God? Do not be deceived: Neither the sexually immoral nor idolaters nor adulterers nor men who have sex with men. (1 Corinthians 6:9)

> [The law is not made] for the sexually immoral, for those practicing homosexuality, for slave traders and liars and perjurers—and for whatever else is contrary to the sound doctrine (1 Timothy 1:10)

We should never forget that Paul is writing within a Greco-Roman social context. We do the Bible an injustice when we read into the Scriptures a modern understanding of sexual intimacy as opposed to the existing cultural ethos of his own time. Throughout the ancient Greek world, pederasty—a sexual relationship between adults and children—was both common and extensively practiced as a type of male initiation rite. Greek sexual customs influenced Roman culture, with the exception that Roman same-sex relationships usually occurred between a master and his slave. It is to this Greco-Roman world that Paul writes his letters. The Greek appearing in these passages, which is usually translated as "homosexual," is "arsenokoites" (with the 1 Corinthians passage also including the Greek word "malakos"). Translating these words to "homosexual," a term that did not exist until the late nineteenth century, has led many to the conclusion that gay men will never inherit the kingdom of God. But "arsenokoites" and "malakos" do not refer to what we today call an intimate homosexual relationship. "Malakos" literally mean "soft," a term that refers to "effeminate boys" when used in other ancient literature. This could also be a reference to a pederasty relationship where a male takes the "soft" or passive position of a woman. "Arsenokoites" is harder to translate because the term appears to have been coined by Paul, not appearing in other ancient literatures nor used by subsequent authors. "Arsenokoite" denotes the passive role taken by male prostitutes. When we consider that there were more than a thousand prostitutes (male and female) working in Corinth out of the Temple of Aphrodite and that male prostitution was extensively practiced in Greece, could 1 Corinthians and 1 Timothy possibly be passages referring to these male prostitutes—specifically, male prostitutes who were still boys? What these biblical passages are condemning is pedophilia and male prostitution (as opposed to female prostitution, which seems to be taken for granted) not a loving relationship between men. We do a disservice to the biblical passage if we are not able to understand that the historical context in which it was written is vastly different than our own. As we read this passage, among others, we must stay attuned to the different attitudes about women that arise as well attitudes about sexual behavior. What is not discussed is this passage is the power of love between two people and the bond that is established based on that love. Nowhere in the Bible will we find examples of loving relationships renounced.

Sex with Angels (2 Peter 2:4–8 and Jude 6—7 NIV)

For if God did not spare angels when they sinned, but sent them to hell, putting them into gloomy dungeons to be held for judgment; if he did not spare the ancient world when he brought the flood on its ungodly people, but protected Noah, a preacher of righteousness, and seven others; if he condemned the cities of Sodom and Gomorrah by burning them to ashes, and made them an example of what is going to happen to the ungodly; and if he rescued Lot, a righteous man, who was distressed by the depraved conduct of the lawless (for that righteous man, living among them day after day, was tormented in his righteous soul by the lawless deeds he saw and heard). (2 Peter 2:4–8)

And the angels who did not keep their positions of authority but abandoned their proper dwelling—these he has kept in darkness, bound with everlasting chains for judgment on the great Day. In a similar way, Sodom and Gomorrah and the surrounding towns gave themselves up to sexual immorality and perversion. They serve as an example of those who suffer the punishment of eternal fire. (Jude 6–7)

In both of these biblical passages, God punishes Sodom and Gomorrah for their "shameless ways" and "unnatural fornication." Because most read their anti-homosexual bias into the text, the shameless ways alluded to are assumed to be homosexuality. Such an assumption misses the point. The 2 Peter passage begins with a reference to sinning angels, while in the Jude passage the subjects are angels who traded "supreme authority" for "spiritual chains." The text is about angels, based on a story that appears in the book of Genesis (6:1–4). In that story, angels came to earth and had sex with mortal women, disrupting the natural order that separates humans from the divine. The "shameless ways," and "unnatural fornication" that the passages 2 Peter and Jude refer to is sex between celestial and mortal beings. Why then mention Sodom and Gomorrah? Because the men of Sodom attempted to gang rape Lot's guests, who were angels.

PART EIGHT

Racism and
Ethnic Discrimination

22

Seeing Dark Bodies[1]

In the U.S. context, those men who are not man enough are those with nonwhite bodies, specifically blacks, Hispanics, Native-Americans, and Asian-Americans. Even though they are emasculated for lacking "what it takes to be a man" they are still feared for having a penis. Because they posses a penis, they are still considered dangerous, for at any time they can threaten white civilization manifested as a white woman. Take the 2006 image used by the anti-immigrant organization Defend Colorado Now. "Wake up Colorado" appears above the image of white woman in a stars-and-stripes Liberty costume reminiscent of a vintage illustration; she is leaning back in a chair, sleeping, vulnerable. She is meant to represent the state itself. Below her are the words "Defend Colorado Now." To me, the image has an unconscious message for the viewer. Colorado, signified by a white woman, must be protected from the danger of Latinos crossing the border, for if she is not, her purity and innocence would surely be sullied.

Euro Americans have historically been taught, through images in popular culture, that male bodies of color are overly sexualized beings who invoke both fascination with and fear of their prowess. We've all heard about the exploits of hot-blooded "Latin Lovers," or the locker room remarks about the larger size of the black penis when compared to whites' (although statistically speaking, all penises, regardless of color, are on average about the same length when flaccid: 4.8 inches). The stereotypical hot Latino Don Juan and the big-membered black signify the image of aggressiveness and carnality. The 1990 documentary *The Bronze Screen: One Hundred Years of the Latino Image in American Cinema* depicts how Latino actors like Ricardo Montalban were portrayed as the stereotypical Latin lover—an image heightened during the 1940s and 1950s as a result of America's "good neighbor" policies with Latin America. Sexual fear and awe of black men is evidenced by the popularity of modern plantation "bodice ripper" novels, and portrayed, to some degree, by the talented actor Paul Robeson in his various photographic poses and films like *The Emperor Jones*. Similarly, the black, brown, red, and yellow female bodies as sensual objects, become available for consumption. The most recognized Asian example is the tragic Puccini opera *Madame Butterfly*, and the stereotypical image of Latinas as hip-swinging hussies was epitomized in the movie roles Carmen Miranda was forced to portray. Such media representations contribute to the cultural image of young white males hoping to learn the "art" of lovemaking from women of color or nonwhite male bodies are at the service of bored white females seeking to spice up their lives with an element of danger by going "slumming."

How did this understanding of dark bodies developed? People of color were historically perceived by white culture as a wild creature devoid of pure white blood; even those who lived in civilized societies were nevertheless seen as part savage. As whites projected their own forbidden desires upon darker bodies, whites could engage in sex with these darker bodies, absolved of any culpability; those who were viewed as being evolutionarily closer to the heat of the jungle were held responsible for compromising the virtues of whites, either through their so-called seductive nature or their "black magic." To engage in sex with these nonwhite bodies gave whites an opportunity to lose themselves to primitive urges, heightening their momentary sexual experience while reinforcing these darker bodies' subjugation....

Owning Black Bodies

Eurocentric sexual norms that oppress people of color [as famously illustrated in] the case of Thomas Jefferson and his slave Sally Hemings. Recent DNA testing confirms the longstanding rumors that Jefferson is the father of the children birthed by Hemings. Although attempts have been made to portray the Jefferson-Hemings relationship as consensual, Hemings inability to withhold consent of her body, which was owned by Jefferson, makes him a rapist.

Under the social system that justified slavery, black women were considered the antithesis of the ideal genteel white woman, who advanced chastity and innocence. White women became symbols of purity and a product of a superior culture, whereas black women were seen as sexual animals to be trained and exploited. On the slave auction block when the bidding slowed down, black women were forced to disrobe to entice possible purchasers to pay a bit more for the nocturnal benefits of owning her body. Black female bodies existed for white male sexual exploitation; white female bodies had to be protected from the black male menace. (This does not discount the oppression of white female bodies—the physical abuse of female black bodies also served to warn white females of a fate that might also wait them if they did not passively submit to patriarchal rule.)

The taking of black female bodies by whites was not considered rape by whites because African women, unlike the properly bred white counterparts, were considered to be closer to the wildness, hence inherently licentious. As sexual savages they were construed as eager to be taken and ravished by any man, white or black. In the final analysis, it was they who were responsible for their own rape. In fact, the culture said black woman really couldn't be raped because they were always the willing whore; it was the rapist who was the true victim for being seduced. As bell hooks reminds us, throughout the South, black slave girls soon after reaching puberty were property at the service of young Southern men needing sexual initiation.[2]

Such practices are not part of some distant past. This became obvious with the public revelation that segregationist leader and civil rights opponent Senator Strom Thurmond had fathered a child with his black maid during his youth. It was, and continues to be, a rite of passage for young white males of privilege to be sexually initiated by women of color, primarily black women. A recent revelation of this privilege can be witnessed over the March 2006 incident concerning Duke University's highly ranked and predominantly white lacrosse team (there is one black member). Several members of the team [were] being accused of raping a black stripper. According to the twenty-seven-year-old alleged victim, she and another black woman were hired as exotic dancers to entertain a group of five men. However, when the women arrived at the house, they encountered more than forty men, all of them white, who proceeded to taunt them with racist epithets.[3] Although [the charges proved to be unfounded,] the point is that these white boys from families of power and privilege hired black women to sexually entertain them, continuing the tradition of assigning darker woman's bodies the role of providing sexual gratification.

According to this view, the "taking" of Black women (and by extension all women of color) could never be defined as rape because due to her seductive nature, she's always "asking for it." Rape only occurred when a white woman was involved. Slave masters were absolved of any blame for sexually "taking" their female through the passage of laws that defined all offspring of a black woman as inheritors of her slave status. As victims of her seduction, white men were not to be held responsible for siring offspring with their slave.

The Bible was masterfully used by those in power to justify the owning of black bodies. This was an easy feat; nowhere in either the Hebrew Bible or the New Testament is slavery categorically condemned. The supporters of slavery in the antebellum South were the ones who had the biblical chapters and verses to quote to justify their way of life. The abolitionists were hard pressed to find any biblical passage that outright condemned the institution of slavery. Even the rape of female slaves found biblical justification and was considered to be ordained by God. Specifically, Numbers 31:18 instructs conquerors as follows: "You shall keep alive all young females who have not had sex with a male for yourselves." This passage was Moses's instructions for treatment of the conquered people of Midian, who were now to be Israel's slaves.

No doubt, with the coming of the civil rights movement, most of these practices of reducing black female bodies for white male consumption came to an end. Today, many Americans believe that the civil rights movement succeeded in eliminating most of our racist past: some now speak about living in a postracial world. But racism and ethnic discrimination persist. Political correctness may abound, but thousands of years of stereotypical attitudes and cultural lessons about bodies of color continue to influence how many whites view them. Consider, for example, the unresolved fate of Natalee Holloway. The blond, blue-eyed graduating honors student from Birmingham, Alabama, was on a senior trip with classmates on the mostly black Caribbean Island of Aruba when she disappeared in May 2005. Her disappearance became a major nationwide news obsession, as the media constantly kept us informed about any developments in this unfolding saga. Unfortunately, she has yet to be found. No one questions this tragic story for the young woman and her friends and family; still, far fewer Americans heard of Latoyia Figueroa, a brown woman who disappeared off the streets of Philadelphia around the same time. Both are young attractive women created in the image of God. Both have worth. Both deserve dignity. But based on the relentless media attention given to Holloway's disappearance, in comparison to the deafening media silence when blacks or Latinas disappear, one can only conclude that skin color determines who has greater worth and deserves more dignity in the eyes of the media. Does this mean the media is racist in its attitudes toward black female bodies—the same attitudes that were prevalent in the pre-Civil Rights America? This is probably the wrong question to ask. What concerns us more here is how our views of darker bodies continue to be constructed after centuries of racist-based "legitimate" ways of understanding black female sexuality.

Blacks as Sexual Deviants

The African men who were shipped to the United States to serve as slaves were also defined as not being *real* men....They could be strong as mules, but they were not considered to be men because they lacked the means of proving their manhood by providing for their family. Our nation's constitution relegated the black man to being just three-fifths of a white man.[4] Of course, we know that these men who labored to the point of death would have been capable of providing for their family had they not been slaves. Obviously, it was their white overlords who reaped the fruits of their labor. But, in a twisted form of logic, the overseer imposed a type of Christian work ethic that blamed the African and Amerindian man of not truly being men because of their impoverished condition. Paradoxically, while the African man was constructed as being less than a man, he was feared for the potential of asserting his lasciviousness, particularly with white women. Hence the stereotypical fear—a fear that still permeates white society—of blacks as rapists, even though most rapes that occur are intraracial, where the victim and perpetrator are of the same race or ethnicity

Labeling blacks (and by extension, all people of color) as morally deficient (evidenced by their so-called overly sexualized demeanor) only confirmed their preference for matters of the flesh over the rational. In the minds of white supremacists, all nonwhite bodies were, and still are, synonymous with unrestrained, primitive, hot sex. Because men of color are ruled by the flesh and not the mind, white control of darker bodies is justified, to ensure, protect, and advance civilization. And how is this control maintained? Black men as sexual predators were controlled by lynching and/or castration. Black women as Jezebels simply got what they deserved and secretly wanted. These sexual acts of terror were justified as effective means of maintaining control over black bodies; blacks were seen as being ultimately responsible for the violence visited upon them.

Sex between a black man and a white woman was perceived as dangerous, if not deadly. The myth of the black man's excessively large penis (when compared to the white man) and the white woman's small clitoris (when compared to the black woman) meant the white woman had to be protected from being not just damaged, but permanently spoiled for white men's use.

On the other hand, the white society that depended on the slavery system constructed reasons to justify white men's having sex with their female slaves. According to a former slave from the Caribbean, "There was one type of sickness the whites picked up, a sickness of the veins and male organs. It could only be got rid of with black women; if the man who had it slept with a Negress he was cured immediately."[5]

These sentiments about blacks as wanton beings lead twentieth-century philosopher Franz Fanon to sarcastically write,

> As for the Negroes, they have tremendous sexual powers. What do you expect, with all the freedom they have in their jungles! They copulate at all times and in all places. They are really genital. They have so many children that they cannot even count

them. *Be careful, or they will flood us with little mulattoes...*One is no longer aware of the Negro but only of a penis; the Negro is eclipsed. He is turned into a penis. *He is a penis.* (italics mine).[6]

Fanon addresses the fears and forbidden desires that are at times projected onto African Americans, as well as other men of color—and the resulting fixation with the black penis that posed a threat to white civilization. The black penis must be kept separate from power and privilege. This is why castration was viewed as an acceptable form of punishment for black men. At times, castration was part of the lynching ritual.

23

Jesús: A Racist? A Sexist?[1]

Is the purpose of Jesús, which includes liberation for the oppressed, truly for all, especially the most marginalized among us? At first glance it seemed as if this is true; but if it is, then Jesús might have had to also learn this lesson. Our faith may tell us that anyone can come to Jesús; that the evangelistic message means no one is turned away. We are supposed to come just as we are, ill and diseased. All who seek healing are supposed to find salvation and liberation in the arms of Jesús, for his unconditional love accepts everyone—regardless of their race or ethnicity. Or does it? Matthew 15:21–28 recounts the story of a Canaanite woman who came to Jesús desperately seeking a healing for her daughter, only to be sent away and called a dog. How many times have Latina/os heard similar remarks? The Canaanites during Jesús' time were seen by Jews as being a mixed race of inferior people, much in the same way that some Euro Americans view Hispanics today, specifically the undocumented. The Canaanites of old—like Latino/as of our time—were foreigners who simply did not belong. They were no better than "dogs." I am old enough to remember restaurant signs throughout the southwestern United States that would say "No dogs, no Mexicans." For this reason, Jesús response to the Canaanite woman is troublesome. When she appealed to Jesús to heal her sick child, Jesús, succumbing to the prevailing xenophobia of his day, responded by saying: "I was sent only to the lost sheep of the house of Israel. It is not good to take the bread of the children and throw it to the dogs."

No matter how much we may try to redeem the text, we cannot ignore the fact that Jesús called this woman of color a dog! We are forced to ask the uncomfortable question: Was Jesús a racist? In this story, Hispanics might find themselves relating more with the Canaanite woman than with Jesús. When states like Arizona passed laws that targeted Hispanics in the name of catching the undocumented (a template for subsequent legislation throughout the country that restricts or denies medical and other services to immigrants who lack documentation), Hispanics are reminded that they are the dogs of

172

society. When politicians like congressman and former presidential candidate Tom Tancredo states that Hispanics are "coming to kill you, and you, and me, and my children and my grandchildren,"[2] Latino/as are reminded that they are the dogs of society. When Latina/os are more likely than the general population to lack basic health coverage, less likely to receive preventive medical examinations, and less likely to receive early prenatal care, they are reminded that they are the dogs of society. And when Latino/as are more likely to live with pollution, exposing them to greater health risks, they are reminded that they are the dogs of society. Jobs, educational opportunities, and social services are for "real" Americans. Instead of taking food away from the children of hardworking "Americans" to throw to the dogs, "they" should just go back to where they came from. Jesús' response was typical for a person acculturated to believe in the superiority of his or her particular ethnicity or race.

How can such abusive words proceed from the mouth of Jesús? In the fullness of Jesús' divinity, he had to learn how to be fully human. His family and culture were responsible for teaching him how to walk, how to talk, and how to be potty-trained. He also learned about the superiority of Judaism and the inferiority of non-Jews, in the very same way that today there are those within the dominant culture, from childhood, who are taught America is number one, superior to other peoples and thus, "exceptional." For some, this superiority takes on a racial component where those with European descent are more advanced than those with Hispanic ancestry. While the minority of Euro Americans who insist on voicing their superiority can easily be dismissed as racist and thus ignored; there remains an unexamined majority who are complicit with social structures that—whether they like it or not—are racist and ethnic discriminatory for them. They may not go to the extreme, like Jesús did, in refusing a medical healing to a woman of color while calling her a dog; nevertheless, the inherent ethic discrimination in the medical establishment accomplishes the same goal. That Latino/as are today's dogs is evident in a quality of health care that ranges from poor to nonexistent.

Nevertheless, for Christians, the imago Dei (the image of God) finds its fullest expression in the personhood of Jesucristo as he turned many "rules" upside down. This is a truth that even Jesús, in his full humanity, had to learn. To deny this woman a healing and calling her a dog reveals the ethnic discrimination that his culture taught him. But Jesús, unlike so many within the dominant social structure of today, was willing to hear the words of this woman of color and learn from her. And thanks to her, Jesús' ministry was radically changed. The Canaanite woman responded by saying, "For even the dogs eat the crumbs that fall from the table of their masters." She was not willing to wait for the crumbs to fall from the master's table; but as biblical scholar Guardiola-Sáenz reminds us, she approached Jesús in a "spirit of protest and reclamation...determined to take the bread from the table of those who displaced her." She refused to stay under the table by insisting to sit at the table as equals. She refused to be a humble dog begging for crumbs. Instead, she was "a dispossessed woman who has awakened from her position as oppressed and now is coming to confront the empire and demand her right to be treated as human."[3] Her remark and attitude shocked Jesús into realizing that faith was not contingent on a person's ethnicity. In fact, Jesús had to admit that this was a woman of great faith. This woman of color had to cross the "border" demarcated by Jesús' culture. It matters little if she belongs. It matters less if she has proper documentation. Her daughter was sick and because of her humanity, she was entitled to a healing. She was more than the dog Jesús called her.

As we consider this story from the Hispanic perspective, we are left wondering if Jesús is here struggling with racism or with assimilation. If we recall that Jesús is a colonized man who is seen by his contemporaries as a *mestizo*, a half-breed, then maybe the cultural norm he is learning to overcome is not the racism of the pureblooded but the strong desire of *mestizos*, then and now, to belong to the dominant culture by becoming whiter than the whites. For some who are oppressed for being "darker," an attempt is made to prove that one really belongs to the dominant culture. Maybe Jesús' dismissal of this woman of color had less to due with the cultural racism taught to him by society and more to do with the desire to assimilate to those who were seen as purer. Regardless as to the reason for Jesús' comment, his mission is changed due to this encounter. How do we know this? Up to this point, the gospel message was exclusively for the Jews. In Matthew 10:5–6, Jesús sends his twelve disciples on their first missionary venture. He clearly instructs them, "Do not turn your steps into other nations, nor into Samaritan cities, rather go to the lost sheep of the house of Israel." Yet five chapters later, Jesus encounters the Canaanite woman who existed on the margins of his society. She challenged Jesús with the good news that healing was not the exclusive property of one ethnic group. Instead, healing should be available to all who come. By the end of his ministry when he gives the Great Commission, he commands his followers to go out to all nations, not just the people of Israel.

It should be noted that not only was the Canaanite woman whom Jesús calls a dog a person of color; but she was also a woman. If we ask if Jesús was a racist, we should also ask if he was a sexist. After all, he chose twelve men to follow him, or did he? The Gospel of Luke tells us that Jesús went to every city and village, preaching with the twelve disciples, along with certain women who he healed of infirmities, among which were María Magdalena, Juana the wife of Chuza who was Herod's steward, Susana, and many others. These women ministered unto him of their substance (8:1–3). Why can't these women who also follow Jesús not be considered disciples, especially when we consider that women in other situations were named as church leaders by Jesús.

Take for example the story of two sisters, Marta and María. During Jesús' travels, he came upon a certain village, where Marta received him into her house. She had a sister named María who chose to sit at the feet of Jesús to hear his words. But Marta was distracted with all the serving and said, "Lord, don't you care that my sister left me alone to serve? Tell her then to help me." Answering her Jesús said, "Marta, Marta, you are anxious and troubled about many things when there is need of only one, and María chose the good part, which shall not be taken from her" (10:38–42). This text has usually been translated as Marta complaining of being overworked. We assume that she is overwhelmed with housework; however, the Greek word used in the text for serving is *diakonia*, a word usually translated as deacon. The work she is doing, and needs help in completing, is in relationship to her role as the deacon of this house church. Unfortunately, her duties and responsibilities as deacon deprive her of the opportunity to "sit at Jesús' feet," as her sister María did.

María, on this day, chose "to sit at Jesús' feet," rather than help Marta with her duties as the house-church deacon. To "sit at Jesús' feet" does not mean that there were no chairs available so she was forced to sit on the floor; to sit at someone's feet was, and still is, a euphemism for a teacher-student relationship. It is the student that "sits at the feet" of the teacher, or in this setting, the rabbi. For example, we are told in Acts 22:3 that Pablo sat "at the feet of Gamaliel" meaning Pablo was a student of Gamaliel. During Jesús' time, women were forbidden to touch Torah, let alone read or study it. Contrary to all social and religious regulations of the time, Luke is telling us that María was Jesús' student and disciple, just like the other twelve men sitting at his feet. In the Gospel of John, Marta and María are portrayed as well-known apostolic figures of the early church that were beloved by Christ (11:5). In the same way that Pedro confesses the messiahship of Jesús (Mt. 16:15–19), so too does Marta as a spokesperson for the early church (Jn. 11:27). And finally, through María's evangelism, many came to believe in Jesús (Jn. 11:45). This interpretation allows us to retell the story, debunking the patriarchy of Jesús' time, as well as our own. Rabbi Jesús was received in the home of one of his apostles named Marta, who also served as founder and deacon of the house church in Bethany in which she proclaimed God's word. On this day her sister María the evangelist sat at the feet of Jesús to study Torah. Marta asked the rabbi to have his student help with the duties required by the deacon, but the rabbi responded that studying Torah was just as important as serving.

We may never really know what occurred in this encounter. Maybe Jesús also learned sexism from his culture in the same way he learned racism until the encounter with the Canaanite woman. Nevertheless, reading Scripture through a liberative lens allows for biblical text that has historically been used to enforce the oppression of women to instead, after carefully delineated, be read to unmask seeds of liberation that challenge patriarchy; regardless of original intention.

24

When Hollywood Gazes
upon Latino Men[1]

Latino men demanding to be treated as an equal risk being dismissed as "aggressive" (if not dangerous), "emotional" (lacking intellectual rigor), and/or "too passionate" (if not overly sensual). But how are these negative depictions of Latinos encoded upon the Latino male body? How are the stigmata of these cultural wounds enfleshed? Members of the Euro American dominant culture, male and female, are privileged with whiteness, creating a tendency to perpetuate the myth that the rules, traditions, institutions, and language of Euro Americans are legitimate and normative. Rejecting this naturalness, we turn to systems of encoding and decoding signs. Semiologist Roland Barthes is helpful here. Relying on the methodology he employs in his book *Mythologies*, this article turns its attention to exploring what Latino male bodies signify to the dominant Euro American culture.

Mythologies consists of a series of brief essays examining common features within popular French culture (i.e., world of wrestling, soap commercials, steak & chips, and striptease) in order to reveal how every cultural phenomenon, regardless of how normative or natural it appears, undergirds ideological assumptions. Norms are naturalized even though they can be construed as the unconscious propaganda of those who benefit from constructing myths. The myth succeeds, not because it is able to mask, but rather because it distorts the glaring contradictions existing within the social system so that they can appear both normal and natural.

The Latino male body as a mental notion ceases to be a symbol, but rather becomes the very ideology defining the Hispanic man who is represented through the signs: (1) greasers, (2) dimwitted, and/or (3) Latin-lovers. Still, the former linguistic sign represented by the Latino body becomes a new "depoliticized" signifier within a new system of meaning, and hence, creates a myth. Emptied from its original meaning, the multiple signs of the Latino male body become new signifiers to a myth, a myth so entrenched within the Euro American mind-set, that its usage becomes second nature. These new signifiers, within this second-order semiological system, now signify Latino men as aggressive, stupid, and sensual. Creating these myths about Latinos has the power to connote a larger sign system that misconstrues society and its intra-relationships.

To understand how Latino male bodies are seen within Euro American culture, we turn to motion pictures where for over a century, Euro Americans have gazed upon Latino bodies depicted on big silver screen. Popular movies entertain us; but more importantly, they reveal society's ethos, a reflection of contemporary Euro American culture. Filmmakers impose upon the viewer what interests them, interests based on their worldviews. How Hispanic men are seen on the big screen provides a unique opportunity to analyze how the dominant culture sees Latino men in the everyday.

Popular movies depicting Latino male bodies exist transhistorically, as intentional signs, as symptoms regulated by something done or by what someone else does. Still, the inherent social structures behind visual art are products of the same social location in which the filmmaker finds him or herself, for they do not exist in a social vacuum. They too are shaped by the socio-historical space that they occupy, a space influencing their works. Movies serve as historical documents expressing the social life they know, including its hopes, its struggles, its disappointments, its joys, and its tragedies. Watching movies allows us to see the constructed reality of the dominant culture. Upon blank film, the filmmaker transforms empty space into ideas, ideas that constructs reality through the normative gaze of those with the power and privilege to make films.

Movies becomes a document that reveals how reality is understood by the dominant culture—male and female—planting in the minds of the viewer the seeds that will eventually blossom into creating an overarching definition of what is a Latino man. Film, as a sign, contains within it the meanings given to it by the dominant culture from where it arises. Consequently, the reality by which we measure a film becomes the recognized referent of a shared illusion. Yet, this illusion becomes a self-contained whole subordinate to its own order and structure. Through the filmmakers' rendition, the inner structure of the movie is capable of surpassing the power structures of reality, transforming those structures by providing a new vision; but all too often it simply creates and reinforces the prevailing normalized gaze and discourse. Consequently, our aim in contemplating popular movies is not to offer insight or feelings about any particular piece, nor is it to provide a critique on story plot.

Depictions of Latino Men

Relying on the documentary *The Bronze Screen: 100 Years of the Latino Image in Hollywood,* we will "see" Latino men on the big screen so that we can glimpse a reality so familiar that its depictions of Latinos are unquestionably believed, even by those who are being depicted. A major contributor to the colonization of Hispanic minds are the movies and television shows that taught those of us who are Latino/as how to play the part of a Hispanic, in effect, constructing our reality. Latinas like Carmen Miranda, Rita Heyward, or Rita Moreno, portrayed as "spicy" or "hot tamale," also deserve our attention, especially if we want to understand how Latinas' bodies are defined to ensure easy appropriation. Unfortunately, for now, our focus will be on how Latino men are portrayed.

Constructing the Latino Greaser

Greaser is a derogative nineteenth century slur for Mexicans whose origins is associated with the labor practice of greasing one's body to facilitate the loading and unloading of cargo and hides. The term soon referred to the Mexican skin tone, connoting the greasy hair associated with being unkempt, unwashed, and unclean. The slur became a common insult for Mexicans during the Mexican-American War. An element of danger was added to the term as demonstrated by the new Anglo invaders of California in their 1855 state statute called the Vagrancy Act, better known as the Greaser Act. The Greaser Act was a so-called anti-vagrancy law, which defined vagrants as "all persons who are commonly known as 'greasers' or the issue of Spanish and Indian blood...and who go armed and are not peaceable and quiet persons."

Hollywood embraced the greaser early during the silent era with such films as *The Greaser's Gauntlet.*(1908), *Tony the Greaser.*(1911), *The Girl and the Greaser* (1913), *The Greaser's Revenge* (1914), *Bronco Billy and the Greaser* (1914), and simply, *The Greaser* (1915). These movies created a neat dichotomy between the good guys, whites, and the bad guys, Mexicans, who were murderous *banditos* and have no qualms in kidnapping white women. The greaser image waned because of a 1922 Latin American boycott of Hollywood films because of how Latino bodies were being portrayed, and the 1930s so-called "Good Neighbor Policy," which acted as a counter to Nazi diplomatic advances in Latin America. The greaser made a comeback in the 1960s as the cowboy's anti-hero, best illustrated by actor Alfonso Arau in the 1969 film *The Wild Bunch.* Greaser evolved to spic as it made its way from westerns to urban jungles in such movies as *West Side Story* (1961, where the leading lady is an Anglo playing a Puerto Rican) and *Scarface* (1983, where the leading man is an Italian-American playing a Cuban). The greaser, spic, becomes a criminal on the run, both repulsive and yet strangely attractive, always looking for trouble. The depiction found in such films as *Boulevard Nights* (1979), *Zoot Suit* (1981), *Colors* (1988), *America Me* (1992), and *Mi Vida Loca* (1994) portrays the Latino man as aggressive and dangerous, someone to fear.

A century of Hollywood depicting Latino bodies as knife-wielding, gang-banging, terrorizing greasers created a myth in the Euro American imaginary that unconsciously (if not consciously) constructs how Latinos are seen by both white men and women. Such men are a menace, more so because they lack the intellectual sophistication to control their passions. A neat dichotomy is created by the cerebral characteristic of white men that occupy an elevated evolutionary space from the less advanced passionate Latino.

Constructing the Latino Dimwit

While conservatives usually question the level of civilized sophistication (i.e., the greaser/spic) of male Hispanics, liberals usually question their level of intellectual prowess. What makes Latino men more dangerous is their lack of the higher powers of rational thinking needed to control their lower base emotions. Not surprisingly, the portrayal of Latinos as dimwitted became a normative depiction on the big screen. Probably the earliest depiction of the clownish Latino was the portrayal of Pancho Villa, by actor Wallace Beery, as savage and animalistic in the 1934 film, *Viva Villa*. Chrispin Martin typifies the roly-poly, corpulent, comic stereotype, playing the buffoon role of Poncho in the 1943 flick, *The Ox-Bow Incident*. It is important to note how the Latino body signifies the dangerous elements associated with the greaser construct coupled with a philistine persona. Latinos intellectual short-failings are also in need of white messiahs—be they men or women. And yet, while the Latino body may be backward, under the surface exists a subdued threat (attraction?), especially for white women. The Latino body may be viewed as the stereotypical domesticated gardener, but one must fear this gentle keeper of our lawns least his true lustful nature erupts.

Constructing the Latin Lover

Thanks to over a century of blockbuster movies, Euro Americans have historically been taught that Latino men are overly sexualized beings invoking both fascination with and fear of their sensual prowess. Hollywood's construct of the hot-blooded Latin lover, and his sexual exploits created a desire to "go slumming" by some white women, as best illustrated by Mae West in the 1933 movie *She Done Him Wrong*, which gave us her now famous description of Latino bodies: dark, handsome, and warm. Latino men's foreign accents are a threat to other men even though they are alluring to "bad" women, as Latino bodies became a commoditized entity for white women consumption. The construction of race and its eroticization is so woven into white America's identity that it has become normalized in the way many whites have been taught by their culture to see Latino male bodies. To question this mind-set as racist only produces an incredulous response of innocence from those who have been socially taught to signify the Latino male body as the receptacle of aggressiveness and carnality.

The construction of the Latin lover came during the era of Rudolf Valentino. Antonio Moreno in *The Spanish Dancer* (1923) and Ramón Novarro in *The Pagan* (1929) were introduced (mainly as a response to the 1922 Latin American boycott of greaser movies) as the first Latin lovers. Probably the most famous Latin lover actor of that time was Ricardo Cortez, aka Jacob Krantz, an Austrian Jew (by now the reader might begin to notice that those who best play Latina/os, according to Hollywood, are usually non-Hispanics).

The image of the Latin lover was heightened during the 1940s and 1950s, mainly as a result of America's "Good Neighbor Policies" with Latin America. Actors like Ricardo Montalban, especially his 1953 movie *Latin Lovers,* created the enduring mode for the stereotypical Latin Lover. Based on the popularity of the literary gene of modern plantation, the "bodice ripper" novels projected white women forbidden desires onto darker bodies, allowing them to engage in sex with these darker bodies, absolved of any culpability. Those viewed as being evolutionarily closer to the heat of the jungle were held responsible for compromising the virtues of whites, due to their so-called seductive nature. To engage in sex with Latino male bodies, white women are given an opportunity to lose themselves to primitive urges, heightening their momentary sexual experience while reinforcing these darker bodies' subjugation.

Over a century of being constantly and consistently harangued by depictions on the silver screen to embrace a naturalized and legitimized Latino male identity has caused psychological damage, as our very minds become sodomized. Movies, as cultural signifiers of the Latino male body, have been used to normalize Latino bodies for U.S. domestication. Whatever liberation looks like, it must begin with liberating our colonized minds that continue to see our bodies through the eyes of the dominant culture, rejecting assimilation to the dominant white culture.

Bow Ties are Cool (and Subversive)

(additional article on topic)

We have come to accept as truth that the closer one can be to the white male ideal, regardless how much one might protest the oppressive social structures constructed designed to privilege white supremacy, the less one struggles for survival. That which is repulsive ironically becomes for many the path toward liberation, even though said liberation is but illusory. Nevertheless, becoming white, assimilating, and not questioning how our minds have been colonized becomes the easiest and most damaging path that many people of color can traverse. This journey toward whiteness begins at times before our very birth. Reflecting on the start of her own journey, Cherríe Moraga recalls that for her mother, on a basic economic level, being Chicana meant being "less." She goes on to observe. "It was through my mother's desire to protect her children from poverty and illiteracy that we became 'anglicized'; the more effective we could pass in the white world, the better guaranteed our future."[2]

When I was about six, we moved away from the slums of Hell's Kitchen to a low-income Irish and Italian neighborhood. My father worked as the stereotypical Latino superintendent of a six-story building. We were among the first (if not the first) Hispanics on the block in Jackson Heights. I was definitely the first Latino enrolled at Blessed Sacrament elementary school. I have joked about the reality of the Irish and Italians taking turns beating me up after school and still carry some of those scars (emotionally as well as physically) on my body. When I look at the scar over my right eye from one particularly vicious fight where I was outnumbered three-to-one or the scar on my upper right thigh (he was aiming higher) when an Irish boy stabbed me with a very sharp pencil (the point broke off and is still visible under the skin), I see a body carrying the stigmata of living in poverty. Pacifism seldom works in the schoolyard—especially during the 1960s where bullying was dismissed as "boys being boys." It is easy being nonviolent from a safe distance. To survive, I often had to throw the first punch. If I ever came home losing a fight, my mother would give me a worse beating for not being "man enough." By the time I was ten, I carried a switchblade (thank you *West Side Story* for showing me what a Latino man is supposed to be like).

Today I resonate with César Chávez's words, "I am not a nonviolent man. I am a violent man who is trying to be nonviolent." Constant violence has a way of pushing one to assimilate. My parents, like Moraga's mother, hoping their beloved child has a better, more secured future, advised me to be American, even though they, as recent arrivals with limited English-speaking abilities, had no way of providing examples on how to do this. By the time I was in my twenties, I was more American than Americans, waving the stars and stripes at every possible opportunity. I changed my name to "Mike," wore no facial hair, parted my hair to the side, stayed out of the sun (a difficult task in Miami), and tried speaking slowly to avoid my heavy accent (I even ran for public office as a conservative Republican). Even though I was still seen as a "spic," my male privilege, along with my lighter skin pigmentation, provided some opportunities (up to a point) that were not relatively available to my *hermanos y hermanas* with darker hues.

While today I abhor assimilation, I wonder if one can "playfully subvert" normative oppressive social signs? That is, can one engage in the performance of *jodiendo* so that a nonconforming conformist approach is employed? Can one wear "whiteness" as a form of self-defense while dismantling the structures that it privileges?

A recent study conducted by Fiona Blaikie concluded that clothes are negotiated expressions of self and visual identity with the body as mediator.[3] Conformity to dress codes (casual for male professors) is usually "driven by a desire to gain social acceptance and status."[4] If clothing is indeed a language unto itself, a collection of signs that signify myths, then can I dress this Latino body in the clothing of power, in effect, "cross-dressing" from what Latino bodies have been signified to represent by society?

Specifically, as a scholar, can I strategize against oppressive norms through dress, realizing that what I wear genders my identity? I found Blaikie's conclusion convincing. "The relationship of oneself to one's body and the presentation of one's body in clothing signifies a sense of ease or dis/ease, a sense of or a repression of the aesthetic, a sense of what is correct and appropriate for dress in relation to one's acceptance by a particular audience, a desire to belong or be accepted by a particular scholarly group, and most of all a sense of oneself."[5]

Using my own body as a canvas, I began in 2011 to exclusively wear bow ties. Why bow ties? One would think that the Roger Kimball quip, "There is something about the combination of denim and tenure that is inherently preposterous,"[6] might hold true; instead, within the academy (and specifically at my institution), an attempt is made by male professors to look as young as the students themselves. T-shirts, jeans, and polo shirts are preferred over jackets and ties because, for example, the necktie is seen as a barrier distancing the professor from the student.[7] To conform to other male professors means creating a state of "eternal adolescence," a wistful attempt to remain the same age as my students. Hence, choosing to wear bow ties along with Western-style "cowboy" boots becomes a nonconformist act for me, even though bow ties have enjoyed a long-term tie to the academy, a tie that appears to have been severed by the casual look.

Working off of Veblen's classical theory of "conspicuous consumption," studies indicate that under certain conditions, deliberate "nonconforming behaviors can be more beneficial than efforts to conform," signifying greater competence and higher status to others.[8] If Elizabeth Wilson is correct, that bodies are biological organisms within an artifact culture whose very boundaries are unclear,[9] then how can a Latino transgress the boundaries and borders created to reinforce the signification by Hollywood of the Latino body as a "greaser," a dimwit, and/or a Latin-lover? Following a cue from genderqueer discourse, I decline to perform the identity assigned by the portrayal of Latinos in movies and other forms of media by engaging in a new identity performance that subverts the established signifiers for my particular Latino body. Performance is here understood to refer "to action that incessantly insinuates, interrupts, interrogates, and antagonizes powerful master discourses."[10]

Consciously, I engage in identity cross-dressing (that is experimenting with identity role-playing) by transgressingly appropriating the costume worn historically by white men with power within the academy. I will argue that wearing a bow tie is a transformative exercise that destabilizes and disrupts the greaser, dimwitted, Latin lover performative identity the dominant culture assigned to the Latino body. Due in part to the dominant culture's gaze fused by a century of racism and ethnic discrimination, the Latino man (as well as all persons of color regardless of gender identity) must dress better in order to be recognized as having the proper academic credentials to teach predominately white students. While my white colleagues can be seen as "cool" for teaching in a T-shirt, the Latino, who constantly has his credibility as a professor questioned, would simply be disrespected and dismissed. For me, wearing a bow tie is not an attempt to assimilate, but rather a professor's costume that provides cover, a survival tactic against rude treatment from students and colleagues whose bigotry easily allows them to write off the Latino as being a credible professional in the classroom.

Since I started wearing bow ties in 2011, an interesting trend developed. My student evaluations significantly rose toward the highest percentile. More important, since wearing bow ties, no further evaluations appeared expressing concerns about my so-called aggressiveness, my so-called lack of academic rigor, or my so-called machismo. And dismissive comments of being an "angry Latino" diminished. It is as if I crossed-dress from the greaser, dimwit, and/ or Latin lover into a dapper, well-learned professor with academic standing. Of course, another variable to consider is that my hair has become grayer (in spite of Grecian Formula). Becoming older, along with the bow tie, I believe, has transformed this once younger and thus more "dangerous and aggressive" Latino body into a tamer version reminiscent of the gentle gardener.

Bow ties, as Christopher Peterson reminds us, are a harmless signature designed (when done correctly) to start a conversation about something that defines one's identity.[11] Although the trend of wearing bow ties declined over the second half of the twentieth century, they have made a comeback. At the lowest point, bow ties were associated with nerds and geeks. Think of the nutty professor played by Jerry Lewis, of deputy sheriff Barney Fife of Mayberry, or Pee-wee Herman.[12] Originally, the bow tie was what one expected reserved stuffy professors or old conservative granddaddies to wear. But today, it gives the wearer a hip, rebellious, metrosexual look, popular with those under forty. Jesse Tyler Ferguson, who plays a gay dad in a same-gender relationship on the ABC series *Modern Family*, and who himself is gay, heads a bow tie movement in solidarity with marriage equality (called Tie the Knot) and helped organized Bow Tie Lobby Day in Springfield, Illinois to repeal the Defense of Marriage Act. Proceeds from the sale of his designer bow ties are donated to the Respect for Marriage Coalition. In this case, the bow tie becomes a symbol of struggling for justice.

Ties, specifically neckties are the "linchpin of the modern wardrobe,"[13] serving no function except to signify masculinity (note to where they point), a garment once exclusively worn by men (with the early exception of Playboy bunnies during the sixties). Neckties as phallic symbol (do you tie them long or short?) can count as sexual harassment in parts of London if a gynecologist's tie touches his patient during an examination.[14] As markers of masculinity, members of the LGBT community, specifically younger lesbians, have begun to wear ties, specifically bow ties, resignifying the bow tie to signal nonconformity, an ambiguous space where masculinity can be performed. In effect, the bow tie becomes identity-bending clothing. A study conducted by Erika Engstrom shows that a major indicator of credibility is one's appearance, which serves as the salient "type of nonverbal cue in forming an impression of a person, and, consequently, personal social identity. We perceive others based in part on what we infer from what they wear."[15] A study conducted at U.S. universities involving 159 subjects (55 percent female) showed that deviance to the clear norms is beneficial on how professors are accessed. Clean-shaven, tie-wearing, dapper male professors were judged to be better teachers and researchers. However, when the university was perceived to be a top-tier school, slouchy appearances earned more points.[16]

Latino/as have historically been stereotyped by Hollywood to dress dangerously: occupying a heavily tattooed body while wearing a white "wife-beater" T-shirt with a plastic rosary as a chain (i.e. the "greaser gang-banger"); humbly: wearing cheap untended and unkempt workman clothes (i.e., the dimwit gardener); or seductively: tight pants, colorful open shirts exposing a hairy chest, and a gold chain hanging down low from the neck (i.e., the flamboyant Latin lover). And yet, Roland Barthes argues that the fashion worn has the liberative potential of playing with multiple identities without the fear of losing oneself.[17] I can wear my *guayabera* when I want to perform *cubanidad* among my most intimate friends and family, but then wear a bow tie when I want to perform serious scholarship, both without the fear of losing myself in white identity. And yet, I also wear boots whenever I wear a bow tie as the "red sneakers" of nonconformity, thus queering any self-construction from becoming too stable. In other words, my bow tie states that I'm playing the game, but my boots subversively suggest that I'm not fully engaged in the game. Ethnicity continues to remain a significant factor in what a Latino can or cannot wear in public, so for the Latino to deliberately construct his own identity as a counter-narrative to the dominant gaze is a deliberate grasp for power. Identity cross-dressing challenges the preconceived biases of the one gazing upon the Latino body.

I argue that placing a bow tie upon my particular Latino body (considering that bow ties are not typically common attire among Hispanics) becomes a disruptive performance act of identity that allows entry into a fluid space where the persistent Latino identity created by Hollywood is bent and subverted. In effect, I am placing an acceptable academic fashion accessory upon an unacceptable Latino body. Basically I am, according to a study conducted by Waggoner and Hallstein, "encouraging perspectives by incongruity," designed to manipulate the structure of the disempowering gaze of the dominant culture. By wearing the quintessential marker of white Eurocentric academic masculinity while simultaneously through praxis destabilizing, disrupting, and deconstructing the very myth the bow tie has historically signified, I am able to cross borders (Latinos seem to be good at crossing borders) at will allowing me to challenge and assert some control over the normative dominant gaze. Bow ties become a costume worn where performance conveys information to others about the role being played, providing those accustomed to gazing upon the Latino body through the eyes of the dominant culture new signs that facilitate their ability to engage in social interactions and which can be bent toward a more equitable exchange. Costume wearing may place one in the spotlight as an object to be gazed, but it is a conscious act that displays the "look" of the object's choosing;[18] providing the object of the gaze subjectivity.

Sadly, regardless of how adept one becomes in role-playing, crossing borders for the Latino never leads "home," for our minds have been so colonized that discovering some true authentic identity can become an exercise in futility. Centuries of colonization where white men and women constructed Latino identity for us have made us forever undocumented sojourners forced to live with an unstable identity always needing to shift so as to survive.

PART NINE

Confronting Racism
and Ethnic Discrimination

25

"Full-Quiver" Theology
Appeals to Race[1]

In a July 27th [2005] interview with *Baptist Press*, Al Mohler, president of Southern Baptist Theological Seminary (my alma mater) insists that couples who choose childlessness are guilty of "rebellion against parenthood [that] represents nothing less than an absolute revolt against God's design." He bases his assertion on Psalm 127:3–5, which reads, "Children are a heritage of the Lord, the fruit of the womb a reward. As arrows in a soldier's hand, so are the sons of the young. Blessed is the man who has filled his quiver with them."

Mohler advocates a "full-quiver" theology, which in some forms disapproves of all forms of contraceptives. Only God can decide when to "open or close the womb." For mere mortals to practice birth control is to supersede the role of divinity. If children are the sign of blessing, then the best that humans can do is have as many children possible, so that a man's quiver can truly be full.

As disturbing as "full-quiver" theology may be, more distressing is Mohler's socio-political reasons for his belief. In an interview he gave to the *Chicago Tribune*, Mohler explained that rather than being concerned with overpopulation, he was more troubled with underpopulation. "We are barely replenishing ourselves," he said. "That is going to cause huge social problems in the future."

According to the U.S. Census Bureau, International Data Base (2005 version) the world population, which was at a little over 6 billion in 2000, is expected to grow to 7 billion by 2013 and to surpass 9 billion by 2050. The U.S. population is also growing, from about 280 million in 2000, to a projected 310 million in 2010, to a little under 400 million by 2040. If these scientifically projected increases are reliable, then we must ask: Why is Mohler concerned about underpopulation? Underpopulation for whom? In other words, who is the "we" that is barely replenishing itself?

The projections concerning U.S. population growth also show that if present trends continue, Euro Americans will cease being the majority race in the United States by about 2050. The combined population growth of communities of color over the next century will make America a predominately nonwhite nation. Hence, the religious call for "full-quiver" theology is white supremacy code language advocating for the increase of white babies. Mohler's call, whether he realizes it or not, is a race-based warning. It is a call for white fecundity, lest America becomes overrun with "colored" children, which would only lead, as Mohler puts it, to "huge social problems in the future."

Regardless of the racist overtures of Mohler's call for productive white sex, children, regardless of their color or ethnicity, can indeed be a joyous product of sex. Still, we cannot lose sight that the ultimate goal of sex is mutual pleasure, not having children. And while reproduction is neither the reason nor purpose for engaging in sex, it does seem fitting that new life can be a product of two becoming one. How right are the words of the psalmist when he or she sings, "Children are a heritage of the Lord, the fruit of the womb a reward" (127:3).

Indeed, as a father of two children myself, I can unequivocally claim that my children are among the greatest blessings of my life. Like brother Al, who also has just two children, we are not in "moral rebellion" against God. But if Mohler insists on imposing a "full quiver," then I suggest he either lead by example or remain quiet.

Still, what about children being God's blessing? It is the height of biblical naiveté to impose modern concepts upon ancient texts. Viewing children as a blessing for their own sake is a relatively modern concept. While the Old Testament declares children are a blessing from the Lord, this blessing was primarily economic. Biblically speaking, children were an asset. Along with women, they were a man's property. If the union failed to produce children, a man had the right to put away his wife and chose another. This was in hopes that the new woman would produce offspring, preferably boys.

In an agricultural-based society, the presence of children literally meant extra hands to work the field. It also provided the parent with a form of social security for the future. Children were necessary to ensure financial support in old age. The more children a man fathered, the more financially secure he became. In modern times, society has turned toward urbanization. Advances in medicine have contributed to longer lives. Population growth has strained resources, and technology reduced the number of people needed to work the soil. As a result, large families have become less the norm.

A disturbing story in the book of Job illustrates how children were viewed as property. Today, it offends our moral sensitivities, but it made perfect moral sense during biblical times. We are told that all of Job's children—seven sons and three daughters—are killed by Satan on God's authority. This is but one of many calamities to befall Job, but no doubt among the most painful. By the end of the book, God restores all of Job's riches and properties, including his children. He fathers seven new sons and two new daughters, replacing those whom he lost earlier in the story.

In a world where children are seen as property, the siring of new children to replace the old dead ones seems fair—kind of like the 14,000 sheep, 6,000 camels, 1,000 oxen, and 1,000 she-donkeys which replaced the livestock destroyed earlier in the story. But if children are a product of love, a quite modern concept, then no amount of additional children can ever make up for loss of a particular child or children. Jesus changes the status of children by making them the ideal by which entrance into God's reigns can occur. No longer is the model one male person benefiting from the power and privilege of being the patriarchal head. Instead, seeking the position of the least among us, the child, becomes the means toward salvation. Children's identity ceased to be property, and instead became a product of love. Jesus returns children (as well as women) to their status as human beings, instead of as property within a patriarchal society.

26

Mad Men, Competitive Women, and Invisible Hispanics[1]

Peggy Olson is the copywriter at the fictitious Madison Avenue advertising firm, Sterling Cooper Draper Pryce in the Emmy award winning television program *Mad Men*, set in the 1960s. In one scene, she is sitting at a bar being wooed by a potential suitor. When Peggy mentions one of her clients, an auto supply firm, her drinking partner informs her of a boycott being waged against that particular company for refusing to hire "Negroes" in their stores down South. Soon the conversation drifts toward the civil rights movement, and the young man questions how Peggy can provide services to the company rather than hold them accountable for their racist policies. Feeling criticized, Peggy responds: "Most of the things Negroes can't do, I can't do either. And nobody seems to care. ... Half of the meetings take place over golf, tennis and a bunch of clubs where I'm not allowed to be a member. Or even enter. The University Club said the only way I could eat dinner there was if I arrive in a cake. I'm sure they can fight their way in[to a job as a copywriter] like I did. Believe me, nobody wanted me there."[2]

The encounter between the fictional character, Peggy Olson and her suitor, reflects the turmoil occurring under the surface of the early 1960s. Peggy symbolizes the millions of women of that era who were competing for a place at the table in a male-dominated world. But simultaneously, African Americans were also striving for their own rights. Peggy's response reveals the tension existing between white women and black men over issues of equality, a historical tension that can be traced back to the friction between Frederick Douglass and Susan B. Anthony[3] and is still present today, as demonstrated during the 2008 Democratic presidential primaries between Barack Obama and Hillary Clinton.[4] But in a black-white and a male-female dualism, this Latino man must ask: Where do my people fit in the equation? Within dichotomies that envision structural injustices as either sexist or racist, Latina/os become the "new white woman," relegated to the passive

191

position occupied by most women during the 1960s. Valerie Saiving may have asked "Where Is the Woman?";[5] but today, I must instead ask: Where Is the Hispanic?

Emma, who lived two floors above us in our tenement building in Queens, New York, during the 1960s, was one of the many Latinas who left for the office buildings in Manhattan at 6 pm each evening to empty trash cans, dust furniture, sweep floors, and mop hallways. If there would have actually been a Sterling Cooper Draper Pryce on Madison Avenue, Emma would have been cleaning up after Peggy Olson. Not surprisingly, there is no character on the show that lifts up Emma's story for the viewers to consider. She, along with most Latino/as remains invisible. True, blacks in the era of *Mad Men*, when Reinhold Niebuhr and Valerie Saiving were writing, lived, and still do, in a society where structural racism exists. And yes, women are forced to operate, then and now, in a society where structural sexism is ever-present. Still, by creating neat dichotomies, not only are Hispanics, along with other communities of color, excluded from the discourse, but the goals of liberation are dwarfed to the benefit of those still grasping for their power and privilege.

Niebuhr, like Peggy Olson's young liberal suitor, was in favor of black civil rights. However, for him, racism was reduced to a manifestation of the sin of pride; an outwork and/or application of his Augustinian anthropology: "All human groups are essentially proud and find that pride very convenient because it seems to justify their special privileges and to explain the sad state of the underprivileged. It is this combination of selfishness and pride which makes the problems of group relationships so difficult."[6] For Niebuhr, humanity is beset by the selfishness of hubris—"will-to-power" dependent upon woman's negation of self. But as Saiving reminded us, the sin for woman is better described as the failure to be a self.[7] Women are particularly tempted to submerge their individuality, their self, to the needs and desires of others[8]—a temptation facilitated by the Niebuhrian private/public dichotomy. She accuses men like Niebuhr of "identify[ing] his own limited perspective with universal truth."[9]

I would add that "sin for Hispanics"—failure to be self—is similar.[10] Nevertheless, Niebuhr insisted that "minorities have developed a pride of their own to compensate for their unconscious inferiority complex."[11] From this perspective, he can paternalistically advise African-Americans in their struggle for civil rights. But such advice, as offered by Niebuhr, was couched within an understanding of the black's placement within a lower evolutionary stage. In calling for boycotts against stores and banks that discriminate against African Americans, Niebuhr advised that "he [the African American] would need only to fuse the aggressiveness of the new and young Negro with the patience and forbearance of the old Negro, to rob the former of its vindictiveness and the latter of its lethargy."[12] For Niebuhr, the Negro's patience and forbearance is not due to religious virtue, but rather racial weakness.[13]

Niebuhr seems to focus more on the disruptive impact that civil rights could have on southern culture than the injustices faced by blacks. He advised African Americans not to make too many demands too quickly. Obtaining civil rights for blacks is good and fine, as long as it does not disrupt order (read as white male privilege). Ethicist Traci West reminds us, "unfortunately Niebuhr did not similarly propose that whites like himself should engage in these tactics in order to challenge racial discrimination at stores and banks that *they* used."[14] It should not be surprising, as West points out, that during the 1950s move toward desegregation, Niebuhr expresses sympathy for those "anxious parents" who opposed school desegregation due to "the cultural differences" of the two races. Niebuhr hoped that someday "the Negro people will have the same advantages as our children,"[15] but not at the price of social order. Order is to be pursued, even at the price of certain inequalities—a proposition incongruent with any marginalized community committed to justice. When writing during his more progressive younger years, Niebuhr made room for these inequalities, a necessity if we wish society to function properly.[16] This position would eventually lead him during the global disarray that followed the Second World War to argue for the need of a stable world order in a nuclear age. Hence Niebuhr makes a preferential option for order and U.S. supremacy, even at the cost of certain inequalities.

Saiving well highlighted the significant differences between masculine and feminine experience, but contended "that there are significant differences between masculine and feminine experience and that feminine experience reveals in a more emphatic fashion certain aspects of the human situation which are present but less obvious in the experience of men."[17] While this may be true, both Saiving and Niebuhr still share white privilege, a concern that Saiving herself recognized during a 1987 interview. "A lot of things I say here may not be true… of poor whites, or black peoples or Chicanos. What I say comes out of not only the middle-class, but the white middle class."[18] And here lies my concern in any equality conversation among white men and white women where people of color (beyond just African-Americans) are not involved in the discourse. Is equality for women, and by extension people of color, achieved by ontologically becoming white males? Saiving admits that many women "were brought up to believe in the fundamental equality of the sexes and who were given the same kind of education and the same encouragement to self-realization as their male contemporaries";[19] nevertheless, it is crucial to realize that this is a privilege denied Latino/as throughout the 1960's, as well as in subsequent decades.

While Saiving argued for the two "tendencies" in human situation, one associated with competitiveness and the other with passiveness,[20] I argue that Hispanics, female and male, are relegated to the role of passiveness. Today's undocumented Latina/os must invisibly live in the shadows, offering themselves up as living sacrifices for the continuous well-being of documented white men and women. The "merely trivial…thousand-and-one routine tasks" that Saiving said women do, which lack "creative drive" but "performed cheerfully" must be done by someone "if life is to go on."[21] Emma, cleaning on Madison Avenue, and my Latino father, mopping floor after floor as a superintendent in the building where Emma lived, both occupy the feminine space Saiving described. The need to survive led them to an anxiety to please: "Si Señor, I am honored to clean after you or pick your produce."

If this is true, then people of color, male and female, become the new white woman, to be domesticated and subdued. For those who historically have been at the pinnacle of hierarchical structures, to be a white male, or to claim equality with white males, implies both domination and protection of those relegated to their underside. Because sexism reflects only one aspect of oppression, it is appropriate to include in our discourse all forms of oppression imposed on those who fail to live up to the manly standards of being at the pinnacle of hierarchical social structures. To incorporate Saiving's concepts today must be as much about race and class as it is about gender. As a Hispanic male, I have been taught that history is forged by male testicles, a view that is reinforced by Niebuhr, especially in his book, *The Structure of Nations and Empires,* an apology for U.S. imperialism. This leads me to wonder how the semiotics of testicles affects a Latino/a reading of both Niebuhr *and* Saiving.

Women, nonwhites, and the poor are marginalized because they lack the testicles to influence history. When white men look into Jacques Lacan's mirror, they recognize themselves as men through the distancing process of negative self-definition: "I am what I am not." The formation of the subject's ego constructs an illusory self-representation through the negation of testicles, now projected upon others, identified as nonmales. Ascribing femininity to the other, regardless of gender, forces the construction of female identity to originate with the white man. In fact, the feminine Object, in and of itself, is seen as nothing apart from a masculine subject that provides unifying purpose.[22] The resulting gaze of the white, elite male inscribes effeminacy upon others who are not man enough to "make" history, "provide" for their family, or "resist" their subjugation. The other, if male, may have a penis, but lacks the testicles to use it. Power and authority exhibit testicles, which are in fact derived from social structures, traditions, norms, laws, and customs created by men who usually are white and wealthy.

From one perspective, no one really has testicles. The white man lives, always threatened by the possible loss of his testicles, while the non-man is forcefully deprived. The potent symbolic power invested in the testicles both signals and veils white, elite male socioeconomic power. Constructing those oppressed as feminine allows white men with testicles to assert their privilege by constructing oppressed others as inhabitants of the castrated realm of the exotic and primitive. Lacking testicles, the other does not exist, except as designated by the desire of the one with testicles. The castrated male (read: race and class Other) occupies a feminine space where his body is symbolically sodomized as prelude to the sodomizing of his mind. While non-men are forced to flee from their individuality, the white man must constantly attempt to live up to a false construction. The non-man becomes enslaved by the inferiority engraved upon their flesh by the U.S. ethos, and as such must move beyond the sin of failing to be self. Likewise, the white man (in other words, Niebuhr and company) is also enslaved to his own so-called superiority, which flows from his testicles, and for them, they must move beyond what Niebuhr recognizes as their sin of pride. Saiving is careful not to fall into the trap of linking liberation to equality with white males; other feminists, unfortunately, have not been so nuance in their analysis.

Those from the dominant culture (Niebuhr and Savings included) and those communities of color relegated to their underside are alienated—both suffer from an obsessive neurotic orientation and both require liberation from their condition. The need for this liberation is best illustrated by the continuing status quo of mad white men, competing white women, and invisible Hispanics.

27

Jesús: Welcoming the Indecent[1]

For the ruler to invite everyone, including the outcasts to the banquet table is considered inappropriate (Mt. 22:1–14). How can we expect the refined to dine with philistines? It is one thing to dine with the uncouth; it is quite another thing to include their voices or perspectives. To seriously do theological and ethical analysis from the social location of the outcast, specifically the sexual outcast is usually considered indecorous if not indecent. It is precisely this indecency that theologian Marcella Althaus-Reid calls for as she seeks a theology that can challenge oppressive social structures. Those most likely to be considered indecent are usually poor women of color. Constructing acceptable theological perspectives of sexuality often ignores the complex set of sexual regulations and gender expectations placed on women. To counter this imposed "decency," she calls for the doing of theology with one's panties off. In other words, she calls for a move beyond what has been constructed as proper behavior, which in reality masks oppressive relationships. The "indecent theology" that she advocates is a perverse and subversive theology that starts with people's experiences without censorship. It is a theology that tells people to come as they are, by first coming out of the closets that constrain and domesticate them.[2]

In a similar way, I argue for an indecent approach to justice-based praxis. The global success of neoliberalism makes any real hope of liberation from global oppressive economic systems unrealistic. The politics of the Euro-American Jesus will not save Hispanics, mainly because we remain complicit with the very neoliberal colonial venture that oppresses the world's marginalized, ignoring or providing justification for the prevailing structures of oppression that remain detrimental to Latino/as. If the Eurocentric politics of Jesus fails to address oppressive structures, then Hispanics must construct the politics of Jesús for their communities, rooted in the Latina/o social context. Those who benefit from the power and privilege accorded by the dominant culture are incapable of fashioning an objective political ethics because their standing within society is protected by the prevailing social structures. If the foundation for the politics of Jesús lies within our cultural context, then I turn to my mother for inspiration as to how this politics is to be constructed.

Mirta—may she rest in peace—was an illiterate country girl from the hills of Santa Clara, Cuba, who was sold as a preteen to a family in the city to work as their domestic maid, where she faced physical and sexual abuse. It was the only way her poverty-ridden family could provide food for themselves. Mirta, a santéra, taught me the ways of the *orishas*, specifically the ways of my *orí*, my head, *Ellegúa*—the trickster.[3] Mirta's faith forged a trickster's ethics needed if one wanted to survive the mean streets of New York City. It is from Mirta's life experiences, and the life experiences of all the Mirtas of the world, that has become the foundation of the ethical thoughts of Mirta's child. I even name this paradigm after the loving and gentle phrase I can still hear *mi mamí*— my mother—constantly say to me: "*Coño Miguelito, no jodas mas!*" This becomes my Caribbean habitus, and it is from her words of wisdom that I advocate what I have come to call an ethics *para joder.*[4] An ethics *para joder* attempts to situate an effective response within the consequences of colonialism, the oppression of normative social structures, and the pain of the domesticated Hispanic. Coining a term to describe an ethical practice already occurring among the marginalized implies that this methodology of *jodiendo* already exists; but as an organic intellectual, I simply am reflecting upon this existing praxis for the purpose of theorizing and theologizing.

To *joder* is a Spanish verb, a word one would never use in polite conversation. Although it is not the literal translation of a certain four-letter word beginning with the letter "F," it is still considered somewhat vulgar because it basically means, "to screw with." Note: it does not mean to screw—but to screw with, an important difference in semantics. The word connotes an individual who purposely is a pain in the rear end, who purposely is causing trouble, who constantly disrupts the established norm, who shouts from the mountaintop what most prefer to be kept silent, who audaciously refuses to stay in his or her place. I have been taken somewhat aback by some who have objected to the use of profanity in describing this ethical political paradigm. But in all reality, what is truly profane is not the word that is used; rather, it is the oppressive death-dealing conditions under which Hispanics are forced to live. An ethics *para joder* is an ethics that "screws" with the prevailing power structures.

Those who are among the disenfranchised, who stand before the vastness of neoliberalism that offers little hope for radical change in their lifetimes, have few ethical alternatives. Regardless of the good intentions of those who are privileged by society, or the praxis they employ to paternalistically save and rescue Hispanics, the devastating consequences of empire will worsen as the few get wealthier and the many sink deeper into the despair of stomach-wrenching poverty. The dominant culture, including progressive ethicists, may be willing to offer charity and to stand in solidarity, but few are willing or able to take a role in dismantling the very global structures designed to privilege them at the expense of the majority of the world's inhabitants.[5] When those who are disenfranchised start to *joder*, it literally creates political instability. An ethics that upsets the prevailing social order designed to maintain empire is an ethics that arises from the margins of society who are disillusioned and frustrated with normative Eurocentric values and virtues. While the majority of all Euro American ethicists insist on social order, marginalized communities must call for social disorder, a process achieved by *jodiendo*. Perhaps, it might lead some within the dominant culture to share in the hopelessness of overcoming the global forces of neoliberalism. If so, it may be the only way that progress is made. A liberative ethics *para joder* can be frightening to those who are accustomed to their power and privilege because hopelessness signals a lack of control. Because those who benefit from the present social structures insist on control, sharing the plight of being vulnerable to forces beyond control will demonstrate how hope falls short.[6]

To *joder* means refusing to play by the rules established by those who provide a space for orderly dissent that pacifies the need to vent for the marginalized, but is designed not to change the power relationships within the existing social structures. If the goal of the politics of Jesús is to bring about change, then it is crucial to go beyond the rules created by the dominant culture, to move beyond what is expected, to push beyond their universalized experiences.[7] In a very real sense, Jesús is a holy *joderon* (a holy screwer). Usually when we think of Jesus, images of a peace loving, gentle pacifist come to mind, at least it did to the mind of John Howard Yoder. Ignored is Jesús the troublemaker, the bringer of conflict, the disrupter of unity. This is a violent Jesús who makes a whip and forcefully drives out the moneychangers in the Temple, overturning their tables (Jn. 3:15). This is a strategic Jesús who prepares his disciples for what is to come. He instructs them that before, when he sent them out without a money belt, bag, or sandals, they lacked nothing. But now, they are to bring their money belt and bag; and if they lack a sword, they are to "sell their cloak and purchase one" (Lk. 22:35–36). Jesús the so-called pacifist is instructing his followers to buy a sword? It would be like today instructing the purchase of a gun. This is a realistic Jesús who warns his disciples that he did not come to bring peace to earth, but division (Lk. 12:51). He did not come to bring peace to earth, but rather a sword. He has come to turn a son against his father, a daughter against her mother, and a daughter-in-law against her mother-in-law. Even a person's enemy will end up being a member of one's own household (Mt. 10:34–36). On the night he was betrayed and arrested, Pedro impulsively drew the sword he had, and struck Malchus, the high priest's slave, cutting off his ear (Jn. 18:10). Jesús responds to this act of violence by stating "All who take the sword will perish by the sword" (Mt. 26:52).

Jesús may be speaking to Pedro, but to whom is he directing his comment? After all, it was Jesús who told his disciples to sell their cloak and buy a sword. In fact, some of the disciples were already armed, for they boasted, "Look Lord, we already have two swords." "That's enough!" (Lk. 22:38). If Jesús' comments are directed to his disciples, then he is contradicting his earlier instructions. No, he was not speaking for the benefit of his disciples, but for those aligned with the colonizer who came to arrest him. Those who are the muscle of the colonizer, picking up the sword to defend the empire will, along with the empire, perish with the sword. We may argue that Jesús abhors violence, but it would be simplistic to argue that he was a pacifist. He calls his disciples to become the recipients of violence, calling them to radical solidarity with a bloody cross. Violence can never be accepted as a necessary evil as per some revolutionaries, nor rejected as antithetical to Jesus as per pacifists. After all, Jesús prophesies about the violence of the Day of Judgment.

History demonstrates the futility of simply denouncing unjust social structures, for those whom the structures privileges will never willingly abdicate what they consider to be their birthright. Not all violence is the same. The violence employed by the marginalized to overcome oppression, is in reality self-defense to the oppressor's violent employment of terror to maintain their subjugation. Unconditional love for the very least among us might lead a person, in an unselfish act, to stand in solidarity with the oppressed in their battle for self-preservation. Protecting a "nonperson" might invite a violent confrontation as the oppressor, feeling backed into a corner, fights tooth and nail to maintain the status quo. To make a preferential option of love for the oppressed means harming the oppressor who has a vested interest on insisting in the use of nonviolence, as the only ethically acceptable methodology, by those who he or she oppresses. The conflict and disruption that comes with following Jesús, whose consequence at times is violence, illustrates the need for an ethical praxis for colonized people that lack the physical or military power to confront or overcome the colonizer. Because the usage of violence all too often becomes the oppressor's excuse to unleash greater violent retaliation, a need to be as wise as serpents but gentle as doves is required. How does one create ethical acts that disrupt structures that support and maintain oppression?

I suggest the need to *joder*; even though the call to *joder*, the call to disrupt the social structures that privileges an elite minority segment of society, might very well brings the unwanted consequence of the sword. Subscribing to this indecent ethics *para joder* recognizes that the prevailing social order exists to legitimize and normalize the privileges of the few at the expense of many. *Joderones* are tricksters who lie so that truth can be revealed. When they lie, cheat, joke, and deceive, they unmask deeper truths obscured by the dominant culture's moralists. These means employed by *joderones* in the struggle for liberation may not be considered moral by the dominant culture, nevertheless, such tricksters are ethical, operating in a realm that moves beyond good and evil, beyond what society defines as being right or wrong.

Joderones are consummate survivors that serve as exemplars for the disenfranchised in need of surviving the reality colonialism constructed for them. By disrupting the empire's equilibrium to create compromising situations for those in power, the *joderon* reveals their weaknesses, exposes what they prefer to remain hidden, and remove their artificial masks of superiority. Disrupted established norms create new situations that provide the marginalized fresh ways of approaching oppression.

The biblical text is full of *joderones*, whether it be Abraham tricking the Egyptian Pharaoh and King Abimelech of Gerar into believing that his wife was his sister, resulting in financial gain (Gen. 12:10–20; 20:1–18); his son Isaac attempting to pull off the same charade with King Abimelech of Gerar (Gen. 26:1–14); or his grandson Jacob who tricked his older brother Esau out of their father's blessings (Gen. 27:1–45). But even the *joderones* can get tricked, as in the case of Laban, Jacob's father-in-law, who tricks Jacob out of seven years of labor and the woman he wants to marry by switching brides on the wedding night (Gen. 29:15–30). During Egyptian captivity, the Hebrew midwives Shiphrah and Puah deceived the Pharaoh to save the lives of the Hebrew babies (Ex. 1:15–21). The Hebrews are then tricked by an elaborate scheme perpetrated by the Gibeonites to enter into a treaty of nonaggression (Josh. 9:3–20). In the book of Judges there is Ehud who tricks Eglon the King of Moab into a secluded room so that he could kill him and free his people from tyranny (Judg. 3:12–30); Jael also frees her people by providing Sisera deadly hospitality (Judg. 4:17–22); and there is Samson, who through his riddles tries to achieve personal gain only to eventually being tricked himself by his wife, Delilah (Judg. 14; 16). Then you have King David, who feigns madness before the King Achish of Gath to preserve his life (1 Sam. 21:11–14). And there is his son King Solomon who tricks the two women fighting over the baby to discover who is being truthful by suggesting he would cut the baby in half (1 Kings 3:16–28). These tricksters, these *joderones*, these screwers with the established order, engaged in deception to achieve personal gain (Jacob), survival (David), salvation of their people (Shiphrah, Puah,

Jael, and Ehud), and discover truth (Solomon).

These holy *joderones* provide a moral justification for the employment of deception as a means of self-preservation for those who face overwhelming odds against surviving. Although a thorough examination of the biblical text for purposes of uncovering the many manifestations of *joderones* and their importance to the development of the Judeo-Christian faith is a worthy project that can serve as a corrective for the prevailing Eurocentric confusion of ethics with personal piety, such an endeavor is beyond the scope of this chapter. For our purposes, we need to focus on just one *joderon*, Jesús, the colonized man. Jesús the liberator screws with the established political and religious authorities by subverting the legitimacy they constructed....For this, he pays the ultimate price of crucifixion, accused of being a heretic. Jesucristo *el joderon*, screws with those who established themselves as the political and religious leaders of the people and from their lofty positions screw the very people they are entrusted to represent, support, and protect. By employing an ethics *para joder*, Jesús literally screwed-up their plans for oppressing the people. Cleansing the Temple becomes a liberative praxis that literally overturns the established tables (Mt. 21:12–13). For those today wishing to be imitators of Christ by following his politics are called to do likewise, to *joder*.[8]

To *joder* is not a praxis in which the disenfranchised engages in out of vengeance or spite. To *joder* is an act of love toward oppressors designed to force them to live up to their rhetoric in the hopes that confronting their complicity with oppressive structures might lead them toward their own salvation. Oppressors are also victims of the structures that are designed to privilege them yet robs them of what it means to be human. Jesús rejects what has been the norm, to love your neighbor and hate your enemy. Instead, he commands his followers to love and pray for those who oppress and persecute. After all, God causes the sun to rise on the evil and good, and sends rain to the just and unjust (Mt. 5:43–45). The wheat and weeds grow together, even though on the day of the harvest, the wheat will be bundled together and burned while the wheat will be brought into the barn (Mt. 13:30). To *joder* is a nonviolent survival strategy based on love designed to liberate the abused from death-dealing social structures that deny them of their humanity, and the abuser whose own humanity is lost through a complicity with these same structures.

Notes

Chapter 1: Testimony on the Blessing of Sex

[1]Originally published in *Genesis: Belief: A Theological Commentary on the Bible* (Louisville: Westminster John Knox Press, 2011), 25–28. This exegesis of the biblical text becomes foundational in all my works dealing with sexual ethics.

[2]Clement of Alexandria, *Christ the Educator*, II: 10:95.

[3]St. Jerome, Letter CCIII to Eustochium, 15:1.

[4]Augustine *The City of God* XIV: 19, 21.

[5]Tertullian, *To His Wife* I: 4

Chapter 2: Unmasking Biblical Justification

[1]Originally published in *Reading the Bible from the Margins* (Maryknoll, NY: Orbis Books, 2002), 82–96. One of the first books I ever wrote that won national awards, I attempted to show how the marginalized read the text, challenging normative interpretations.

[2]It is not within the scope of this book to reconcile what many Christians notice as being two separate accounts of Creation. The first creation story (Gen. 1:1—2:4) lists the order of creation as follows: Day 0: formless void; Day 1: light; Day 2: the heavens; Day 3: land and vegetation; Day 4: the sun and moon; Day 5: the living creatures in the water and air; Day 6: the living creatures on the land and humans (both male and female); Day 7: God rested. By contrast, the second creation story (Gen. 2:5–25) lists the order as Day 1: there is land; Day 2: water surfaces onto the land; Day 3: man; Day 4: Eden (plants); Day 5: animals; Day 6: woman.

[3]Although it is important to note that some feminist biblical scholars maintain that "the" *adam*, the first creation, was neither male or female, but both, separated in Genesis 2:21–22 when God creates Eve. See Phyllis Trible, *God and the Rhetoric of Sexuality* (Philadelphia: Fortress Press, 1978), 73.

[4] Trible, *Texts of Terror: Literary-Feminist Readings of Biblical Narratives* (Philadelphia: Fortress Press, 1984), 65–87.

[5] Elsa Tamez, "The Woman Who Complicated the History of Salvation," in *New Eyes for Reading: Reading and Theological Reflections by Women from the Third World*, ed. John S. Pobee and Bärbel Von Wartenberg-Potter (Oak Park, IL.: Meyer-Stone Books, 1986), 5–17; Renita J. Weems, *Just a Sister Away: A Womanist Vision of Women's Relationship in the Bible* (San Diego: LuraMedia, 1988), 1–19; and Delores S. Williams, *Sisters in the Wilderness: The Challenge of Womanist God-Talk* (Maryknoll, NY: Orbis Books, 1993).

Chapter 3: Orthoeros

[1]Originally published in *Professional Sexual Ethics: A Holistic Ministry Approach*, ed. Patricia Beattie Jung and Darryl W. Stephens (Minneapolis: Fortress Press, 2013), 87–97. The chapter constructs an ethical paradigm upon which to engage in healthy sexual relationships.

[2]This chapter is based on my earlier book, *A Lily Among the Thorns: Imagining a New Christian Sexuality* (San Francisco: Jossey-Bass, 2007).

[3]Pope Benedict XVI, *God is Love*, I: 6

[4]Marvin M. Ellison, *Erotic Justice: A Liberating Ethics of Sexuality* (Louisville: Westminster John Knox Press, 1996), 12.

Chapter 4: Physical Union & Spiritual Rapture

[1]Originally published in *A Lily Among the Thorns: Imagining a New Christian Sexuality* (San Francisco: Jossey-Bass, 2007), 59–69. This chapter section attempts to show how the biblical text celebrates the body and its pleasures, lost for most of Christian history.

[2]*Mishnah*, "Tractate Yadayim," 3:5.

[3]Ramban, Iggeret HaKodesh, 2.

4Carey Ellen Walsh, *Exquisite Desire: Religion, the Erotic, and the Song of Songs* (Minneapolis: Fortress Press, 2000), 65, 88.

[5]Ibid., 124–25, 130.

[6]Ibid., 66, 101.

[7]Ibid., 86, 106–09, 125, 128.

[8]Michael Le Page, "Orgasms: a Real 'Turn-off' for Women," *New Scientist*, no. 2505 (June 25, 2005): 14.

[9]Meredith McGuire, *Religion: The Social Context* (Belmont, CA: Wadsworth Publishing Company, 1997), 66.

[10]*The Spiritual Canticle*, 23 & 27.

[11]*Ascent of Mount Carmel*, 1:4:3–4.

[12]*The Spiritual Canticle*, 13:2.

[13]*Ascent of Mount Carmel*, 2:32:2.

[14]Teresa de Ávila, *Life of St. Teresa*, trans. J. M. Cohen (Harmondsworth, England.: Penguin, 1957), 210.

[15]Teresa de Ávila, *Life of St. Teresa*, 27.

[16]Miguel A. De La Torre, *Doing Christian Ethics from the Margins* (Maryknoll, NY: Orbis Books, 2004), 36–37.

Chapter 5: Jesús: Androgyous?

[1]Originally published in *The Politics of Jesús: A Hispanic Political Theology* (Lanham, MD: Rowman & Littlefield, 2015), 71–73. This chapter section argues for Jesus Christ's intersexuality.

[2]Gary M. Burge, Lynn H. Cohick, and Gene l. Green, *The New Testament in Antiquity: A Survey of the New Testament within its Cultural Context* (Grand Rapids, MI: Zondervan, 2009), 143-44.

[3]Edward L. Kessel, "A Proposed Biological Interpretation of the Virgin Birth," *Journal of the American Scientific Affiliation* (September, 1983): 129–36.

Chapter 6: Why Does God Need a Penis?

[1]Originally published in *A Lily Among the Thorns: Imagining a New Christian Sexuality* (San Francisco: Jossey-Bass, 2007), 15–18. This chapter section questions why we insist on making God male.

[2]Mary Daly, *Beyond God the Father: Toward a Philosophy of Woman's Liberation* (Boston: Beacon, 1973), 19.

Chapter 7: Fifty Shades

[1]Originally published as an op-ed on my blog *Our Lucha* (https://ourlucha.wordpress. com/about/) on February 21, 2015. Bothered by the film *Fifty Shades of Grey* for failing to advocate for a healthy sexuality, I responded with this article.

[2]Pope Gregory, *Dialogues* 2:2.

[3]Nedarim, 15b.

[4]Mishnah Torah, Issurei Biah, 21:9.

[5]This op-ed is derived from my book *A Lily Among the Thorns: Toward a New Christian Sexual Ethics* (San Francisco: Jossey-Bass, 2007).

Chapter 8: Private Sin

[1]Originally published in *A Lily Among the Thorns: Imagining a New Christian Sexuality* (San Francisco: Jossey-Bass, 2007), 119–23. This chapter section attempts to liberate the act of masturbation from culturally induced shame.

[2]Brian Alexander, "Unleashing your Wild Side," MSNBC, May 31, 2005.

[3]"Lectures on Genesis," *Luther's Work* VII.

[4]For a complete review of clitoridectomy procedures within English-speaking Western nations, see Mary Daly, *Gyn/Ecology: The Metaethics of Radical Feminism* (Boston: Beacon Press, 1978), 240–45.

[5]http://www.amnesty.org/ailib/intcam/femgen/fgm1.htm.
[6]"Masturbation Cuts Cancer Risk," BBC, July 16, 2003.
[7]Babylonian Talmud Niddah, 13 a-b.
[8]Mishnah Niddah, 2.1.

Chapter 9: First Man and Woman

[1]Originally published in *Genesis: Belief: A Theological Commentary on the Bible* (Louisville: Westminster John Knox Press, 2011), 57–63. This exegesis of the biblical text celebrates the becoming of one as an alternative to what has come to be known as the traditional biblical marriage.
[2]Phyllis Trible, *God and the Rhetoric of Sexuality* (Philadelphia: Fortress Press, 1978), 161.
[3]Tertullian, *De pudicitia* 21.16.
[4]Babylonian Talmud, *Sanhedrin* 58a.
[5]Augustine, *The Literal Meaning of Genesis* IX:5, 9.

Chapter 10: War on Women

[1]Originally published in *Doing Christian Ethics from the Margins*, 2 ed. (Maryknoll, NY: Orbis Books, 2014), 283–312. The chapter attempts to explore the interconnectedness of institutionalized abuse and violence toward women.
[2]Brian Stelter, "Limbaugh Apologies for Attack on Student in Birth Control Furor," *Times*, March 3, 2012.
[3]Rosalind S. Helderman, "A Todd Akin Defense," *Washington Post*, August 20, 2012.
[4]Annie Groer, "Indiana GOP Senate Hopeful Richard Mourdock Says God 'Intended' Rape Pregnancies," *Washington Post*, October 24, 2012.
[5]Christine Roberts, "Pennsylvania Senate Hopeful Says Pregnancy from Rape 'Similar' to 'Having Baby Out of Wedlock,'" *New York Daily News*, August 27, 2012.
[6]Steven Harmon, "Leader of California Republican Group Steps into Rape Pregnancy Controversy," *Mercury News*, March 1, 2013.
[7]Aaron Blake, "GOP Congressman: Rate of Pregnancies from Rape Are Very Low," *Washington Post*, June 12, 2013.
[8]Jonathan A Gottschall and Tiffani Gottschall, "Are Per-Incident Rape-Pregnancy Rates Higher Than Per-Incident Consensual Pregnancy Rates?" *Human Nature* 14, no. 1 (2003): 1.
[9]A.M. Gomez, "Sexual Violence as a Predictor of Unintended Pregnancy, Contraceptive Use, and Unmet Needs Among Female Youth in Columbia," *J Women Health* 20, no. 9 (September 2011): 1349–56.
[10]Sara Shute, "Sexist Language and Sexism," in *Sexist Language: A Modern Philosophical Analysis*, ed. Mary Vetterling-Braggin (Boston: Littlefield, Adams, and Company, 1981), 27.
[11]Ariane Hegewisch, Claudia Williams, and Vanessa Harbin, *Fact Sheet: The Gender Gap by Occupation*, (Washington, DC: Institute for Women's Policy Research, 2012), 6.
[12]The wage gap, according to the U.S. Census Bureau, differs from state to state with Wyoming paying women the least at 67 cents for every dollar made by a man, and Vermont paying the most at 87 cents for every dollar paid to a man. See Ariane Hegewisch and Maxwell Matite, *Fact Sheet: America's Women and the Wage Gap* (Washington, DC: National Partnership for Women & Family, 2013), 1.
[13]Caroline Dobuzinskis, *News Release: Statement from IWPR President Dr. Heidi Hartmann on the 50th Anniversary of the Equal Pay Act* (Washington, DC: Institute for Women's Policy Research, 2013), 1.
[14]National Partnership for Women & Family, *Fact Sheet: African American Women and the Wage Gap* (Washington, DC: National Partnership for Women & Family, January 2013), 1; *Fact Sheet: Latinas and the Wage Gap* (Washington, DC: National Partnership for Women & Family, April 2013), 1.
[15]Ibid., 2.
[16]Stephanie Coontz, "Progress at Work, But Mothers Still Pay a Price," *New York Times*, June 8, 2013.
[17]Hegewisch and Matite, *Fact Sheet: America's Women and the Wage Gap*, 1.
[18]Ibid.
[19]Wendy Wang, Kim Parker and Paul Taylor, *Breadwinner Moms: Mothers Are the Sole or*

Primary Provider in Four-in-Ten Households with Children; Public Conflicted about the Growing Trend (Washington, DC: Pew Research Center, 2013), 1.

[20]"The Unstoppable Climb in C.E.O. Pay," *New York Times*, June 30, 2013.

[21]Stephanie Coontz, "The Myth of Male Decline," *New York Times*, September 30, 2012.

[22]Aldo Svaldi, "Men Winning More Jobs than Women in Economic Recovery," *Denver Post*, August 10, 2012.

[23]Robert Pear, "Gender Gap Persists in Cost of Health Insurance," *New York Times* March 19, 2012.

[24]Stephanie Coontz, "Why Gender Equality Stalled," *New York Times*, February 17, 2013.

[25]Ibid.

[26]Catherine Rampell, "U.S. Women on the Rise as Family Breadwinners," *New York Times*, May 29, 2013.

[27]Shannan Catalano, Erica Smith, Howard Snyder, and Michael Rand, *Female Victims of Violence* (Washington, DC: U.S. Department of Justice, Bureau of Justice Statistics, 2009), 2–3.

[28]Centers for Disease Control and Prevention, "Adverse Health Conditions and Health Risk Behaviors Associated with Intimate Partner Violence," *Morbidity and Mortality Weekly Report* (February 2008): 113–17.

[29]Katrina Baum, Shannan Catalano, Michael Rand, and Kristina Rose, *Stalking Victimization in the United States* (Washington, DC: U.S. Department of Justice Bureau of Justice Statistics, 2009), 3.

[30]Catalano et. al. *Female Victims of Violence, 3.*

[31]Jeani Chang, Cynthia J. Berg, Linda E. Saltzman, and Joy Herndon, "Homicide: A Leading Cause of Injury Deaths Among Pregnant and Postpartum Women in the United States, 1991–1999," *American Journal of Public Health* 95, no. 3 (2005): 471–77.

[32]Michael Rand, *National Crime Victimization Survey: Criminal Victimization* (Washington, DC: U.S. Department of Justice, Bureau of Justice Statistics, 2008), 1.

[33]Although all rapes are in a sense forcible, making the usage of this adverb troublesome; it is used nonetheless so as to remain faithful to the legal distinction used in the data collection.

[34]Vangie A. Foshee et. al., "The Safe Dates Project: Theoretical Basis, Evaluation Design, and Selected Baseline Findings," *American Journal of Preventive Medicine, Supplement* 12, no. 5 (1996): 39–47.

[35]Rand, *National Crime Victimization Survey*, 4.

[36]Shannan Catalano, *Intimate Partner Violence in the United States* (Washington, DC: U.S. Department of Justice Bureau of Justice Statistics, 2007), 12–13.

[37]Rand, *National Crime Victimization Survey*, 4.

[38]David Murphey, *What Do We Know about the High School Class of 2013?* (Bethesda, MD: Child Trends, 2013), 1–2.

[39]Thomas H. Cohen, and Tracey Kyckelhahn, *Felony Defendants in Large Urban Counties* (Washington, DC: U.S. Department of Justice, Bureau of Justice Statistics, 2006), 3.

[40]Mary Louise Roberts, *What Soldiers Do: Sex and the American G.I. in World War II France* (Chicago: University of Chicago Press, 2013), 9.

[41]Ibid., 10.

[42]While the focus will remain on women, it should be recognized that women are not the only victims of sexual violence, so too are men. According to the a Pentagon report, 6.1 percent of active women in the military and 1.2 percent of active men experienced sexual assault in 2012, an increase over the 2010 report that documented 4.4 percent of women and less than 0.9 percent of men experienced sexual assault. Because men represent the largest proportion of armed service personal (85 percent), the majority of the 26,000 service members who experienced unwanted sexual contact were men. See United States Department of Defense, *Department of Defense Annual Report on Sexual Assault in the Military: Fiscal Year 2012* (Washington, DC, Department of Defense, 2012), 2.

[43]Ibid., 3, 12, 71.

[44]James Risen, "Military Has Not Solved Problem of Sexual Assault, Women Say," *New York Times*, November 2, 2012; "Air Force Leaders Testify on Culture That Led to Sexual Assaults of Recruits," *New York Times*, January 24, 2013.

[45]Thom Shanker, "Women Were Secretly Filmed at Wes Point, the Army Says," *New York Times*, May 22, 2013.

[46]Jennifer Steinhauer, "Sexual Assaults in Military Raise Alarm in Washington," *New York Times*, May 7, 2013; "Military Courts Are Called Outdated on Sex Crimes," *New York Times*, May 8, 2012.

[47]Detis Duhart, *Violence in the Workplace, 1993–99* (Washington, DC: Bureau of Justice Statistics, 2001), 1–2.

[48]Steven Luke, "San Diego Domestic Violence Victim Fired from Teaching," *San Diego NBC 7*, June 13, 2013.

[49]Denis Yost, "Hale: 'I've Never Thought My Sexual Orientation Is a Sin'," *NBC 4 News, WCMH*, May 24, 2013.

[50]*States Enact Record Number of Abortion Restrictions in 2011* (New York: Guttmacher Institute, 2012), 1.

[51]*2012 Saw Second-Highest Abortion Restrictions Ever* (New York: Guttmacher Institute, January 2, 2013), 1.

[52]Arizona, Michigan, and Virginia.

[53]Arizona, Mississippi, and Tennessee. The Mississippi law closes down the state's only remaining abortion clinic that relies on traveling doctors.

[54]Alabama, Arizona, Florida, Kansas, Louisiana, Mississippi, Texas, and Virginia.

[55]John Schwartz, "Texas Senate Approves Strict Abortion Measure," *New York Times*, July 14, 2013.

[56]Erik Eckholm, "Arkansas Passes a 12-Week Limit in Abortion Law," *New York Times*, March 7, 2013.

[57]Fernanda Santos, "Arizona Law Struck Down as Restricted," *New York Times*, May 22, 2013.

[58]Associated Press, "House Republicans, Taking on Own Leaders, Promote Legislation to Ban Abortion After 20 Weeks," *Washington Post*, May 22, 2013.

[59]Jeremy W. Peters, "House Panel Advances Bill to Restrict Abortions," *New York Times*, June 13, 2013; "Unfazed by 2012, G.O.P. Is Seeking Abortion Limits," *New York Times*, June 18, 2013. It should be noted that because Democrats control the Senate and White House, the bill had no chance of becoming law; nevertheless, its purpose was to satisfy a vocal constituency of the Republican base. Also, Republican-controlled legislatures in Arkansas and North Dakota already passed more restrictive bans on abortions while South Carolina, Texas, and Wisconsin are considering similar bans as the U.S. House.

[60]Jeremy W. Peters, "In Partisan Vote, House Approves Ban on Abortions after 22 Weeks," *New York Times*, June 19, 2013.

[61]Women's lives are endangered by the difficulty, and sometimes refusal, to perform medically necessary terminations. Also, many women would resort to unsafe solutions if they are unable to access safe and legal abortions.

[62]"The Campaign against Women," *New York Times*, May 19, 2012.

[63]James Trussell, "Contraceptive Failure in the United States," *Contraception* 83, no. 5 (2011): 398.

[64]William D. Mosher and Jo Jones, "Use of Contraception in the United States: 1982-2008," *Vital and Health Statistics* 23, no. 29 (2010): 7, 22.

[65]Lawrence B. Finer and Mia R. Zolna, "Unintended Pregnancy in the United States: Incidence and Disparities, 2006," *Contraception* 84, no. 5 (November, 2011), 478.

[66]*U.S. Teenage Pregnancies, Births and Abortions, 2008: National Trends by Race and Ethnicity* (New York: Guttmacher Institute, February 2012) 2, 7.

[67]Ibid., 3.

[68]John S. Santelli, Laura Duberstein Lindberg, Lawrence B. Finer, and Susheela Singh, "Explaining Recent Declines in Adolescent Pregnancy in The United States: The Contribution of Abstinence and Improved Contraceptive Use," *American Journal of Public Health* 97, no. 1 (2007): 150.

[69]Alexander McKay and Michael Barrett, "Trends in Teen Pregnancy Rates from 1996–2006: A Comparison of Canada, Sweden, USA and England/Wales," *Canadian Journal of Human Sexuality* 19, no. 1–2 (March, 2010): 45-46, 59-60.

[70]Pam Belluck and Emily Ramshaw, "Women in Texas Losing Options for Health Care," *New York Times*, March 8, 2012. It should be noted that Presidents Truman, Eisenhower, and Johnson all served as honorary co-chairmen of the fund-raising committee of Planned Parenthood.

[71]Since 2011, Kansas, Indiana, New Hampshire, North Carolina, and Wisconsin have tried to stop family planning and cancer screening funds.

[72]Pam Belluck and Emily Ramshaw, "Women in Texas Losing Options for Health Care," *New York Times*, March 8, 2012.

[73]Kansas, Wisconsin, North Carolina, New Hampshire, Tennessee, Indiana, and Texas

[74]Arizona and North Carolina.

[75]*2012 Saw Second-Highest Abortion Restrictions Ever* (New York: Guttmacher Institute, 2013), 1.

[76]"The Politics of Religion," *New York Times*, May 27, 2012

[77]Julie Rover, "When Religious Rules and Women's Health Collide," *NPR News*, May 8, 2012.

[78]On June 28, 2013, U.S. District Judge Joe Heaton ruled that Hoppy Lobby would not be subjected to the $1.3 million in daily fines until their hearing scheduled for July 2013. See Associated Press, "Judge: Hobby Lobby Won't Have to Pay Fines," *NPR News*, June 28, 2013.

[79]Employment Division, Department of Human Resources of *Oregon v. Smith.*

[80]It should be noted that the Hyde Amendment bars the use of federal money for abortions except in the case of rape, incest, or when the life of the woman is endangered.

[81]"Sex Trafficking and the First Amendment," *New York Times*, April 3, 2012.

[82]The International Violence Against Women Act (I-VAWA) is proposed legislation intended to address violence against women through the foreign policy of the United States, specifically, by providing best practices that prevent violence, protect victims, and prosecute offenders.

[83]The Trafficking Victims Protection Act provides the U.S. government with the tools to combat worldwide and domestic trafficking of persons.

[84]Nicholas D. Kristof, "Is Delhi So Different From Steubenville?" *New York Times*, January 13, 2013.

[85]United Nations Resources for Speakers on Global Issues, "Ending Violence Against Women and Girls," see: http://www.un.org/en/globalissues/briefingpapers/endviol/index.shtml.

[86]Mayy El Sheikh and David D. Kirkpatrick, "Rise in Egypt Sex Assaults Sets Off Clash Over Blame," *New York Times*, March 26, 2013.

[87]United Nations Resources for Speakers on Global Issues, "Ending Violence Against Women and Girls," see: http://www.un.org/en/globalissues/briefingpapers/endviol/index.shtml.

[88]Hiroko Tabuchi, "Japanese Politicians Reframes Comments on Sex Slavery," *New York Times*, May 27, 2013.

[89]Gardiner Harris, "India's New Focus on Rape Shows Only the Surface of Women's Perils," *New York Times*, January 13, 2013.

[90]United Nations Resources for Speakers on Global Issues, "Ending Violence Against Women and Girls," see: http://www.un.org/en/globalissues/briefingpapers/endviol/index.shtml.

[91]Rod Nordland, "Moral 'Crimes' Land Afghan Women in Jail," *New York Time*, March 29, 2013; Graham Bowley, "Afghan Prosecutors Faces Criticism for Her Pursuit of 'Moral Crimes,'" *New York Times*, December 29, 2012.

[92]Meghan Davidson Ladly, "Defying Parents, Some Pakistani Women Risk All to Marry Whom They Choose," *New York Times*, September 12, 2012.

[93]Kyle Almond, "Malala's Global Voice Stronger than Ever," *CNNWorld*, June 17, 2013.

[94]"Pakistan Blast Kills Female Students," *BBC News*, June 15, 2013.

[95]United States Department of State, *Trafficking in Persons Report* (Washington, DC: Department of State, 2012) 7, 45.

[96]Suzanne Daley, "In Spain, Enslaved by a Boom in Brothel Tourism," *New York Times*, April 6, 2012.

[97]Howard W. French, "A Village Grows Rich Of Its Main Export: Its Daughters," *New York Times*, January 5, 2005.

[98]United States Department of State *Trafficking in Persons Report*, 8.

[99]United Nations Resources for Speakers on Global Issues, "Ending Violence Against Women and Girls," see: http://www.un.org/en/globalissues/briefingpapers/endviol/index.shtml.

[100]Juan Forero, "Acid Attacks in Colombia Reflect Rage," *Washington Post*, August 3, 2012.

[101]Iran, Russia, and the Vatican failed in their attempt in excluding the language that appears as paragraph 14 of the 2013 document for *The Elimination and Prevention of all Forms of Violence against Women and Girls*.

[102]"Unholy Alliance," *New York Times*, March 11, 2013.

[103]Catherine Rampell, "U.S. Women on the Rise as Family Breadwinners," *New York Times*, May 29, 2013.

[104]Lectures on Genesis, Luther's Works, I.

[105]Miguel A. De La Torre, "Beyond Machismo: A Cuban Case Study," *Sexuality and the Sacred: Sources for Theological Reflection*, 2nd ed. (Louisville: Westminster John Knox Press, 2010), 222.

[106]Mary Daly, *Beyond God the Father: Toward a Philosophy of Women's Liberation* (Boston: Beacon, 1973) 19.

[107]Paul Tillich and Paul Ricoeur assert that one can only speak of, or describe God through the use of symbols, connecting the meaning of one thing recognized by a given community that is comprehensible (i.e., father) with another thing that is beyond our ability to fully understand (i.e., God). See Ricoeur, *Interpretation Theory*, 1976, and Tillich, *Theology of Culture*, 1959. As important as symbols are to better grasp the incomprehensible essence of the Divine, they are incapable of exhausting the reality of God. To take symbolic language literally (i.e., God is exclusively male or female) leads to the absurd (i.e., God has a penis or vagina) and borders on idolatry (the creation of hierarchies in relationships by who is closer to the Divine ideal).

[108]Miguel A. De La Torre, *A Lily Among the Thorns: Imagining a New Christian Sexuality* (San Francisco: Jossey-Bass, 2007), 16–17.

[109]Elizabeth Grosz, *Jacques Lacan: A Feminist Interpretation* (London: Routledge, 1990), 115–45.

[110]Miguel A. De La Torre, "Mad Men, Competitive Women, and Invisible Hispanics," In *Journal of Feminist Studies in Religion* 28, no. 1 (Spring, 2012): 125.

[111]For example, in the *Gospel of Mary*, Mary of Magdala is referred to as the Apostle of the Apostles, specifically for her rousing sermon to the despondent disciples after Christ's ascension.

[112]Historically, men have argued that this hierarchy is the divine order of things. Others maintain that the man and woman being naked yet feeling no shame (Gen. 2:25) is the correct pre-Fall divine order of things and the verse stating that the man will rule over the woman (Gen. 3:16) refers to the consequence of sin, not the will of God.

[113]De La Torre, *A Lily Among the Thorns* , 18–22.

[114]*On Married Life*, Weimarer Ausgabe, X:2 .

[115]De La Torre, *A Lily Among the Thorns*, 22–24.

[116]Clement of Alexandria, *Christ the Educator*, II:10:95.

[117]De La Torre, *A Lily Among the Thorns*, 24–27.

[118] *Summa Theologica* 1:92:1.

[119]De La Torre, *A Lily Among the Thorns*, 27–29.

[120]The Apparel of Women, I:1:2.

[121]Edward Wong, "Forced to Abort, Chinese Woman Under Pressure, *New York Times*, June 27, 2012.

[122]Ma Jian, "China's Brutal One-Child Policy," *New York Times*, May 21, 2013.

[123]Jennifer Steihauer, "House Rejects Bill to Ban Sex-Selective Abortions," *New York Times*, June 1, 2012.

[124]Associated Press, "One Region in Myanmar Limits Births of Muslims," *New York Times*, May 25, 2013.

[125]Iowa: Court Upholds Firing of Woman Whose Boss Found Her Attractive," *New York Times*, December 22, 2012.

[126]Alissa J. Rubin, "Painful Payment for Afghan Debt: A Daughter, 6," *New York Times*, April 1, 2013.

[127]Alissa J. Rubin, "Afghan Who Agreed to Trade His Daughter to End a Debt Says It Was Paid," *New York Times*, April 2, 2013.

[128]Other Latin American countries with total bans on abortions are Chile and Nicaragua.

[129]Karla Zabludovsky, "A Salvadoran at Risk Tests Abortion Law," *New York Times*, May 28, 2013.
[130]Karla Zabludovsky and Gene Palumbo, "Salvadoran Court Denies Abortion to Ailing Woman," *New York Times*, May 29, 2013.
[131]Karla Zabludovsky, "A High-Risk Pregnancy Is Terminated. But Was It an Abortion?" *New York Times*, June 4, 2013.

Chapter 11: Open Mind, Faithful Heart

[1]Review of Bergoglio, Jorge Mario, (Pope Francis). *Open Mind, Faithful Heart: Reflections on Following Jesus*. Trans. Joseph V. Owens, SJ. New York: Crossroad Publishing Co., 2013. Originally published in the *Journal of the American Academy of Religion* 82, no. 2 (Spring 2014): 548–51. In the midst of global praises concerning the Pope's liberationist call to stand in solidarity with the oppressed, this book review argues that the Pope remains complicit with oppressive structures, specifically sexism.

Chapter 12: Lot's Wife

[1]Originally published as an op-ed in *Ethics Daily* on June 17, 2010. The op-ed challenges how Lot's wife been historically interpreted—as unfaithful.

Chapter 13: Sarah

[1]Originally published in *Genesis: Belief: A Theological Commentary on the Bible* (Louisville: Westminster John Knox Press, 2011), 206–10. This exegesis of the biblical text recognizes how in spite of so-called "biblical marriage," Sarah, the matriarch of the faith, was betrayed.
[2]Nina Bernstein, "Immigration Officer Guilty in Sexual Coercion Case," *New York Times*, April 14, 2010.
[3]Very Rev. James Alberione, S.S.P., S.T.D., *Woman: Her Influence and Zeal as an Aid to the Priesthood*, trans. Daughters of St. Paul (Boston: St. Paul Editions, 1964), 40.
[4]Nina Bernstein, "An Agent, A Green Card, and a Demand for Sex," *New York Times*, March 21, 2008.

Chapter 14: Dinah

[1]Originally published in *Genesis: Belief: A Theological Commentary on the Bible* (Louisville: Westminster Knox Press, 2011), 285-93. This exegesis of the biblical text wrestles with the sexual abuse of rape and the deafening silence of God in the midst of this abuse.
[2]Joy A. Schroeder, *Dinah's Lament: The Biblical Legacy of Sexual Violence on Christian Interpretations* (Minneapolis: Fortress Press, 2007), 51.
[3]Athalya Brenner, *I Am…Biblical Women Tell Their Own Stories* (Minneapolis: Fortress Press, 2005), 25.
[4]Lyn Bechtel, "What if Dinah Is Not Raped (Genesis 24)," *Journal for the Study of the Old Testament* 62 (June, 1994): 19–36.
[5]Eight out of every ten rape cases involved a perpetrator known by the victim, as per a Department of Justice report. See Patricia Tjaden and Nancy Thoennes, *Full Report of the Prevalence, Incidence, and Consequences of Violence Against Women Survey* (Washington D.C.: U.S. Department of Justice, 2000) 1–2.
[6]Bava Batra 15b.
[7]*Rabbah* 19:12. 67

Chapter 15: Medieval Witches

[1]Coauthored with Albert Hernandez, this chapter section was originally published in *The Quest for the Historical Satan* (Minneapolis: Fortress Press, 2011), 157–69. Today's abuse of women can be traced to the witch crazes and trails of the medieval age where women were perceived to be close with the devil.
[2]Heinrich Kramer, and Jakob Sprenger, *Malleus Maleficarum*, ed. and trans. Montague Summers (New York: Dover Publications, 1971 [1486?]), 158–59.
[3]Gareth J. Medway, *Lure of the Sinister: The Unnatural History of Satanism* (New York: New York University, 2001), 56.

⁴Alain Boureau, *Satan the Heretic: The Birth of Demonology in the Medieval West*, trans. Teresa Lavender Fagan (Chicago: University of Chicago Press, 2006), 93–118.

⁵Julio Caro Baroja, *The World of the Witches*, trans. O.N.V. Glendinning (Chicago: University of Chicago Press, 1965 [1961]), 17, 21, 65.

⁶Pope Innocent VIII, *Summis Desiderantes*, 1484.

⁷Brian P. Levack, *The Witch-Hunt in Early Modern Europe* (London: Longman Group, 1987), 19–22.

⁸Kramer and Sprenger, *Malleus Maleficarum*, 42.

⁹Ibid., 43-44. The misogyny that undergirds the *Malleus Maleficarum*, especially Part 1, Question 6 (41–54), helps explain the sadistic persecution of women that took place during the late medieval witch hunts. One is also struck with how many pages are dedicated to issues dealing with sexuality.

¹⁰Tertullian, *The Apparel of Women*, I: 1:2

¹¹Accused witches were usually stripped naked before their male judges who were looking for the devil's concealed mark made upon her body to signify their pact. The mark was usually on her left side and at times consisted of a claw mark.

¹²Kramer and Sprenger, *Malleus Maleficarum*, 11.

¹³Ibid., 238.

¹⁴Ibid., 77, 82.

¹⁵Ibid., 8.

¹⁶Ibid., 89–91.

¹⁷Ibid., 118.

¹⁸Thomas Aquinas, *Summa Theologica*, I: 51, 3, 6.

¹⁹Augustine, *De Trinitate*, III

²⁰Kramer and Sprenger, *Malleus Maleficarum*, 114.

²¹Ibid., 134.

²²Martin Luther, *A Commentary of St. Paul's Epistle to the Galatians*, ed. Edwinus London; trans. George Roerer (London: Matthews and Leigh, 1807 [1531]), 126.

²³John Calvin, *Institutes*, I: XIV: 18.

²⁴Ibid.

²⁵Elaine Pagels, *The Origin of Satan* (New York: Vintage Books, 1996), 180.

²⁶Martin Luther, *Weimar Edition*, XVI, 551

²⁷Martin Luther, A Commentary of St. Paul's Epistle to the Galatians.

²⁸John Calvin, *Institutes*, I: XIV: 17

²⁹Kramer and Sprenger, *Malleus Maleficarum*, 116.

³⁰John Calvin, *Institutes*, I: XIV: 18

³¹René Girard, *The Scapegoat*, trans. Yvonne Freccero (Baltimore: The Johns Hopkins University Press, 1986), 12.

³²René Girard, *Things Hidden since the Foundation of the World*, trans. Stephen Bann and Michael Metteer (London: Athlone Press, 1987), 23–30.

³³Girard, *The Scapegoat*, 15.

³⁴Ibid., 12–15.

³⁵For a more complete analysis of how Girard's concept of scapegoat applies to the marginalized communities, see Miguel A. De La Torre, *Liberating Jonah: Forming an Ethics of Reconciliation* (Maryknoll, NY: Orbis Books, 2007), 69–72.

³⁶Medway, *Lure of the Sinister*, 73.

Chapter 16: Beyond Machismo

¹Originally published in the *Journal of the Society of Christian Ethics* under its previous name *The Annual of the Society of Christian Ethics* 19 (1999): 213–33. The article was written when I was a graduate student and represents both my first presentation at my guild and my first peer-reviewed journal article.

²Edward W. Said, *Culture and Imperialism* (New York: Vintage Books, 1994), 14, 96, 228–30.

³According to Shute, sexism names social structures and systems where the "actions, practices, and use of laws, rules and customs limit certain activities of one sex, but do not limit those same activities of other people of the other sex." See Sara Shute, *Sexist Language*

and Sexism, Sexist Language: A Modern Philosophical Analysis, ed. Mary Vetterling-Braggin (Boston: Littlefield, Adams, and Company, 1981), 27.

⁴*Mujerista* Theology and Latina Feminist Theology are a response to the sexism existing within our Hispanic community and to the racial, ethnic, and class prejudice existing within an Anglo feminist community that ignores the fundamental ways white women benefit from the oppression of women of color. These Latina theologies attempt to find a Hispanic community that obliterates those institutions that "generate massive poverty, systematic death, and immense inhumane suffering" so that all, women and men, can find fullness of "life, justice, and liberation." See the works of Pilar Aquino and Ada María Isasi-Díaz. Absent from the discourse is the privileged position occupied by Exilic Cuban Latinas. Obviously Exilic Cuban women still face discrimination, especially outside of Dade County. But the existence of an ethnic enclave facilitated Exilic Cuban women in obtaining higher status jobs otherwise unavailable. Recently arriving Latinas often obtain employment characterized as dangerous, low paying, and degrading. This was also the case with Cuban women arriving in the 1960s. Cuban women were able to gain employment faster than their male counterparts, because the market in unskilled jobs preferred women, who could be given lower wages. By 1970, Exilic Cuban women constituted the largest proportionate group of working women in the United States. Their role as wage-earners was more a response to economic survival than a response to the feminist movement for equality. See María Cristina García, *Havana USA: Cuban Exiles and Cuban Americans in South Florida, 1959–1994* (Berkeley: University of California, 1996), 109. Eventually, the establishment of the economic ethnic enclave of Miami shielded more recent arrivals from the predicament still faced by other non-Cuban Latinas. Among some Exilic Cuban women, status and social prestige are measured by the ability to hire *una negrita* (a black girl—regardless of age) or *una india* (a *mestiza*) to come and clean house. Missing from a *mujerista* discourse is how race and class impacts intra-Latina location and oppression.

⁵*Machismo* has recently become a popularized term. Although it is used synonymously with sexism, it originally referred to a celebration of conventional masculinities. The term *machismo,* unlike *machista,* is neither solely associated with the oppression of women, nor solely used in a pejorative sense. *Machismo* described the values associated with being a man, a *macho.* Similarly, the celebration of female attributes is known as *hembrism.* See Ian Lumsden, *Machos, Maricones and Gays: Cuba and Homosexuality* (Philadelphia: Temple University Press, 1996), 217. A popular Cuban saying is *"soy tan hembra como tú macho"* (I am as much woman as you are man).

⁶Antonio Maceo, Cuba's black general during the Wars for Independence, not only symbolized the hopes of Cuba's blacks, but embodied the *macho* qualities of honor, bravery, patriotism, and the best that Cubans can hope to be. His exploits on and off the battlefield served as testimony to his testosterone creating the Cuban compliment *"Como Maceo"* (Like Maceo) said while upwardly cupping one's hand as if to weigh the enormity (of one's *cojones*). Blacks who demonstrate white qualities of *machismo* may receive admiration and praise even while being denied earned positions of power and privilege within Cuban society. Likewise, women who demonstrate *macho* attributes will receive praise for their manliness while being denied positions of responsibility. For example, José Martí, father of Cuban independence, honored Maceo's mother, Mariana Grajales Maceo, for impressive procreation of male patriots while glossing over, if not totally ignoring the efforts of Cuban women of all colors who raised funds, aided refugees, outfitted insurgent forces, attracted Anglo support, fought as *mambisas* (female freedom fighters), and served as spies and couriers. Women in *Cuba Libre* were to serve as a repository of inspiration, beauty, purity and morality lest the unleashed powers of female passion generate the destructive passion of men. For a brief history of Martí's attitudes toward women and their role in *Cuba Libre,* see Nancy A. Hewitt, "Engendering Independence: Las Patriotas of Tampa and the Social Vision of José Martí," *José Martí in the United States: The Florida Experience,* ed. Louis A. Pérez Jr. (Tempe: Arizona State University Center for Latin American Studies, 1995), 23–32.

⁷Elizabeth Grosz, *Jacques Lacan: A Feminist Interpretation* (London: Routledge, 1990), 115–45.

⁸According to Fidel Castro, "[Revolutionary Cuba] needed strong men to fight wars, sportsmen, men who had no psychological weakness." Additionally, in a 1965 interview

with *El Mundo,* Samuel Feijoo, one of Cuba's most prominent revolutionary intellectuals stated, "No homosexual [represents] the revolution, which is a matter for men, of fists and not of feathers, of courage and not of trembling." See Lumsden, *Machos, Maricones and Gays,* 53–54, 61. Likewise, Exilic Cubans consider *patria* building the task of real men of valor. During an interview with the *Miami Herald,* Miriam Arocena, wife of a convicted Exilic Cuban terrorist responsible for several bombings, told the reporter, "This [her husband's terrorist actions] is a thing for men of valor, not for weaklings like you." See Joan Didion, *Miami* (New York: Simon and Schuster, 1987), 99.

[9]Between 1965 and 1968, thousands of artists, intellectuals, hippies, university students, Jehovah's Witnesses, and homosexuals were abducted by the State Secret Police and interned, without trial, in Military Units for Assistance to Production (U.M.A.P.), reeducation labor camps. Because they were dissidents from the normative point of view, they were constructed as homosexuals as illustrated by the slogan posted at the camp's entrance: "Work will make men of you."

[10]Ruth Behar, Introduction, *Bridges to Cuba,* ed. Ruth Behar (Ann Arbor: University of Michigan Press, 1995), 12.

[11]Mirta Mulhare de la Torre (no relation) (doctoral dissertation, University of Pittsburgh, 1969), who studied Cuban sexuality, wrote: "The dominant mode of behavior for *el macho,* the male, [was] the sexual imperative…A man's supercharged sexual physiology [placed] him on the brink of sexual desire at all times and at all places." See Lumsden, *Machos, Maricones and Gays,* 31.

[12]Gustavo Pérez Firmat, *Life on the Hyphen: The Cuban-American Way* (Austin: University of Texas Press, 1994), 41–45.

[13]Frantz Fanon, *Black Skin, White Masks,* trans. Charles Lam Markmann (New York: Grove Press, 1967), 63.

[14]For Fanon, the fantasy of the colonized man is to occupy the space of power and privilege belonging to the colonizer. McClintock points out that the desire of the colonizer differs between the man and the woman. The white male has the luxury of *seizing* any woman of color, while the white woman who sexually engages the man of color *accepts* him. Instead of seizing, it is giving. See Anne McClintock, *Imperial Leather: Race, Gender and Sexuality in the Colonial Contest* (New York: Routledge, 1995), 362.

[15]For a more detailed discussion on the construction of Cuban homosexuality, see Lourdes Arguelles and B. Ruby Rich, "Homosexuality, Homophobia, and Revolution: Notes Toward an Understanding of the Cuban Lesbian and Gay Male Experience," in *Hidden from History: Reclaiming the Gay and Lesbian Past,* ed. Martin Bauml Duberman, Martha Vicinius and George Chauncey (Markham, Ontario: New American Library, 1989); Henk van de Boogaard and Kathelijine van Kammen, "Cuba: We Cannot Jump over Our Own Shadow," in IGA Pink Book, 1985: *A Global View of Lesbian and Gay Oppression and Liberation* (Amsterdam: COC, 1985); Lumsden, *Machos, Maricones and Gays;* and Flavio Risech, "Political and Cultural Cross-Dressing: Negotiating a Second Generation Cuban-American identity," in *Bridges to Cuba: Puentes a Cuba,* ed. Ruth Behar (Ann Arbor: University of Michigan Press, 1995).

[16]Missing from this analysis is the space occupied by lesbians, known by Cubans as *tortilleras* (derogatory term translated as dyke). While *maricones* constitute a "scandal" as men forsaking their manhood, *tortilleras* are usually ignored due to the overall machismo of the society that grounds its sexuality on the macho's desires, repressing finite sexuality. Tolerance of lesbians is partly due to their unimportance to the macho's construction of sexuality. They simply have no space in the dominant construction. For lesbians, as well as homosexual men, the adage "*se dice nada, se hace todo* (say nothing, do every)" remains the accepted closeted norm of the Cuban community.

[17]Carlos Franqui, *Family Portrait with Fidel: A Memoir,* trans. Alfred MacAdam (New York: Random House, 1984), 150.

[18]Several postcolonialist scholars who analyze the gendering of nationhood and land are Peter Mason, *Deconstructing America: Representations of the Others* (New York: Routledge, 1990); Anne McClintock, *Imperial Leather: Race, Gender, and Sexuality in the Colonial Contest* (New York: Routledge, 1995); David Spurr, *The Rhetoric of Empire: Colonial Discourse in Journalism, Travel Writing and Imperial Administration* (Durham: Duke University Press, 1993); and Tzvetan Todorov, *The Conquest of America: The Question of the Other,* trans. Richard Howard (New York: Harper & Row, 1984).

[19]Spaniards' understanding of racism was unlike the North American that passed laws prohibiting racial mixing. For Spaniards sexual relations were as natural as breathing or eating. Spaniard men took indigenous women as bed-partners, concubines, or wives. The children of these unions, claimed by the Spaniards as their own, took their father's name. It is estimated that by 1514, 40 percent of Spanish colonizers had indigenous wives. By 1570, in accordance with the Council of Trent elevation of marriage to a sacrament, the Crown forbade married men from traveling to the Americas for more than six months without their family. This resulted in more single men heading west, stimulating a rise of a miscegenate population. See Magnus Mörner, *Race Mixture in the History of Latin America* (Boston: Little, Brown, 1967), 35–52; Carl Ortwin Sauer, *The Early Spanish Main* (Berkeley: University of California Press, 1966), 199.

[20]Mörner, *Race Mixture in the History of Latin America*, 35–52.

[21]Todorov, *The Conquest of America*, 48–49.

[22]Ibid., 16

[23]McClintock, *Imperial Leather*, 30.

[24]The entry in his travel diary for Thursday, October 11 reads: Immediately [the morning of Friday the 12th, after land was sited at 2:00 a.m.] they saw naked people, and the admiral went ashore in the armed boat…The admiral called two captains…and said they should bear witness and testimony how he, before them all, took possession of the island…They [the land's inhabitants] all go naked as their mothers bore them, and the women also…they were very well built, with very handsome bodies and very good faces. See Christopher Columbus, *The Journal of Christopher Columbus*, trans. Cecil Jane (New York: Clarkson N. Potter, 1960), 22–24.

[25]Columbus records indigenous accounts about an island called Matino, believed to be entirely peopled by women. See Columbus, *The Journal*, 150–51. Rather than visiting it, Columbus returns to Spain, possibly indicating that he and his crew have had their fill of native, erotic women.

[26]Mason, *Deconstructing America*, 170.

[27]Luis N. Rivera Pagán, *A Violent Evangelism: The Political and Religious Conquest of the Americas* (Louisville: Westminister/John Knox Press, 1992), 11.

[28]Mason, *Deconstructing America*, 56–57.

[29]Francisco López de Gómez, *Historia General de las Indias (1552), Biblioteca de Autores Españoles*, ed. Enrique de Vedía (Madrid: Ediciones Atlas, 1946) 2:155.

[30]Pagden also quotes Cieza de León who wrote, "Many of them (as I have been reliably informed) publicly and openly practiced the nefarious sin of sodomy." Also, he quotes Gonzalo Fernández de Oviedo as stating, "[They even wore jewels depicting] the diabolical and nefarious act of sodomy." See Anthony Pagden, *The Fall of Natural Man: The American Indian and the Origins of Comparative Ethnology* (Cambridge: Cambridge University Press, 1982), 174–76.

[31]Mason, *Deconstructing America*, 67, 173.

[32]Pagden, *The Fall of Natural Man*, 135.

[33]Sven Lovén, *Origins of the Tainan Culture, West Indies*, trans. anonymous (Göteborg: Flanders Bokryckeri Akfiebolag, 1935), 529.

[34]Diana Iznaga, "Introduction," Fernando Ortiz, *Los Negros Curros* (La Habana: Editorial de Ciencias Sociales, 1986), xviii–xix.

[35]Mason, *Deconstructing America*, 56.

[36]Bartolomé Las Casas, *History of the Indies* superiority of Protestantism over Catholicism for Anglos, covering attention from the treatment of the indigenous population of North America. Regardless of how the Black Legend was constructed for Anglo consumption, it cannot be denied that within one lifetime, an entire culture of a people, developed upon the Islands of the Caribbean, was exterminated. Those few Taínos who physically survived were assimilated within the dominant Spanish culture.

[37]Pagán, *A Violent Evangelism*, 49.

[38]Las Casas, *History of the Indies*, 156.

[39]In spite of *machismo* positioning the black man as a woman, it must be noted that within Cuban African culture, sexism also is prevalent. Ibos girls are taught to obey and serve men while boys learn to look down at their mothers. The *machista* ethos of the *abakuá* only allow intercourse if the man is on top and is the only one who is active. See Lumsden, *Machos, Maricones and Gays*, 47, 221-22; Enrique Sosa, *El carabalí* (La Habana:

Editorial Letras Cubanas, 1984), 50–51; and Manuel Martínez Casanova and Nery Gómez Abréu, *La sociedad secret abakuá* (Santa Clara: University Central de Las Villas, n.d.), 16–17. The *bantú* uses the word "man" to solely apply to the members of their nation. All other Africans are not men. See Fernando Ortiz, *El engaño de las razas* (La Habana: Editorial De Ciencias Sociales, 1975), 37.

[40]Ortiz, *El engaño de las razas*, 60, 88.

[41]Lumsden, *Machos, Maricones and Gays*, 50.

[42]Franklin W. Knight, *Slave Society in Cuba During the Nineteenth Century* (Madison: University of Wisconsin Press, 1970), 76–78; Louis A Pérez, *Essays on Cuban History: Historiography and Research* (Gainesville: University Press of Florida, 1995), 87.

[43]White Cubans constructed an illness that could only be cured by having sex with a black woman. Former Cuban slave Esteban Montejo wrote: There was one type of sickness the whites picked up, a sickness of the veins and male organs. It could only be got rid of with black women; if the man who had it slept with a Negress he was cured immediately. See Esteban Montejo, *The Autobiography of a Runaway Slave*, ed. Miguel Barnet, trans. Jocasta Innes (New York: Pantheon Books, 1968), 42.

[44]Ortiz, *El engaño de las razas*, 325–30.

[45]Quoting Gunnar Myrdal, *An American Dilemma*, Ortiz shows how the myth of the black man's overly extended penis (when compared to the white man) and the white woman's small clitoris (when compared to the black woman) creates a need for precautions least the white woman be damaged, as well as spoiled. See Ortiz, *El engaño de las razas*, 87–88.

[46]See Fanon, *Black Skin*, 57–59, 170. Fanon continues by asking: Is the lynching of the Negro not a sexual revenge? We know how much of sexuality there is in all cruelties, tortures, beatings. One has only to reread a few pages of Marquis de Sade to be easily convinced of the fact (Ibid., 159).

[47]Lourdes Casal, "Race Relations in Contemporary Cuba," *The Cuban Reader: The Making of a Revolutionary Society*, ed. Philip Brenner, William M. LeoGrande, Donna Rich, and Daniel Siegel (New York: Grove Press, 1989), 472.

[48]I use the word *Coolie* to refer to the Chinese laborer because this word best describes their social location of oppression. The word *Coolie* is composed of two Chinese characters, *coo* and *lie*. *Coo* is defined as "suffering with pain;" *lie* means "laborer." Hence the Coolie is the "laborer who suffers with pain," adequately describing their condition in Cuba.

[49]The first shipment of Coolies by Waldrop and Company sailed from Amoy on February 7, 1853, with 803 Chinese and arrived in La Habana with only 480. In 1859, the Spanish frigate *Gravina* embarked with 352 Coolies and arrived with 82. See Duvon Clough Corbitt, *A Study of the Chinese in Cuba, 1847–1947* (Wilmore, KY: Asbury College, 1971), 16, 54. For a graphic documented description of the suffering and humiliation caused by their brutal treatment by "civilized" Cuban, see Ch'ên Lanpin, *Chinese Emigration: The Cuba Commission Report of the Commission sent by China to Ascertain the Condition of Chinese Coolies in Cuba*, trans A. MacPherson and A. Huber (Shanghai: The Imperial Maritime Customs Press, 1876); also Rebecca J. Scott, *Slave Emancipation in Cuba: The Transition to Free Labor, 1860–1899* (Princeton: Princeton University Press, 1985), 3, 124.

[50]Hugh Thomas, *Cuba: The Pursuit of Freedom* (New York: Harper & Row, 1971), 188.

[51]By 1942, the Chinese Consulate in Cuba had 18,484 Chinese registered, of which 56 were women. Social and legal regulations forbade African (or white) and Asian intermarriage. Duvon Clough Corbitt, *A Study of the Chinese in Cuba, 1847–1947* (Wilmore, KY: Asbury College, 1971), 114–15.

[52]Fernando Ortiz, *Los negros brujos: Apuntes para un estudio de etnología criminal* (Miami: New House Publishers, 1973), 19.

[53]Verena Martinez-Alier, *Marriage, Class and Color in Nineteenth Century Cuba: A Study of Racial Attitudes and Sexual Values in a Slave Society* (London: Cambridge University Press, 1974), 79. Early during Castro's regime, China sent over a shipment of "socialist" condoms. *Machos* refused to use them claiming they were "too small," thus contributing to both the myth of the Chinese's small penis and to a national rise in pregnancy. See Franqui, *Family Portrait with Fidel*, 146.

[54]Ignacio Ellacuría, "The Crucified People," *Mysterium Liberationis: Fundamental Concepts of Liberation Theology*, ed. Ignacio Ellacuría and Jon Sobrino, trans. Phillip Berryman and Robert R. Barr (Maryknoll, NY: Orbis Books, 1993), 580–81.

[55]Jon Sobrino, *Jesus the Liberator: A Historical-Theological Reading of Jesus of Nazareth,* trans. P. Burns and F. McDonagh (Maryknoll, NY: Orbis Books, 1993), 259–60.

[56]Knight, *Slave Society in Cuba During the Nineteenth Century,* 88–89; James S. and Judith E. Olson, *Cuban Americans: From Trauma to Triumph* (New York: Twayne Publishers, 1995), 13; and Pérez, *Essays on Cuban History,* 135, 152.

[57]Robert L. Paquette, *Sugar is Made with Blood: The Conspiracy of La Escalera and the Conflict between Empires over Slavery in Cuba* (Middletown, CT: Wesleyan University Press, 1988), 48, 91.

[58]The lyrics of a slow rumba sung in Matanzas by slaves after emancipation serve as a hidden-transcript describing the new economic reality for both the ex-slaves and the poor whites:

En el año 44, yo 'taba en el ingenio
In the year '44 (year of a preemptive violent repression toward a supposed slave revolt) I was on the sugar mill
En el año '44, negra, yo 'taba en el ingenio
In the year '44, *negra,* I was on the sugar mill
Ahora, ahora
Now, now,
negro con blanco, chapea cañaverá.
Black with white weeding in the cane field.

See Rebecca J. Scott, *Slave Emancipation in Cuba: The Transition to Free Labor, 1860–1899* (Princeton: Princeton University Press, 1985), 255.

[59]Pérez, *Essays on Cuban History,* 39.

[60]José Martí, *"Manufacturer's" Do We Want Cuba? Our America by José Martí: Writings on Latin America and the Struggle for Cuban Independence,* ed. Philip S. Foner, trans. Elinor Randall, Juan de Onís, and Roslyn Held Foner (New York: The Monthly Review Press, 1977), 229.

[61]Martí found it necessary to defend Cuban *machismo.* In *A Vindication of Cuba,* he responds:

Because our half-breeds and city-bred young men are generally of delicate physique, of suave courtesy, and ready words, hiding under the glove that polishes the poem the hand that fells the foe are we to be considered as the *Manufacturer* does consider us an "effeminate" people?…These "effeminate" Cubans had once courage enough, in the face of a hostile government, to carry on their left arms for a week the mourning-band for Lincoln. (Ibid., 236.) In an interesting pre-Lacanian analysis, Martí accuses the United States of transferring negative characteristics onto Hispanics so as to define the Anglo subject "I" through the negation of the Hispanic Object. In *The Truth About the United States,"* Martí writes: Those structural qualities which, for their constancy and authority, demonstrate two useful truths to our America: the crude, uneven, and decadent character of the United States, and the continuous existence there of all the violence, discord, immorality, and disorder [are] blamed upon the peoples of Spanish America. See *idem, The Truth about the United States, Inside the Monster by José Martí: Writings on the United States and American Imperialism,* ed. Philip S. Foner, trans. Elinor Randall, Luis A. Baralt, Juan de Onís, and Roslyn Held Foner (New York: Monthly Review Press, 1975), 54.

However, Martí is also guilty of seeing the Cuban Other as effeminate. In a May 2, 1895 letter "To the New York Herald," *Our America,* he wrote, "The harsh and jealous Spanish possessions allied 400 years ago against the harsh but effeminate Moor." (See Ibid., 429).

Chapter 17: Rebekah

[1]Originally published in *Genesis: Belief: A Theological Commentary on the Bible* (Louisville: Westminster John Knox Press, 2011), 226–32, the story explores how matriarchy can be a biblical alternative to patriarchal structures.

[2]Barbara J. Essex, *Bad Girls of the Bible: Exploring Women of Questionable Virtue* (Cleveland: United Church Press, 1999), 24–25.

Chapter 18: Tamar

[1]Originally published in *Genesis: Belief: A Theological Commentary on the Bible* (Louisville: Westminster John Knox Press, 2011), 305–14. The text presents Tamar as a trickster who seeks justice through prostitution.

[2]Thomas Aquinas, *Summa Theologica* II:2

[3]Johanna W. H. Bos, "Out of the Shadows: Genesis 38; Judges 4:17–22; Ruth 3," in *Reasoning with the Foxes: Female Wit in a World of Male Power,* ed. J. Cheryl Exum and Johanna W. H. Bos, *Semeia* 42 (1988): 37–67.

[4]L. William Countryman, *Dirt, Greed & Sex: Sexual Ethics in the New Testament and their Implications for Today* (Philadelphia: Fortress Press, 1988), 164.

[5]Sir James George Frazer, *The Golden Bough: A Study in Magic and Religion* (New York: The Macmillian Company, 1951), 12.

[6]Richard Lewinsohn, *A History of Sexual Customs,* trans. Alexander Mayce (New York: Fawcett Premier Book, 1958), 69, 135.

[7]Augustine, *On the Good of Marriage,* 8, 12.

[8]Aquinas, *Summa Theologica,* II:2.

[9]Richard Lewinsohn, *A History of Sexual Customs,* trans. Alexander Mayce (New York: Fawcett Premier Books, 1958), 157.

Chapter 19: When the Bible Is Used for Hate

[1]During my tenure at Hope College, I would write bimonthly editorials in the *Holland Sentinel,* a local newspaper with a daily circulation of about 10,500. The first op-ed, *When the Bible is Used for Hate,* was published on February 1, 2005. The editorial criticized James Dobson, founder of Focus on the Family, for a speech he gave in Washington, D.C., where Dobson claimed the cartoon character SpongeBob SquarePants was gay friendly. Within a week, Dobson responded to my editorial with his own, ending his op-ed with "I do worry…about the students who sit under his [De La Torre] liberal tutelage at Hope College. I'm glad my son and daughter are not among them." A firestorm erupted with both my institution pressuring me to resign my tenure and a major portion of the community calling for my ouster, demanding that I apologize. On March 15, 2005, I did apologize, but not to them. The second op-ed *An Apology to Homosexuals* attempted to raise the community consciousness. After months of turmoil, I resigned my tenure and left Hope College after the president of the institution wrote in a March 14, 2005, letter to me stating: "Hope is dependent on enrollment and gifts to drive the college financially…you [have] lost my trust and confidence." The continuous community harassment finally led to the Holland Sentinel stating on May 21, 2005: "The resignation of Hope College professor…has generated more letters to this page than any other topic in 2005…we do not intend to publish any more letters on the subject." A few months afterwards, and a few days after resigning, I accepted a position at the Iliff School of Theology in Denver.

Chapter 20: From Basher to Ally

[1]This chapter appeared in *Out of the Shadow and into the Light: Struggling with the Sin of Heterosexuality* (St. Louis: Chalice Press, 2009), 59–75, a book I edited based on a 2007 conference held in Colorado Springs funded by the Gill Foundation. I organized the conference to provide a forum to facilitate open discussion of gay and lesbian topics in the context of the Church and the Christian Bible. One could argue God has a sense of humor, as I organized the conference in the backyard of Focus on the Family, the organization most responsible for my relocation from Holland, Michigan to Denver, Colorado. My contribution to the discourse explored my own complicity with heterosexism.

[2]Marvin M. Ellison, "Practicing Safer Spirituality," in *Out of the Shadow and into the Light: Struggling with the Sin of Heterosexuality* ed. Miguel A. De La Torre (St. Louis: Chalice Press, 2009), 1–18.

[3]Martin Luther King, Jr., *Why We Can't Wait* (New York: A Mentor Book, 1964), 77.

[4]Edward W. Said, *Culture and Imperialism* (New York: Vintage Books, 1994), 96, 228–300.

[5]Jacques Lacan, Écrits: *Culture and Imperialism,* trans. Alan Sheridan (New York: W.W. Norton, 1977), 286.

[6]Marcella Althaus-Reid, *From Feminist Theology to Indecent Theology: Readings on Poverty, Sexual Identity and God* (London: SCM Press, 2004), 30–31.

[7]Ian Lumsden, *Machos, Maricones and Gays: Cuba and Homosexuality* (Philadelphia: Temple University Press, 1996), 31.

[8]Marvin Leiner, *Sexual Politics in Cuba: Machismo, Homosexuality, and AIDS* (Boulder: Westview Press, 1994), 22.

[9]Rafael L.Ramírez, *What it Means to be a Man: Reflections on Puerto Rican Masculinity*, trans. Rosa E. Casper (Piscataway, NJ: Rutgers University Press, 1999), 45.

[10]Paulo Freire, *Pedagogy of the Oppressed* trans. Myra Bergman Ramos (New York: Continuum, 1994), 28–31.

[11]Elizabeth Grosz, *Jacques Lacan: A Feminist Interpretation* (London: Routledge, 1990), 115–45.

[12]Lourdes Arguelles and B. Ruby Rich, "Homosexuality, Homophobia, and Revolution: Notes toward an Understanding of the Cuban Lesbian and Gay Male Experience, Part I," *Signs: Journal of Women in Culture and Society* 9, no. 4 (Summer 1984): 687.

[13]Reinaldo Arenas, *Before Night Falls* trans. Dolores M. Koch (New York: Viking, 1993), 280–81.

[14]Ibid., 108.

[15]This is not to assert that homosexuals do not face violence within the Hispanic community because of their orientation. Just as the Cuban poet Reinaldo Arenas faced persecution by the Castro government, so too have gays living in the United States experienced violence at the hands of the Latino/a community. For example, Manolo Gomez, who attempted to create a counter-organization to the mid-1970 Anita Bryant crusade against homosexuals, found himself fired from his job at a monthly periodical, and suffered a severe beating from unknown assailants. He eventually left Miami, Florida, fearing for his life. See Lourdes Arguelles and B. Ruby Rich, "Homosexuality, Homophobia, and Revolution: Notes toward an Understanding of the Cuban Lesbian and Gay Male Experience, Part II," *Signs: Journal of Women in Culture and Society* 11, no. 1 (Winter 1985): 127.

Chapter 21: The Bible

[1]This section is part of a bilingual book I wrote for Unid@s, The Human Rights Campaign, and Institute for Welcoming Resources. *A La Familia: Una Conversación Sobre Nuestras Familias, la Biblia, la Orientación Sexual y la Identidad de Género* (Human Rights Campaign, 2011), 66–83. The book, which is also available online (www.hrc.org/files/documents/A_La_Familia.pdf), was geared to a more conservative church audience to guide discussion in the event a family member "comes out" of the closet. Because the book is bilingual, different generations can read along and discuss its contents. This section deals with the biblical texts that have been used to condemn queer folk.

Chapter 22: Seeing Dark Bodies

[1]Originally published in *A Lily Among the Thorns: Imagining a New Christian Sexuality* (San Francisco: Jossey-Bass, 2007), 40–41, 43–47. This chapter section explores the interconnectedness of racism and Euro American sexual mores.

[2]bell hooks, *Ain't I a Woman: Black Women and Feminism* (Boston: South End Press, 1981), 28–29.

[3]Joe Holley and Christian Swezey, "Rape Accusation Against Lacrosse Players Roils Duke," *Washington Post*, March 30, 2006.

[4]U.S. Constitution, article 1, section 2.

[5]Esteban Montejo, *The Autobiography of a Runaway Slave*, ed. Miguel Barnet, trans. Jocasta Innes (New York: Pantheon Books, 1968), 42.

[6]Frantz Fanon, *Black Skin, White Masks* trans. Charles Lam Markmann (New York: Grove Press, 1967), 157–59, 170.

Chapter 23: Jesús: Racist? Sexist?

[1]Originally published in *The Politics of Jesús: A Hispanic Political Theology* (Lanham, MD: Rowman & Littlefield, 2015), 124–29. In our rush to deify Jesus, we seldom pause long

enough to struggle with some of the texts that prove to be more problematic, specifically those texts that seems to reveal a Jesús complicit with racism and sexism.

[2]Dan McLean, "Immigration's Tancredo's Top Topic," *New Hampshire Sunday News*, June 12, 2005.

[3]Leticia Guardiola-Sáenz, "Reading from Ourselves: Identity and Hermeneutics among Mexican-Americans Feminists," in *A Reader in Latina Feminist Theology: Religion and Justice* ed. María Pilar Aquino, Daisy L. Machado, and Jeanette Rodríguez (Austin: University of Texas Press, 2002), 94–95.

Chapter 24: Hollywood and Latino Men

[1]Both were originally published as op-eds on my blog *Our Lucha* (https://ourlucha. wordpress.com/about/). The first article, published on November 14, 2015, examined how Latino male bodies are constructed on the big screen, shaping reality for a white audience. The second article, published September 12, 2015, is connected to the first, for it explores how does one dress the male body to subvert the reality created for white audiences on the big screen.

[2]Cherríe Moraga, "La Güera," *This Bridge Called My Back: Writings by Radical Women of Color*, ed. Moraga, Cherríe and Gloria Anzaldúa (New York: Women of Color Press, 1981), 28.

[3]*Education & the Arts* 10, no. 8 (March 16, 2009): 1.

[4]Silvia Bellezza, Francesca Gino, and Anat Keinan, "The Red Sneakers Effect: Inferring Status and Competence from Signals of Nonconformity," *Journal of Consumer Research* 41, no. 1 (June 2014): 35.

[5]Fiona Blaikie, "Knowing Bodies: A Visual and Poetic Inquiry into the Professoriate," *International Journal of Education & the Arts* Vol. 10, No. 8 (March 16, 2009): 1.

[6]Roger Kimball, "Whose Enlightenment is It?" *The New Criterion* (April 1996): 4–5.

[7]Joseph Epstein. "Hats Off" *The Weekly Standard* 5, no. 9, (Nov 15, 1999): 4.

[8]Bellezza et. al, "The Red Sneakers Effect," 35–36.

[9]Elizabeth Wilson, *Adorned in Dreams*, (London: Virago, 1985), 2.

[10]Homi K. Bhabha, *The Location of Culture* (New York: Routledge, 1994), 32.

[11]Christopher Peterson, "Bow Ties and Other Signatures," *Psychology Today* (September 9, 2011).

[12]Glenn O'Brien, "Why the Bow Tie's Not for Schmucks," *Gentleman Quarterly* (2003).

[13]Nicholas Antongiavanni, *The Suit: A Machiavellian Approach to Men's Style* (New York: HarperBusiness, 2006), 143.

[14]James Owen Drife, "Bow? Wow!" *British Medical Journal* 307, no. 6909 (October 9, 1993): 943.

[15]Erika Engstrom, "Audiences' Perceptions of Sources' Credibility in a Television Interview Setting," *Perceptual and Motor Skills* 83 (1996): 579.

[16]Bellezza et. al, "The Red Sneakers Effect," 42–43.

[17]Roland Barthes, *The Fashion System*, trans. Matthew Ward and Richard Howard (New York: Hill and Wang, 1983), 255–56.

[18]Catherine Egley Waggoner and D. Lynn O'Brien Hallstein, "Feminist Ideologies Meet Fashionable Bodies: Managing the Agency/Constraint Conundrum," *Text and Performance Quarterly* 21, no. 1 (2001): 33, 35-36.

Chapter 25: "Full-Quiver" Theology

[1]Originally published as an op-ed in *Ethics Daily* on December 14, 2005. The op-ed was a response to Dr. Al Mohler, president of Southern Baptist Theological Seminary, who advocates parents having as many children as possible, an argument that I claim is race-based.

Chapter 26: Invisible Hispanics

[1]Originally published in the *Journal of Feminist Studies in Religion* 28, no. 1 (Spring 2012): 121–126. The article was part of a larger roundtable discussion that explored Valerie Saiving Goldstein's feminist critique of Reinhold Niebuhr. In this article I tried to move the discussion beyond a neat white male-female dichotomy by focusing on who is usually left out of the discussion.

[2]"The Beautiful Girls," *Mad Men*, Episode 9, AMC, premier September 19, 2010.

[3]A close friend of Susan B. Anthony, Frederick Douglass advocated for the rights of women, even participating at the first Women's Rights Convention held in Seneca Falls in 1848 and signing the Declaration of Sentiments. Nonetheless, the relationship between the two leaders was strained after the Civil War over the issue of passage of the Fourteenth and Fifteenth Amendments. Anthony refused to support the Fifteenth Amendment because it excluded women, while Douglass believed it was important to first secure the rights of African-American males before working to achieving the rights of women. As Douglas said, "When women, because they are women, are dragged from their homes and hung upon lamp-posts…then they will have an urgency to obtain the ballot." After the Fifteenth Amendment was ratified in 1870, Douglass resumed his work for women's rights.

[4]Although Hillary Clinton later served as President Barack Obama's secretary of state, their differences during the primaries manifested themselves in disturbing ways. For example, Clinton made the claim that it took a Lyndon Johnson to make a Martin Luther King's dream a reality. The message was clear. King and Obama can give great speeches, but it takes white presidents to bring about effective change.

[5]Valerie Saiving Goldstein, "Where Is the Woman?" *Theology Today* 19, no. 1 (April, 1962): 111.

[6]Reinhold Niebuhr, "The Confession of a Tired Radical," *Christian Century* 45, no. 35 (August 30, 1928): 1046.

[7]Valerie Saiving Goldstein, "The Human Situation: A Feminine View," *Journal of Religion* 40, no. 2 (April, 1960): 109–11.

[8]Ibid.

[9]Ibid.,100.

[10]It should be noted that many Latinas, in unison with other women of color, have spoken on and written about the need for them to respond to the sexism existing within their own communities of color and to the racial, ethnic, and class prejudice existing within the Anglo feminist communities that ignores the fundamental ways white women benefit from the oppression of women of color.

[11]Niebuhr, "The Confession of a Tired Radical," 1046.

[12]Reinhold Niebuhr, *Moral Man and Immoral Society: A Study in Ethics and Politics* (New York: Charles Scribner's Sons, 1932), 254.

[13]Ibid., 268.

[14]Traci C. West, *Disruptive Christian Ethics: When Racism and Women's Lives Matter* (Louisville: Westminster John Knox Press, 2006), 13.

[15]Ibid., 15.

[16]Niebuhr, *Moral Man and Immoral Society*, 128.

[17]Saiving, "The Human Situation: A Feminine View," 101.

[18]"A Conversation with Valerie Saiving," *Journal of Feminist Studies in Religion* 4 (Fall 1988): 99–115.

[19]Saiving, "The Human Situation: A Feminine View," 108.

[20]Ibid., 104–05.

[21]Ibid., 109.

[22]Elizabeth Grosz, *Jacques Lacan: A Feminist Interpretation* (London: Routledge, 1990), 115–45.

Chapter 27: Jesús: Welcoming the Indecent

[1]Originally published in *The Politics of Jesús: A Hispanic Political Theology* (Lanham, MD: Rowman & Littlefield, 2015), 158–65. Since 2007, with the publication of *Liberating Jonah*, I have been struggling to articulate an indecent ethics that reflects the indecent conditions the disenfranchised are forced to endure. This section is the most recent articulation of my attempt to construct an ethics *para joder*.

[2]Marcella Althaus-Reid, *Indecent Theology: Theological Perversions in Sex, Gender and Politics*, (London: Routledge, 2000), 1–9.

[3]Santería is an Afro-Cuban religion to which many, not just Cubans, follow and practice. The *orishas* are quasi-deities to whom all of humanity belongs as children. These *orishas* watch over each human head. The *orisha* of my head (*orí*) is *Ellegúa*, known as the

trickster. The trickster figure becomes an important component of the ethics that I propose. For a better understanding of *Santería*, see my award-winning book *Santería: The Beliefs and Rituals of a Growing Religion in America* (2004).

[4]Miguel A. De La Torre, "Doing Latina/o Ethics from the Margins of Empire: Liberating the Colonized Mind," *Journal of the Society of Christian Ethics* 33, no. 1 (2013): 11.

[5]Miguel A. De La Torre, *Latina/o Social Ethics: Moving Beyond Eurocentric Moral Thinking* (Waco, TX: Baylor University Press, 2010), 92.

[6]Ibid., 94.

[7]The *ethics para joder* which I advocate that arises from the underside of society is an ethics which: (1) disrupts the social order and equilibrium; (2) employs the cultural Hispanic symbol of the trickster in the formation of praxis; (3) looks toward the biblical text for narratives of figures who played the role of trickster; (4) moves beyond the Civil Right's concept of civil disobedience toward the Sanctuary Movement's concept of civil initiative; and (5) roots itself in the pastoral which is linked to a communal, not individualistic ethos of the marginalized. Space prevents a thorough exploration of all of these components; nevertheless, a full elucidation of these components can be found in De La Torre, *Latina/o Social Ethics*, chap. 4.

[8]De La Torre, *Latina/o Social Ethic*, 114–15.

Index

Scripture Index

CPSIA information can be obtained
at www.ICGtesting.com
Printed in the USA
LVHW021926230720
661378LV00020B/2292

9 780827 221796